Antonia Clare • JJ Wilson • Stephanie Dimond-Bayir

speakout

2ND EDITION

Intermediate
Flexi Course Book 1

with DVD-ROM

BBC

Pearson Education Limited
Edinburgh Gate
Harlow
Essex CM20 2JE
England
and Associated Companies throughout the world.

www.pearsonelt.com

First published 2015
This edition published 2016
ISBN: 978-1-292-14931-8

Set in Aptifer sans 10/12 pt
Printed in China by Golden Cup

Acknowledgements
The Publisher and authors would like to thank the following people and institutions for their feedback and comments during the development of the material: **Australia:** Erica Lederman; **Hungary:** Eszter Timár; **Mexico:** Hortensia Camacho Barco; **Poland:** Konrad Dejko; **Spain:** Sam Lanchbury, Victoria O'Dea; **UK:** Lilian Del Gaudio Maciel, Joelle Finck, Niva Gunasegaran.

Text acknowledgements
We are grateful to the following for permission to reproduce copyright material:
Extract on page 25 from "Fraud Fugitive in Facebook Trap", 14/10/2009, http://news.bbc.co.uk/1/hi/world/americas/8306032.stm, copyright © BBC Worldwide Limited; Extracts on pages 37, 70, 161 from *Longman Active Study Dictionary*, 5th edition, Pearson Education Ltd, copyright © Pearson Education Limited, 2010; Extract on page 44 from "Millionaires prefer Gap to Gucci" 05/10/2003, http://www.bbc.co.uk/print/pressoffice/pressreleases/stories/2003/10_october/05/mind_millionaire.shtml, copyright © BBC Worldwide Limited; Extract on pages 44-45 from "Have you Got What it Takes to be Millionaire ?", *The Telegraph*, 05/06/2014 (Shirley Conran), copyright © Telegraph Media Group Limited; Extract on page 80 adapted from 'The secret of success' interview with Malcolm Gladwell, BBC Focus, Issue 197, 01/12/2008, p.23. Presenters Jenny Osman & Ian, copyright © Immediate Media Company Bristol Ltd; Extract on page 105 from "12 Giant leaps for mankind" by Rob Attar, *BBC History Magazine*, Vol.10, no.7, pp.42-47, copyright © Immediate Media Company Bristol Ltd; Extract on pages 116-117 adapted from "I am the Ethical Man" by 22/02/2006 and "We are all ethical men and women now" 13/04/2007 by Justin Rowlatt, http://news.bbc.co.uk/1/hi/programmes/newsnight/4736228.stm, http://www.bbc.co.uk/blogs/newsnight/2007/04/we_are_all_ethical_men_and_women_now.html, copyright © BBC Worldwide Limited; and Extract on page 121 adapted from "Top Ten New Restaurants in East London", *Traveller*, 09/05/2013, source: http://www.cntraveller.com/recommended/food/top-10-new-restaurants-east-london/viewall. Reproduced with permission from Conde Nast.

Illustration acknowledgements
Fred Blunt: 29, 66, 90, 159, 160; Lyndon Hayes: 26, 27, 74, 75; Eric Smith: 129, 133, 135, 137, 140, 149, 150, 151, 152, 153, 154, 157.

Photo acknowledgements
The Publisher would like to thank the following for their kind permission to reproduce their photographs:

(Key: b-bottom; c-centre; l-left; r-right; t-top)

123RF.com: 123vector 37 (car), 86br, agencyby 84/8, Diego Alies 37 (Book), andersonrise 148 (young girl with brown hair), AnnSunnyDay 37, Andrey Bayda 44tl, Jacek Chabraszewski 148 (young girl), Brian Eichhorn 148r (grandma), Elena Elisseeva 148 (son), Warren Goldswain 148 (mature man), Gabriel Gonzalez 121, goodluz 148 (father), Paul Michael Hughes 148 (young boy), Ihor Obraztsov 46r, jehsomwang 37 (wind), kritchanut 116-117 (background), Kurhan 148 (aunty), 148 (uncle), lammeyer 148 (mother), Lightwave Stock Media 32l, lightwise 117t, Roman Malyshev 37 (microscope), nazlisart 37 (Flag), Sean Nel 84/9, nyul 148 (brother), 148 (cousin), 148 (husband), Photoroad 8-9 (background), Aigars Reinholds 148 (grandpa), rido 148 (man), robinsphoto 148 (young woman), serezniy 84/1, Dmitriy Shironosov 148 (daughter), Andrei Shumskiy 7b (icon), 19b (icon), 31b (icon), 43b (icon), 55 (icon), 67b (icon), 79b (icon), 91b (icon), 103b (icon), 115b (icon), sima 148 (grandma), Eric Simard 148 (ME), sjenner13 96, David Smith 43r, 52-53 (balloon), Eunika Sopotnicka 33, stylephotographs 148 (mother-in-law), tetyanka 45 (car), veralub 84/3 (a), Mikhail Vorobiev 12b, Wavebreak Media Ltd 7l, 8c, Cameron Whitman 148 (sister), 148 (young man) , Lisa Young 148r (grandpa); **Alamy Images:** Vincent Abbey 87b, ableimages 48t, Agencja Fotograficzna Caro 94br, Arterra Picture Library 157/1, Anatolii Babii 62/C, Peter Barritt 103r, Creation of Adam fresco on the ceiling of the Sistine Chapel by Buonarroti Michelangelo Vatican Museum Rome Italy Europe 112-113b, Blend Images 59 (F), Catchlight Visual Services 91cr, 98tr, Cultura Creative (RF) 48b, Cultura RM 60, culture-images GmbH 65b, David J. Green - lifestyle 2 91cl, Deborah Ernest 61, Everett Collection Historical 103l, Garry Gay 43l, Ian Goodrick 55cr, 62/B, Tim Graham 110bl, Thierry Grun 87c, Heritage Image Partnership Ltd 104c, Images-USA 117 (bus), Isowork Images 62/E, Eddie Linssen 151t, LondonPhotos / Homer Sykes 108tr, M. Timothy O'Keefe 62/D, David Pearson 110tr, Davide Piras 43cl, 47/C, Pixellover RM 8 97, StreetStock 67cl, 71, The Illustrated London News Picture Library. Ingram Publishing. Alamy 110br, Gregg Vignal 10; **BBC Photo Library:** Hladik, Martin 36; **BBC Worldwide Ltd:** 16 (inset), 28 (inset), 40 (inset), 52l (inset), 55r, 64 (inset), 76 (inset), 100 (inset), 124r (inset); **Comstock Images:** 99; **Corbis:** 68 / Ocean 25 (background), 25cl, Amelie-Benoist / Bsip 31t, Andersen Ross / Cultura 52-53, Bettmann 23b, 81tr, 103cr, Edgar Su / Reuters 35l, Hemant Mehta / India Picture 87t, Jon Hrusa / Epa 24, Ingo Bartussek / Westend61 50r, Lan 80t, LWA / Larry Williams 16-17, Photo Media 67l, Photo Media / Classicstock 108l, Arnie Sachs / CNP / AdMedia 104l; **Fotolia.com:** 118, arphoto 44 (notes), Banana Republic 44-45 (background), Andrey Burmakin 79cr, Cifotart 80-81 (background), cunico 38tr, dominiquelavoie 151c, Dp3010 76 (cake), Esolla 77 (flowers), Eyematrix 56 (background), Fontanis 84/6, Joe Gough 84/11, Kaesler Media 38l, karandaev 84/10, Login 110 (background), Monkey Business 38r, nacroba 67cr, photorealistic 51, Željko Radojko 44 (watch), Raven 38 (food icon), Robsonphoto 76-77 (heart background), Maksim Striganov 44 (ring), sumnersgraphicsinc 77 (cork), surasaki 76-77 (flower background), Taiga 67r; **Getty Images:** 68/C, 112-113t, Frank Barratt 103cl, BBC News & Current Affairs / Jeff Overs 116l, Al Bello / Staff 88-89 (background), Bilderlounge 31cr, 38tc, Fotog 59/C, FPG 67t, George Hoyningen-Huene / RDA / Contributor 21 (F), Jeff Giniewicz 31r, 40-41, Tim Graham 163, Judith Haeusler 56b, Hero Images 34b, 47/A, Stan Honda / Staff 79r, 88-89 (foreground), iStock / Getty Images Plus 35c, Vincenzo Lombardo 115cr, Massive 68/A, Buda Mendes 91t, Tatiana Morozova 69/E, Zhang Peng 119r, Philip Game / Lonely Planet Images 91r, 100-101, Photo 12 110tl, Photonica World 115cl, 119l, Tom C. Robison 43t, Terry Fincher 107, Westend61 68/B; **Nicola Krebill:** 56t; **NASA:** NASA / JPL / ASU 95; **Pearson Education Ltd:** Sophie Bluy 63; **Photolibrary.com:** Sugar Gold Images. Denkou Images 68/D; **Plainpicture Ltd:** Julian Love / Cultura 43cr; **Press Association Images:** Fiona Hanson 65cr; **Reuters:** Chip East 161, Dylan Martinez 79t; **Rex Features:** 19cl, 21 (B), 21 (G), 23t, 52r (inset), 80cr, 80bl, 104r, Agencia EFE 110cl, Ron C Angle 80br, Stuart Clarke 110cr, Cultura 84/3 (b), Cultura / REX 32r, Design Pics Inc 7r, 16b, Everett Collection 21 (D), I Love Images 115l, ITV 111, KeystoneUSA-ZUMA 81tl, Franck Leguet 21 (A), Geraint Lewis 83b, Steve Meddle / ITV 72, Scott Myers 21 (C), Niviere / Villard 21 (E), PictureGroup 79l, Brian Rasic 108br, Ron Sachs / Pool via CNP 21 (H), Solent News 47/B, Universal History Archive / Universal Images Group 81bl, 81br, WestEnd61 98tl; **Robert Harding World Imagery:** Nick Bonetti 93, Fernanda Preto 94cl, P. Schickert 911, 92; **Science Photo Library Ltd:** Amelie-Benoist / Bsip 35r, David A. Hardy 31cl; **Shutterstock.com:** 06photo 122, 48c (butterfly), auremar 86tr, bikeriderlondon 86tl, Franck Boston 84/12, Andrey Burmakin 103t, damato 84/7, Zeynep Demir 19t, EpicStockMedia 59/E, Greg Epperson 84/5, FloridaStock 115r, 124-125, Stanimir G.Stoev 44 (coins), Jaroslaw Grudzinski 76 (rings/rose), InesBazdar 19cr, Inga Ivanova 151b, Shaun Jeffers 64-65, Christopher Kolaczan 157/5, Olivier Le Queinec 105r, M. Shcherbyna 157/2, mhatzapa 84/4 (b), Monkey Business Images 73, Vladimir Mucibabic 69/F, nobeastsofierce 104-105, Ollyy 12t, Pakhnyushcha 49, pixeldreams.eu 79cl, 83 (background), Graham Prentice 59/D, RG-vc 55cl, Rido 84/4 (a), robcocquyt 62/A, Sailorr 59/A, Sozaijiten 59/B, Ssuaphotos 157/3, Dan Thornberg 117 (flag), Three one five 157/4, Tupungato 94bl, Kiselev Andrey Valerevich 84/2, Roman Vanur 115t, Wavebreakmedia 311, Chamille White 55t, Zurijeta 50l; **SuperStock:** Blend Images 98tc, Cultura Limited 7t, Cultura Ltd 14b, Cusp / Cusp 19r, 28-29, F1 Online 14t, RubberBall 7cr, Science Photo Library 7cl, 11l, 11r; **The Kobal Collection:** Warner Bros. / James, David 19l; **TopFoto:** 2005 155, Ronald Grant Archive / ArenaPAL 23c; **www.playpumps.co.za:** 55l, 56c

All other images © Pearson Education

Every effort has been made to trace the copyright holders and we apologise in advance for any unintentional omissions. We would be pleased to insert the appropriate acknowledgement in any subsequent edition of this publication.

speakout 2ND EDITION

Intermediate
Students' Book

with DVD-ROM

Antonia Clare • JJ Wilson

BBC

CONTENTS

GRAMMAR

1 Read the text and find examples of …

1 the past simple *he saw*
2 the past continuous
3 the present perfect
4 the past perfect
5 a modal verb
6 a superlative
7 a relative clause
8 a passive

There have been some amazing coincidences throughout history, but this might be the best. In 1900 King Umberto of Italy was dining in a restaurant when he saw that the owner looked exactly like him. The man, who was also called Umberto, was born in Turin on the same day as the king and, like the king, married a woman called Margherita. Amazingly, their weddings had been on the same day. The king invited the restaurant owner to an athletics meeting the next day. As the king sat down, he was told that the other Umberto had died in a mysterious shooting accident. Just as the king heard this news, an anarchist shot him dead.

PRONUNCIATION

2 A Find pairs of words that have the same vowel sound.

B L.1 Listen and check your answers.

C Work in pairs. Think of other words in English that use the same sounds.

VOCABULARY

3 A Complete the common phrases below using the correct verb from the box.

~~have~~ take check watch chat go meet play do (x2)

1 *have* a meeting
2 ______ your email
3 ______ out with friends
4 ______ some sport
5 ______ a colleague
6 ______ some work
7 ______ on the internet
8 ______ a break
9 ______ a DVD
10 ______ some music

B Add phrases 1–10 above to the word webs below.

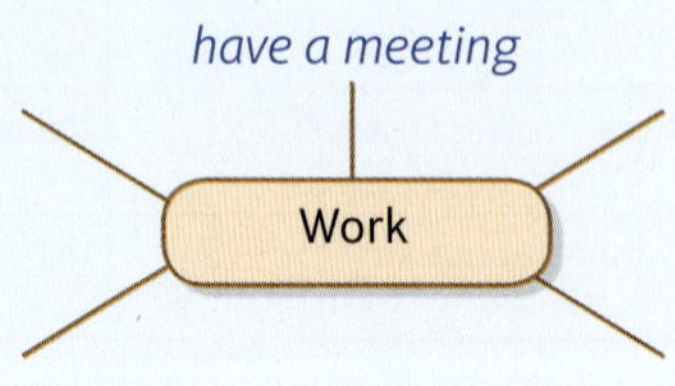

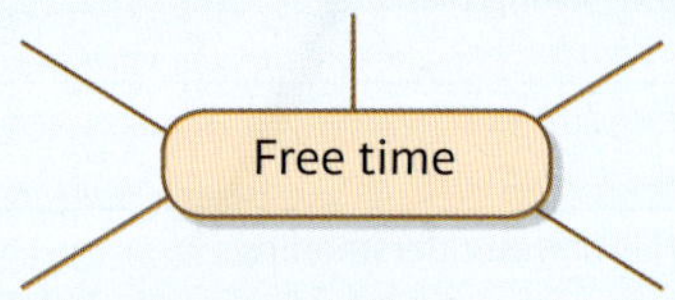

C Can you add any more phrases to the word webs? Which of these things do you do on a normal day?

COMMON ERRORS

4 A Correct the mistakes.

1 She likes listening music.
2 I am architect.
3 Are you feeling allright?
4 When I can visit your house?
5 Let's discuss about this tomorrow.
6 He don't come here often.
7 We come from germany.
8 Where you go yesterday?
9 I live in this town all my life.
10 My wife is a really good cooker.

B Which mistakes are connected with …

a) verb–noun agreement *6*
b) spelling
c) verb tense
d) punctuation/capitalisation
e) prepositions
f) articles
g) vocabulary
h) word order
i) missing auxiliary verb
j) extra words

1 identity

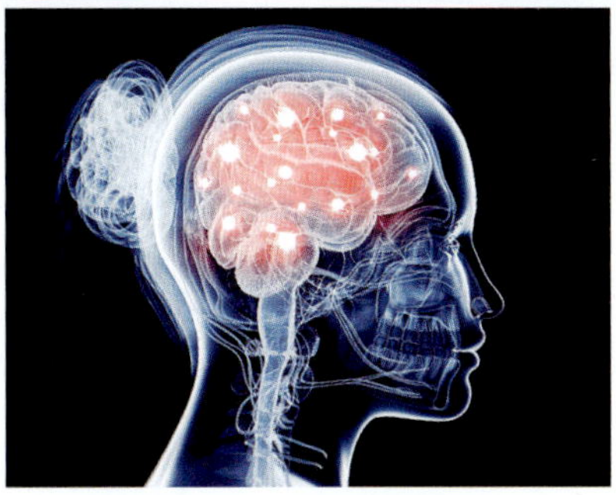

SPEAKING **1.1** Talk about important dates in your life **1.2** Talk about the differences between men and women **1.3** Role-play an interview **1.4** Speak about yourself for 60 seconds

LISTENING **1.2** Listen to a set of instructions and do a test **1.3** Listen to three interviews **1.4** Watch a BBC documentary about a blind artist

READING **1.1** Read about bilingualism **1.3** Read tips on doing successful interviews

WRITING **1.1** Write an email of introduction **1.4** Write a personal description

BBC INTERVIEWS

What does family mean to you?

1.1 ME AND MY LANGUAGES

G question forms
P intonation: *Wh-* questions
V language

VOCABULARY

LANGUAGE

1 A Read questions 1–10. What do the words in bold mean? Check with other students or your teacher, then think about your answers to the questions.

1 Why are you learning English? For work, exams, travel, etc.?
2 Do you speak any languages apart from your **mother tongue** and English?
3 Who is the best language learner in your family?
4 Did you use any **learning strategies** when studying your second language? Which?
5 When was the first time you used a **foreign** language outside the classroom?
6 Do you have the chance to speak/write to **native speakers** regularly?
7 Is it important for you to learn **slang** or **jargon** in English, or do you only want to learn standard English?
8 Which is more important to you when you learn to speak a language: **fluency** or **accuracy**?
9 Which **skill** is the hardest for you: speaking, listening, reading, or writing? Which is the easiest?
10 Do you know anyone who is **bilingual**? What advantages might they have in life?

B Work in groups. Discuss your answers to questions 1–10.

2 Answer the questions.

1 Which words in bold in questions 1–10 have silent letters?
2 What are the silent letters in these words: *science, talk, listen, know, right, wrong, hours, guess*?
3 Which statement (a or b) do you think is true?
  a Most words in English are spelt differently to how they are pronounced.
  b Under twenty percent of words in English are spelt differently to how they are pronounced.

speakout TIP

Around fourteen percent of English words have irregular spelling; they are spelt differently to how they are pronounced. When you learn new words, try to hear them. Watch out for silent letters!

BILINGUALS: EXOTIC BIRDS OR EVERYDAY PEOPLE?

by Johan Acosta

Grandpa shouts, "Dinner's ready" in Danish. My mother asks me in English to lay the table. As I do so, I catch the theme tune of the Brazilian soap opera on TV in the living room, where my sister is relaxing. She speaks perfect Portuguese. My father asks her to record the programme in his native Spanish, and we take our places at the table. And what's on the menu? Italian meatballs.

We know we aren't a normal family. At any moment, you might hear conversations in four different languages, and almost everyone understands almost everything. But what is normal these days? My mother is half-Danish, half-English, and my father, who is from Bolivia, speaks Spanish and Guaraní. Because of my mother's work (she's now retired), we lived in Brazil, Italy and Germany, so we picked up three more languages. Now as adults, my sister and I both speak six languages.

READING

3 A Read the title of the text. What do you think it will discuss? Read to find out.

B Read the text again and answer the questions.

1 What six languages do you think the writer and his sister speak?
2 How do you think the writer learnt each of his languages?
3 How many of the world's people are thought to be bilingual?
4 What are those who learn their second language as children better at compared to those who learn a second language as adults?
5 What health benefit of being bilingual is mentioned in the text?

Being bilingual, or in our case multilingual, has so many advantages. All the recent research suggests we benefit in many ways: social, cultural, economic, academic, and intellectual. The research has also destroyed some of those persistent myths.

One of the myths is that bilingualism is uncommon, as if we bilinguals are like rare, exotic birds. The truth is that around fifty percent of the world's inhabitants are bilingual. The continents with the most linguistic diversity are Asia and Africa. In Nigeria alone, 500 languages are spoken, in India 400.

Some people believe that you have to learn both languages as a child to be truly bilingual. My sister and I are fortunate in this respect, but we know countless people who have mastered a second language as adults. They may not have such perfect pronunciation as those who acquire their second language as children, but they are still completely fluent and accurate.

Another myth about bilinguals concerns identity. Some people think we have split personalities. As kids, my sister and I were often asked "But where are you really from? Don't you get confused?" Not at all. I am me, the product of many cultures. I can switch languages easily, according to where I am and who I'm with, and this seems completely natural to me.

As for the benefits, bilinguals do better on certain tests, are better protected against mental illnesses such as Alzheimer's, gain insights into other cultures, have access to more of the world's information, and are in some contexts more employable. Being bilingual has made me who I am, and for that I'm grateful.

‘One of the myths is that bilingualism is uncommon, as if we bilinguals are like rare, exotic birds.’

C Underline words or phrases in the text that match meanings 1–6 below.

1 relating to the language you grew up speaking (paragraph 1)
2 learnt by listening/watching other people (paragraph 2)
3 speaking many languages (paragraph 3)
4 false ideas that people continue to believe and repeat (paragraph 3)
5 learn without needing to try hard, e.g. a language (paragraph 5)
6 understand important truths about a subject (paragraph 7)

D Discuss the questions with other students.

1 Do you agree with the writer's list of the advantages to being bilingual?
2 Do you think there any disadvantages to being bilingual?
3 Do you know any families that are bilingual or multilingual? Are they similar to the family in the text?

GRAMMAR

QUESTION FORMS

4 A Read sentences 1–6 and answer questions a)–e).

1 Do you speak other languages?
2 Did you use any learning strategies?
3 Who did you talk to?
4 What happened?
5 What did you talk about?
6 Who is the best language learner in your family?

a) Underline the main verb in each question. (The first has been done for you.)
b) Circle the auxiliary verbs. Which auxiliary refers to the past? Which refers to the present?
c) Which two questions are yes/no questions?
d) Which two questions end in a preposition: *of*, *by*, etc.?
e) Which two questions use *wh-* words to refer to the subject (the person who does the action, or the action itself) and don't use an auxiliary verb?

▷ page 68 **LANGUAGEBANK**

B ▶ 1.1 **INTONATION: *wh-* questions** Listen to the questions in Exercise 4A. Are the question words (*wh-* words) in 3–6 said in a higher or a lower voice?

C Listen and say the questions at the same time.

5 A Put the words in the correct order to make questions.

1 do / every / you / day / study ?
2 your / any / did / languages / teach / parents / you / other ?
3 is / learner / who / the / best / you / language / know ?
4 was / teacher / your / English / first / who ?
5 do / do / you / remember / what / English / to / words / in ?
6 languages / you / what / do / to / like / listening ?
7 do / what / watch / you / English / in / TV / programmes?
8 foreign / did / speak / first / when / language / a / you ?

B Choose three of the questions to ask other students.

SPEAKING

6 A Write four dates, four names and four places that are important to you.

Dates: *7 May 2008 – My son was born.*
Names:
Places:

B Work in groups. Take turns to explain what you wrote. As you listen, think of questions to ask afterwards.

WRITING

EMAILS OF INTRODUCTION; LEARN TO WRITE FORMAL AND INFORMAL EMAILS

7 A When would you write a letter or email to introduce yourself?

B Read the emails. Why are the people writing? Which sentences tell us?

To: ramirezh@languagestar.nett   Subject: Spanish conversation class

Hi Hernan,

My name's Julia Brown. I heard from my friend Nichola Lazarus that you're running a Spanish conversation class. She said you'd be happy to accept a few more people. My mother tongue is English but I picked up some Spanish years ago when I was travelling in Latin America. I really want to develop my fluency and accuracy, so I'd love to join the class. Hope to hear from you soon.

All the best,

Julia 😃

To: GND staff   Subject: Greetings

Dear Colleagues,

As you probably know, next month I will start work as the new director of the Language Teaching Education Programme. For those of you who don't know me, I would like to take this opportunity to introduce myself. Since 2010, I have worked at the School of Education at Borodive University. I have been involved in a number of language teacher education projects across Europe and I worked extensively on the Star Placement Initiative that placed six thousand native speakers in language classrooms in eight countries. I am married with two children and my family is bilingual in English and Turkish.

I look forward to working with you.

Yours sincerely,

Talya Osman

8 Read the five steps for good email writing. Do you think the emails in Exercise 7B follow steps 1–3?

1 Aim for your audience: think about who you are writing to. Is the email formal or informal?
2 Be brief: try not to use too many words. Emails shouldn't go on for pages.
3 Communicate clearly: use simple, clear language and simple sentence structure.
4 Do two drafts: write a first version and then rewrite.
5 Edit everything: check grammar, vocabulary, spelling and punctuation before sending.

9 A Look at the emails in Exercise 7B again. Which one is formal and which is informal? How do you know?

B Answer questions 1–4 with formal (F) or informal (I).

1 Which email uses full forms of verbs (*I will*, *I would*) instead of contractions (*you're*, *I'd*)?
2 Which email leaves out words (e.g. *Hope to …* instead of *I hope to …*)?
3 Which email sounds more like spoken English?
4 Which email uses longer, more complex sentences?

C Complete the notes with phrases from the email.

Greeting
(formal): 1 _______.
(informal): Hi/Hello.

Introduction
(formal): I would like to take this 2 _______.
(informal): My name's …

Final message
(formal): I look forward to …
(informal): 3 _______.

Goodbye
(formal): 4 _______.
(informal): All the best.

10 Choose a situation below and write an email. Think about who you are writing to, the reason for writing and the style: formal or informal.

Situation 1
You are going to join an English conversation class. Write an email introducing yourself to the teacher and the class. Mention your experience of learning and speaking English and say why you want to join the class.

Situation 2
Next week you start a new job in a multinational company. Your colleagues speak over twenty languages, and all of them read English. Write to introduce yourself. Mention your previous work experience and the languages you know, and add something personal.

VOCABULARY

RELATIONSHIPS

1 A **Work in pairs. Think of all the people you have talked to in the last 24 hours. What relationship do they have to you?**

B **Look at the words in the box and answer the questions.**

~~boss and employee~~ classmates partner team-mates member godfather and godmother mentor and pupil fiancée and fiancé

1 Which pair works together? *boss and employee*
2 Which pair promises to help guide a child through life?
3 Which pair is going to get married?
4 Which pair involves one person learning from the other?
5 Which word describes people who play in the same sports team?
6 Which word describes people who go to the same class?
7 Which word describes a person who is part of a club?
8 Which word is a general word for 'someone who you do something with'?

C 1.2 **Listen to six sentences. Tick the words in the box in Exercise 1B which you hear.**

D **WORD STRESS** **Six of the words have two syllables. Find the words and underline the stressed syllable. Say the words aloud, putting the stress on the correct syllable.**

▷ page 78 **VOCABULARYBANK**

speakout TIP

Remember: most two-syllable words in English have the stress on the first syllable. Hold a hand under your chin. Say the word slowly. The jaw (the bottom part of your chin) drops more on the stressed syllable.

2 **Work in groups. Discuss the questions.**

1 Can you think about one man and one woman who have played important roles in your life? Who were they? Why was the relationship important?
2 Do you think men and women are different in these roles? How?

LISTENING

3 A **Read the text. Discuss. Do you think male and female brains are different? How? What are the stereotypes of men and women in your country?**

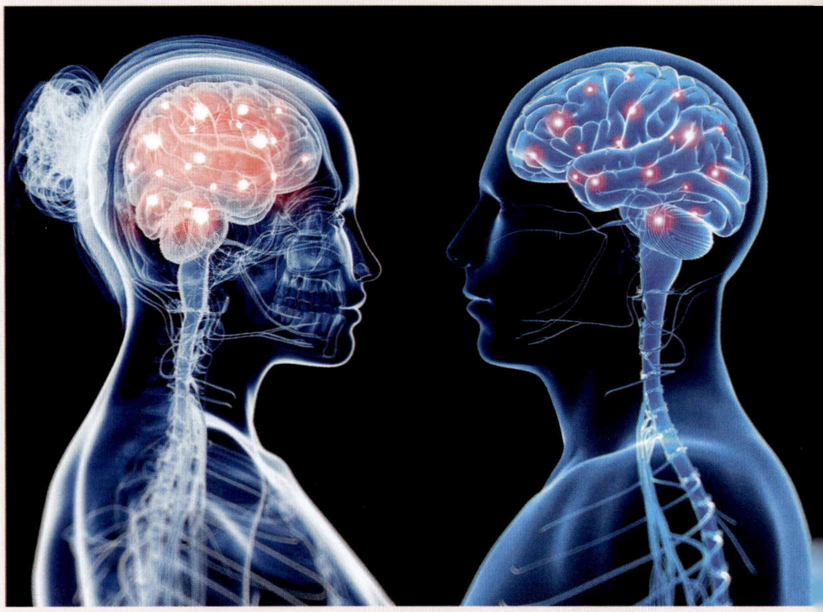

Are men's and women's brains wired differently?

Is it true that men are from Venus and women are from Mars? Some researchers think that male and female brains are wired differently, with male brains wired from back to front, and female brains wired from side to side. This might explain why men are good at performing a single task, like cycling or navigating, whereas women might be better at multi-tasking. Other researchers disagree, however. What do YOU think? Try the bike test to find out if your brain is male or female.

B 1.3 **Take a piece of paper. Listen to Part 1 and 2 and follow the bike test instructions.**

C 1.4 **Listen to the explanation in Part 3. Turn to page 83 and check your picture. How many parts did your bike have? Could it work? Does it have a person on it? Compare your picture with other students'.**

D **Discuss the questions.**

1 Was the explanation correct for you?
2 Do you agree with the presenter's views about men and women?

"Women think people are important. Men, on the other hand, are more interested in getting the machine right."

SPEAKING

4 A Read the information. Which comments do you agree/disagree with? Can you think of any opinions to add?

Are men & women really different?

We asked for comments and this is what you said.

"Absolutely! Men can't watch sport on TV **and** talk to their girlfriend at the same time."

"WOMEN DON'T KNOW HOW TO READ MAPS."

"Women remember **every outfit they've worn** for the past twenty years. Men **can't remember** what they were wearing yesterday without looking on the floor."

"Men can buy a pair of shoes on the internet in **90 seconds**. Women like to take three weeks."

"A baby is crying, a dog is barking, a doorbell is ringing, but the man of the house is sleeping. **Men can sleep through anything**. Women can't."

"Men speak in sentences. Women speak in **paragraphs**."

B Do the men and women in your life conform to the normal stereotypes? Why?/Why not?

GRAMMAR

REVIEW OF VERB TENSES

5 A Match the underlined verbs below with the tenses a)–d).

1 We asked for comments and this is what you said.
2 Men can't remember what they were wearing yesterday.
3 Women remember every outfit they've worn for the past twenty years.
4 A baby is crying.

a) present simple
b) present continuous
c) past simple
d) past continuous

B Complete the rules with the correct tenses a)–d).

RULES

1 We use ______ for actions, events or situations that are finished.
2 We use ______ for things that are going on at a particular moment in the present.
3 We use ______ for habits, routines and things that are always true.
4 We use ______ when someone was in the middle of an action at a particular moment in the past.

C Read about state verbs. Underline three examples in the text above.

RULES

Some verbs are not usually used in the continuous, e.g. want, like, remember, understand, know. These are called 'state verbs'.

▷ page 68 **LANGUAGEBANK**

6 A Read the text below and put the words in brackets into the correct tense.

My name is Matsuko Tamazuri. I am twenty-three and I [1]________________ (be) a student. I study French and Spanish at university in Osaka, where I [2]________________ (grow up), but at the moment I [3]________________ (learn) English in New York. When I first [4]________________ (get) here, everything [5]________________ (seem) different: the food, the clothes and the weather. Now I [6]________________ (enjoy) it and it feels like home! I have a boyfriend called Josh. I [7]________________ (meet) him three weeks ago when I [8]________________ (look) for an internet café! My hobbies [9]________________ (be) surfing the net and singing. I [10]________________ (sing) every day, usually in the bathroom!

B Work in pairs. Ask questions and write your partner's personal profile. Use the profile above to help.

VOCABULARY PLUS

COLLOCATIONS

7 A Work in pairs and do the quiz.

B Turn to page 83 and read the text to check your answers.

8 A Look at the quiz again. Find and circle five expressions using *take, get, do* and *go*.

B Write the expressions in italics in the correct places in the word webs below.

1 *~~on a diet~~, home, off something, for a drink/a walk/ a meal, grey*

go
- *on a diet* (start something)
- ________ (become)
- ________ (move to a place)
- ________ (other expressions)

2 *responsibility for, after someone, part in something, a taxi*

take
- ________ (go in a vehicle)
- ________ (join in)
- ________ (phrasal verbs)
- ________ (other expressions)

3 *married, a job/degree, on with someone, here*

get
- ________ (become)
- ________ (obtain)
- ________ (go somewhere)
- ________ (phrasal verbs)

4 *exercise, research, housework, someone a favour*

do
- ________ (activity)
- ________ (responsibilities and tasks)
- ________ (find information)
- ________ (help someone)

▷ page 78 **VOCABULARYBANK**

SPEAKING

9 A Think about your classmates. Write down the name of someone who:

- never gets angry.
- does research for his/her job.
- took a test in the last six months.
- went for a meal last weekend.
- took up a new hobby recently.
- always gets here early.
- went for a walk today.
- got a new job recently.

B Work in groups. Ask the other students to check if they agree with your ideas.

What women **really** think

Stella magazine commissioned YouGov, a research agency, to interview over 1,000 women in the UK about everything from their eating habits to their relationships and family values, to find out what they really think.

How do you think they responded?

1 How many women in the UK would prefer to have a male boss?

a) less than 30% b) about 50% c) over 70%

2 How many women spend more than seven hours a week doing exercise?

a) 4% b) 15% c) 30%

3 What is the biggest challenge for women today?

a) staying healthy b) making enough money

c) balancing home and work life

4 What do women think is the best age to get married?

a) between 21 and 24 b) between 25 and 29

c) over 30

5 What do 59% of women think fathers should take more responsibility for?

a) their children b) doing the housework

c) organising holidays

6 According to women, how much housework do they do?

a) more than 50% b) over 75% c) nearly all of it

7 How many women aged 45–54 met their husbands through the internet?

a) 1% b) 9% c) 16%

8 How many women have gone on a diet in the past?

a) 20% b) between 35% and 45% c) over 50%

F talking about yourself
P intonation: sounding polite
V interview advice

5 Tips to help you do well at interviews

How do you get into the university or the job of your dreams? Even before the interview, you might need to catch someone's attention. The Dean of Admissions at Harvard University says he often receives flowers and chocolates from potential students. One student sent references every day for three months. Eventually, he even sent a letter from his dentist saying how nice his teeth were. He didn't get an interview.

For those of you who do make the interview stage, here are five top tips:

1 Be prepared. Do some research about the university or company so you know what questions to ask.

2 Dress appropriately. You don't have to dress smartly but you should look clean. And don't wear 'bling' (large pieces of jewellery).

3 Arrive on time. Fifteen minutes early is OK.

4 Shake hands firmly and make eye contact. First impressions are important.

5 Speak clearly and try to offer full answers rather than short responses. This shows your enthusiasm.

SPEAKING

1 A Look at the photos. What types of interview could this be? Choose from the list below.

- job interview
- interview for a place at university
- newspaper/magazine interview
- interview for a talk show/radio programme
- placement interview for a language course

B Look at the list of interview types above. Answer questions 1–3.

1 Which types of interview above have you experienced?
2 Which will you experience in the future?
3 Do you think it is possible to show 'the real you' in a short interview? Why?/Why not?

VOCABULARY

INTERVIEW ADVICE

2 A Work in pairs. What should/shouldn't you do in an interview? Think of as many things as you can in two minutes.

You should try to ask questions.

B Look at topics 1–3 below and match them to the expressions in the box.

dress smartly *3* speak clearly answer briefly shake hands firmly send references arrive on time avoid eye contact be prepared do some research show enthusiasm

1 Should do during an interview
2 Shouldn't do during an interview
3 Might do before an interview

3 Read the text and answer the questions.

1 What type of things do some people do to get an interview at Harvard University?
2 According to the text, what should you do before and during an interview? Do you agree with the advice?

FUNCTION

TALKING ABOUT YOURSELF

4 A 1.5 **Listen to three extracts from interviews and answer the questions.**

1 What types of interview are they?
2 Which interviewee doesn't follow the five tips? What does he/she do wrong?

B Answer questions 1–6. Listen again to check.

Interview 1
1 What does the student want to practise?
2 What types of classes are in the afternoons?

Interview 2
3 What did the girl organise on the summer camp?
4 What 'can be difficult' according to the interviewer?

Interview 3
5 What does the man want to know?
6 Why are online courses more difficult than face-to-face courses, according to the interviewer?

5 A Read the extracts from the interviews. Underline the expressions that introduce a question.

Extract 1
T: OK … Is there anything else?
S: Could I ask a question?

Extract 2
I: There are a couple of things I'd like to ask about. Your CV says you have some experience of looking after children?
A: Yes, I was a tutor on a summer camp last year.
I: Can I ask you about that? What type of things did you do?

Extract 3
I: I think that's about it. Do you have any questions? Any queries?
S: Um, yes, actually I do have a query.

B Read the extracts below and underline the expressions that are used to introduce an opinion.

Extract 1
S: I've … spent time in Britain, but that was a few years ago. So for me the most important thing is to just refresh …

Extract 2
I: OK. And you enjoyed it?
A: Yes.
I: What aspect, what part did you enjoy, would you say?
A: I suppose I'd have to say I liked the games best …
I: … We often find that different ages together can be difficult.
A: It depends. In my opinion, you can usually get the older children to help the younger ones.

Extract 3
S: So I wouldn't need to attend classes?
I: Not for the online courses. But … well, one thing I'd like to say is that the online courses are, in many ways, more difficult than face-to-face courses.

▷ page 68 LANGUAGEBANK

6 Put the words in the correct order to make sentences or questions.

1 query / I / a / have / do
2 I / a / could / question / ask / ?
3 like / couple / of / are / about / I'd / things / to / a / ask / there
4 ask / you / I / can / that / about / ?
5 true / this / opinion / my / isn't / in
6 to / I'd / I / agree / have / say
7 thing / that / like / I'd / one / say / is / to / is / course / the / difficult
8 is / thing / important / most / for / the / me / to / study

LEARN TO

USE TWO-WORD RESPONSES

7 A Match expressions 1–5 with expressions a)–e).

1 Of course.	a) Please continue.
2 That's right.	b) You're correct.
3 I see.	c) You're welcome.
4 No problem.	d) Yes, definitely.
5 Go ahead.	e) I understand.

B Which expressions in Exercise 7A are more formal? Read audio script 1.5 on page 87 to see how the expressions are used.

C 1.6 **INTONATION: sounding polite Listen to the expressions in Exercise 7A. Notice how the speaker begins the expression with a high pitch to sound friendly. Listen again and repeat.**

SPEAKING

8 Role-play an interview in pairs. Follow instructions 1–5.

1 Either choose one of the interview types in Exercise 1A, or Student A: turn to page 83 and Student B: turn to page 86.
2 Decide on your roles.
3 Interviewer: think of questions. You can make notes if you wish. Interviewee: guess what type of questions the interviewer will ask and prepare answers.
4 Practise your role-play.
5 Perform it in front of other students.

1.4 THE BLIND PAINTER

DVD PREVIEW

1 A Work in pairs and discuss the questions.

1 What creative or sporting activities are important to you? How would you feel if you couldn't do them any more?'

2 Which creative or sporting activities would be particularly difficult if you were blind? What problems do you think a blind person would have?

B Read about the programme. What caused Sargy Mann to go blind? What happened after he went totally blind?

The Blind Painter

BBC

Sargy Mann painted all of his professional life, first as a teacher and later as a professional artist. In his mid-30s he developed cataracts on both eyes, eventually leading to total blindness. He continued to paint. Twenty-five years later, Sargy's work was very popular with art collectors, with paintings regularly selling for more than £50,000 (US$80,000). He spoke to BBC News about his life and how he continued to work.

DVD VIEW

2 Watch the DVD. What does Sargy use to help him paint? What do you think of his paintings?

3 A Answer the questions.

1 What do you know about Sargy Mann after watching the clip?

2 Why did Sargy start to paint again after he went blind?

3 How does he use Blu-Tack to help him paint?

4 Who buys his artwork?

B Look at the quotes from the DVD. Try to complete the phrases using the words in the box.

sensation	go	edgy	coordinates	landscape	nonsense

1 The idea of painting when you were totally blind seemed a ______ to me.

2 I wonder what would happen if I give that a ______.

3 I had the most extraordinary ______.

4 Pre total blindness, I would say I was a ______ painter.

5 Now the thing about these bits of Blu-Tack of course is that what they are actually is ______.

6 They are ______, dangerous. They tell stories, they're full of impact through colour.

C Watch the DVD again to check your answers.

D Match the words and expressions from Exercise 3B with a)–f) below.

a) a very strange or unusual feeling

b) an artist who paints the countryside and scenery

c) experimental or avant-garde

d) numbers or information used to indicate a point

e) looked like a silly idea

f) (to) try something

4 Discuss the questions.

1 Do you think that Sargy Mann would have been such a successful artist if he was not blind?

2 Can you think of other people who have achieved great things despite physical disabilities?

speakout 60 seconds about you

5 A 1.7 Listen to Monica talking about herself. Which questions does she answer from the questionnaire below? What does she say?

Who are you?

1 What three words best describe you?
2 What is your idea of perfect happiness?
3 What possession is most important to you?
4 What is your greatest achievement?
5 What do you like most/least about your lifestyle?
6 What is your favourite sound, smell and taste?
7 What do you always carry with you?
8 Who would be your perfect dinner date? Why?
9 What's your favourite month and why?
10 If you could change one thing about the past, what would it be?

B Listen again. Complete the phrases Monica uses.

KEYPHRASES

I'm going to tell you ______ about myself.
I think three words that describe me would be ______, talkative and hard-working.
One of the things I ______ about my lifestyle …
I suppose that's one ______ I don't like.
In the summer, I love to ______ to the coast …
It makes me feel ______.

C Prepare to talk about yourself for 60 seconds. Choose two or three questions from the questionnaire in Exercise 5A. Plan your answers. Practise and time your presentation to check you can say it all in just 60 seconds.

D Work in pairs and take turns to give your presentation. Take notes on your partner's presentation. What do you have in common?

writeback a personal description

6 A Read the text. What do you think are Stephan's main achievements?

Stephan Wilding in 100 words:

Stephan decided to change his degree from pharmacology to studying Thai at the School of Oriental Studies in London. When he finished university, he spent six months in Thailand teaching English before coming back to the UK. Unsure of his next move, he spent his evenings and weekends teaching himself how to code. He then got together with some friends to start up their own software business. It was a huge adventure and they learnt a lot very quickly. They have recently won a contract to build a computer platform for a design company, so the future is looking good.

B Work in pairs. You are going to write a short description of your partner. Check your notes from Exercise 5D and ask your partner questions if you think you need more information. Then use the text in Exercise 6A to help you write your description(100 words).

V LANGUAGE

1 A Read the advice from a 1950's English course book. Complete the sentences with the words in the box.

foreign strategy jargon bilingual native speakers ~~fluency~~ slang accuracy skill mother tongue

1 Using the right method, *fluency* in the target language is possible after just a few weeks.
2 Students should talk with ______ ______ only. Exposure to other learners will result in new errors.
3 To improve ______, the student should copy out several pages from the textbook every day.
4 The student's biggest problem is translating every word of English into his ______ ______.
5 The best ______ is for the student to imitate the recordings for an hour at a time.
6 It is unnecessary to learn ______ words unless the learner needs them for a specific job.
7 It is impossible to become ______ unless the second language was learnt in childhood.
8 Students should avoid ______ because it isn't proper English.
9 To improve the listening ______, the student should listen daily to the radio.
10 The ______ student needs to be corrected every time he makes a mistake.

B Which advice is still useful? Change any advice you disagree with. Compare your ideas with a partner.

G QUESTION FORMS

2 A Find and correct the mistakes in the questions below. Four of the questions are correct.

1 When you started studying English?
2 Who did helped you to learn English?
3 What annoys you about your job or your studies?
4 Did you to learn anything important at school?
5 Do you be enjoy learning languages?
6 In your job or studies, is there anything you are not happy with?
7 When you imagine the perfect career, what do you think of?
8 What keeps you awake at night?

B Ask your partner four of the questions.

V RELATIONSHIPS

3 A Put the letters in the correct order to find the names of twelve types of people.

1 tomdogher	5 ceanife	9 sobs
2 niface	6 breemm	10 emeyloep
3 ilupp	7 stamcasel	11 trenom
4 nraterp	8 dethagorf	12 maatteme

B Work in pairs. Which of these people do you know or have in your life? Which of these are you?

G REVIEW OF VERB TENSES

4 A Find and correct the mistakes. Five of the underlined verbs are incorrect.

12.10.09

I [1]was walking to work this morning when I [2]was seeing Mr Gonzalez, my old Spanish teacher. He [3]was wearing a leather jacket and carrying a guitar. I [4]ask him how he was. He said, 'Fine. I [5]go to my band practice.' I said, 'What band?' He replied, 'I [6]don't teach any more. It [7]wasn't really the best job for me. A few years ago I [8]was starting a band called The Big Easy. We [9]don't make much money, but I [10]'m liking the lifestyle.' I asked him where he lived and he said, 'I [11]'m living in my caravan at the moment. I [12]travel a lot. I'm a child of the sixties!'

B Write a short diary entry about an interesting or unusual day.

F TALKING ABOUT YOURSELF

5 A Complete the conversations. Write an expression from the box in the correct place in the sentence.

~~query about~~ like to to say you about I ask thing I'd

1 A: I have a *query about* the class. Do I have to bring a pen?
B: No, it's a computer class.

2 A: Could a question? Where does the tennis class meet?
B: At the tennis courts.

3 A: I'd have I'm not sure you're qualified. Why should we employ you for the library position?
B: Because I'm good with children and animals.

4 A: There are a couple of things I'd ask. Firstly, can you work on Saturdays?
B: Is that at the weekend?

5 A: One like to say is that you look good for your age. How old are you?
B: Thirty.

6 A: Can I ask your latest film, *Philadelphia*? Where is it set?
B: In Philadelphia.

B Work in pairs. Write an interview (a job, a place on a course, a magazine interview). Use the expressions in Exercises 5 and 7 on page 15 to help.

C Work in groups and take turns to role-play your interviews.

2 tales

FACT OR FICTION? p20

WHAT REALLY HAPPENED? p23

I DON'T BELIEVE IT! p26

HUSTLE p28

SPEAKING **2.1** Talk about life stories **2.2** Talk about an important news event **2.3** Tell a true story or a lie **2.4** Tell a narrative

LISTENING **2.1** Listen to a radio programme about films **2.2** Listen to news reports **2.3** Listen to a woman telling a story **2.4** Watch a BBC drama about an art thief

READING **2.2** Read an article about conspiracy theories; **2.3** Read a text about lying

WRITING **2.2** Write a news report **2.4** Write a newspaper article

BBC INTERVIEWS

When is it ok to tell a lie?

2.1 FACT OR FICTION?

G present perfect and past simple
P weak forms: *have*
V types of story; prepositions

SPEAKING

1 A Work in groups and discuss. Can you think of a film you have seen that has taught you about a person/event in history?

B Work in pairs and do the quiz. Decide if the information is fact, fiction or partly true. Then check your answers on page 83.

C Discuss. Do you think it is all right for film-makers to change the facts of a story? Why?/Why not?

HOLLYWOOD versus history

Can you tell your facts from fiction?

1 In the film *The Last Samurai*, Tom Cruise plays a US army captain who joins the samurai warriors in Japan in 1876. Was Captain Nathan Algren a real figure from history?

2 In *Shakespeare in Love*, William Shakespeare is inspired to write *Romeo and Juliet* by his real-life relationship with a young actress. Did this happen in real life?

3 In the film *Braveheart*, Mel Gibson plays the character William Wallace, leading an army of men with painted faces, and wearing kilts* as he battles to free Scotland from the English. How much truth is there in the story?

4 In the 1995 adventure, *Apollo 13*, we hear the pilot saying the famous words 'Houston, we have a problem.' But were these his exact words?

* kilt – a type of skirt traditionally worn by Scottish men

VOCABULARY

TYPES OF STORY

2 A Look at the types of film stories in the box below. Match the types of story with the descriptions a)–i).

a biopic   a docudrama   a disaster movie
a romantic comedy   a period drama
a fantasy film   a science fiction film
a psychological thriller   an action/adventure film
a mystery   a crime film

a) Heroes chase and fight each other.
b) The main character has mental problems.
c) A story about the science of the future.
d) Things that happen in the life of a real person.
e) The good guy (the detective) finds the bad guy (the criminal).
f) People dressed up in old-fashioned costumes.
g) Funny things happen. Two people fall in love.
h) Terrible things happen, but people survive.
i) A documentary made more interesting with some parts acted.
j) Strange things happen in an imaginary world.
k) Somebody gets murdered and a clever detective tries to find out who did it.

B Read the opinion below. What type of films does the writer enjoy? Why?

"I love watching romantic comedies. I enjoy sitting down and watching a couple find each other and fall in love. It's really easy watching. I find it relaxing because I don't have to think. It's funny how my taste in films has changed. When I was younger I enjoyed action films, like *Terminator 2*. But now I guess my interests are different."

C Work in pairs and answer the questions.

1 Which types of film do you enjoy watching? Have your tastes changed over the years?
2 Can you name films which match each type of story? Have both of you seen them? Are your opinions about them the same or different?

LISTENING

3 A 2.1 Listen to the first part of a radio programme about films and answer the questions.

1 What type of film does the programme talk about?
2 Why are these films so popular?

B Work in pairs and discuss. Look at the photos of actors who have played the roles of famous people in films. How do you think they prepared for the roles?

C 2.2 Listen to the second part of the radio programme. Are the sentences true (T) or false (F)?

1 Helen Mirren won an Oscar for her role as the Queen.
2 Will Smith met Muhammad Ali but they didn't get on.
3 Josh Brolin talked to himself in a Texan accent all day.
4 Audrey Tautou watched films of Coco Chanel.

4 A 2.3 Listen to the whole programme and complete the information.

1 Hollywood has always used ______ ______ in its films.
2 Hollywood began making films in the ______s.
3 Some of the best films in recent years have been based on ______ ______.
4 From these films we've learnt about the ______ lives of some of the biggest music legends.
5 Many of these actors have won ______ for their roles.
6 Helen Mirren met the Queen for ______ .
7 Josh Brolin phoned hotels in Texas, to listen to their ______ .
8 Tautou wanted to look like Coco Chanel, so that we would recognise her ______ .

B Check your answers in the audio script on page 87.

A Helen Mirren
B Queen Elizabeth I

C Will Smith
D Muhammad Ali

E Audrey Tautou
F Coco Chanel

G Josh Brolin
H George Bush

GRAMMAR

PRESENT PERFECT AND PAST SIMPLE

5 A Read the sentences in Exercise 4A and underline examples of the present perfect and past simple.

B Complete the rules with present perfect or past simple.

RULES

1 Use the ______ to talk about experiences or things that happened before now. The time is not specified or important.
2 Use the ______ to talk about recent events, or an action which started in the past and continues now.
3 Use the ______ to talk about a specific event in the past (we know when the event happened).
4 Use the ______ to talk about an action which started and finished at a specific time in the past.

C Look at the sentences in Exercise 4A again and match them with one of the rules above.

▷ page 70 **LANGUAGEBANK**

6 A Read the text. What changed Chris Gardner's life?

Chris Gardner is a successful businessman and a millionaire. But things [1]______ always ______ (not be) easy. He [2]______ (not meet) his father until he was twenty-eight years old. This experience made him sure about one thing: he was determined to be a good father to his own children. As a young man, Gardner [3]______ (experience) hard times. His wife [4]______ (leave) him, he [5]______ (lose) his job, and at one stage he and his two-year-old son [6]______ (sleep) in train stations and airports. He [7]______ (come) a long way since then. His life changed when he [8]______ (meet) a man driving a red Ferrari and asked him what job he did. The man was a stockbroker, so Gardner asked him out to lunch, and the Ferrari driver introduced Gardner to the world of finance. Since he became successful, he [9]______ (spend) a lot of money helping homeless people, and he [10]______ also (write) books about his experiences. His story was told in the film *The Pursuit of Happyness*, starring Will Smith.

B Complete the text with the correct form of the verbs in brackets.

7 A ▶ 2.4 **WEAK FORMS: *have*** Listen to the pairs of phrases. Notice the difference.

1 I lived / I've lived
2 we met / we've met
3 he decided / he's decided
4 they spent / they've spent

B ▶ 2.5 Listen and write the sentences.

C Listen again and check. Then listen and repeat.

8 A Work in pairs. Student A: write *Have you ever … ?* questions using the prompts in the box below. Student B: turn to page 83.

be on TV/in a newspaper   watch film at an outdoor cinema
do something embarrassing in public   write a poem/story
go to a country on a different continent
collect something as a hobby   see someone commit a crime

B Take turns to ask and answer questions. Try to find five things that you have done and your partner hasn't done.

SPEAKING

9 A Imagine you are going to make a film about your life. Choose five events you would like to include. Write some notes in the film strip below.

B Work in pairs. Take turns to talk about the film of your life.

C Think of three questions to ask your partner about the film of their life. Ask and answer the questions

Why did you choose to … ?
What happened when you … ?
What did you enjoy best about … ?

VOCABULARY *PLUS*

PREPOSITIONS

10 PREPOSITION + EXPRESSIONS OF TIME Complete the word webs with expressions in the box.

Saturday	the weekend	Monday morning	New Year's Day
July	the winter/the summer	the twenty-first century	lunchtime

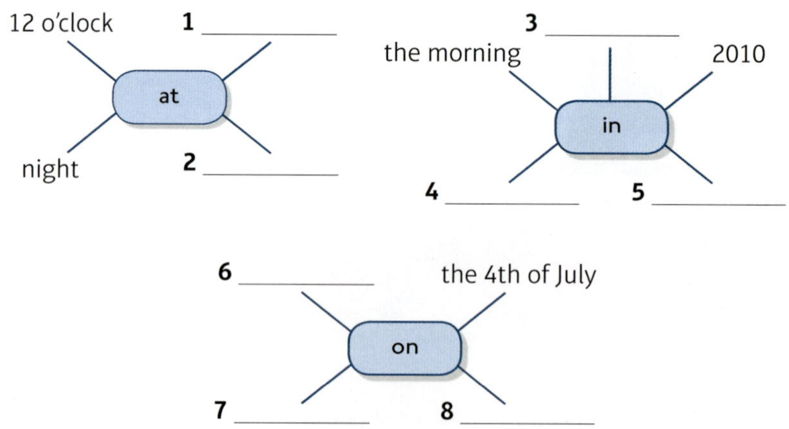

speakout TIP

To help you remember which preposition of time to use, try to memorise this: ***on** Monday; **in** winter; **at** that time.*
on = for specific days, *in* = for time periods, *at* = for specific times

▷ Page 79 **VOCABULARYBANK**

11 PREPOSITION + NOUN Complete the phrases with the correct preposition: *on*, *for* or *by*.

1 It's a book ____ Dan Brown, a film ____ Steven Spielberg, a song ____ Amy Winehouse.
2 I saw it ____ TV. I heard it ____ the radio. I spoke to him ____ the phone.
3 We went ____ a walk, ____ a drive, ____ a run, ____ a swim.
4 They travelled ____ boat, ____ plane, ____ coach, ____ train.

12 A FIXED EXPRESSIONS Match the fixed expressions in bold in sentences 1–10 with meanings a)–j).

1 I dropped it **by mistake**.
2 I saw the film **on my own**.
3 He's here **on business**.
4 We met **by chance**.
5 It was made **by hand**.
6 We got there **in the end**.
7 She said it **on purpose**.
8 We arrived **on time**.
9 I'll do that **in a moment**.
10 They're **in a hurry**.

a) finally
b) cannot wait
c) by a person, not a machine
d) it was not a mistake
e) alone, not with other people
f) not early, not late
g) in a very short time
h) accidentally
i) not on holiday, but for work
j) it was not planned

B Look at Exercise 12A again. Write 6–8 questions with phrases with prepositions.

*Do you usually arrive **on time**, or are you sometimes late?*
*Do you prefer to live with someone, or live **on your own**?*

C Work in pairs. Take turns to ask and answer the questions.

SPEAKING

1 A Discuss the questions.

1 How do you keep up-to-date with the news?
2 What have been the most important stories in the last five years?

B 2.6 Listen to the excerpts from news reports. Which stories can you see in the photos?

READING

2 A Work in pairs. Read the definition and look at the photos below. Then answer the questions.

> **a conspiracy theory:** /kənˈspɪrəsi ˈθɪəri/ a theory or belief that there was a secret plan behind a major event

From Longman Active Study Dictionary.

1 What do you think the conspiracy theories were about (the events in the photos)?
2 Which story do you think involved a real conspiracy, according to official reports?

B Read the article to check your answers.

3 A Read the article again and answer the questions.

1 Who died in their bathroom?
2 Who was shot?
3 Who was arrested?
4 Who was murdered?
5 Who were the suspects?
6 Who was photographed?

B How are these words and phrases related to the stories?

> shadows fans stars painkillers photographs a studio hospital the FBI (Federal Bureau of Investigation) a man with a gun a flag

C Work in pairs. Answer the questions.

1 What do you think? Do you believe the official reports or the conspiracy theorists?
2 Do you know any other conspiracy theories? What happened?

The World's best-known conspiracy theories

Man on the Moon We've seen the photos, but many people claim that Neil Armstrong's 'giant leap for mankind' never really happened. They suspect that the astronauts Neil Armstrong and Buzz Aldrin never left earth, but acted out the scene and took photographs in a studio. Conspiracy theorists say there were strange shadows falling in the photos, and surprisingly no stars are visible. They point out that the US flag, planted by Buzz Aldrin, was apparently waving, although there is no wind on the Moon. However, these doubts can be explained logically. The lighting conditions on the Moon were complicated, and the flag only appears to 'flutter' because the astronauts moved it.

The King is Dead When Elvis Presley was found lying unconscious on his bathroom floor at his home *Graceland*, his family and friends desperately tried to save him. An ambulance was called and Elvis was rushed to hospital where a special room had been prepared for him. However, the 'King of Rock'n'Roll' was already dead when he arrived there. At first, doctors said that Elvis died because his heart had stopped, but later they claimed that drugs were involved. Elvis had taken painkillers because he had toothache and he couldn't sleep. However, for years his fans refused to believe that Elvis was gone, and there were numerous sightings of 'Elvis' around the world. There is even a website elvis-is-alive.com dedicated to finding out the truth.

The Death of a President President John F. Kennedy was assassinated on 22nd November 1963. He was riding through crowds in his car when a gunman shot him once in the head. Lee Harvey Oswald was arrested almost immediately after Kennedy's death, and charged with killing him. He was murdered two days later. A report in 1964 concluded that Oswald had acted alone. But conspiracy theorists have doubts, and believe more people were involved. Suspects include the CIA, the FBI and the Cuban leader Fidel Castro. In 1979, a new report agreed that Oswald had killed Kennedy, but also concluded that the President was killed 'as a result of conspiracy' by unknown people.

GRAMMAR

NARRATIVE TENSES

4 A Read the summary. Find and underline examples of the past simple and the past continuous and answer the questions.

In 1963, President Kennedy and his team were preparing for the next presidential campaign. In Dallas, he was riding through crowds in his car when a gunman shot him.

1 Which tense is used to talk about the main events in a story?
2 Which tense is used to give background information in a story?

B Read the conclusion and answer the questions.

Lee Harvey Oswald was arrested for the crime. A report later agreed that Oswald had killed Kennedy, but also concluded that there had been a conspiracy by a number of unknown people.

1 Which of the underlined verbs is in the past simple?
2 Which of the underlined verbs is in the past perfect?
3 Which tense describes the event(s) that happened first?

C Underline the correct alternative to complete the rule.

RULES	Use the past perfect to talk about actions which happened *before the past time event we are talking about/a very long time ago.*

D 2.7 **WEAK FORMS: *had, was, were*** **Listen to the news summary. Notice how *was*, *were* and *had* are pronounced. Listen again. Try to shadow read the text (read at the same time as the recording).**

were preparing /wə/ not /wɜː/
was riding /wəz/ not /wɒz/
had killed /həd/ not /hæd/

▷ page 70 LANGUAGEBANK

5 Read an account of an important news event. Complete the text with phrases a)–h).

a) He had been in prison
b) one of the branches broke
c) we heard some shots
d) 50,000 people were waiting
e) to hear what Mandela was saying
f) When he finally arrived
g) were talking to each other
h) many people had climbed onto it

11 February 2000: Nelson Mandela's release from prison

I was in the crowd on the parade in Cape Town that day. It was a hot day, and [1]_______ to see Mandela walk free from the prison. [2]_______ for twenty-seven years. At one point [3]_______ but most people stayed calm. People [4]_______ and singing songs. There was a great feeling of solidarity. There was a large tree in the middle of the parade, and [5]_______ to get a better view. Suddenly, [6]_______ and people fell to the ground. But nobody wanted to leave. Nobody wanted to miss the chance of seeing Mandela for the first time. [7]_______ there was a huge cheer. From where I was standing, it was difficult [8]_______ but I knew I was there for an important moment in our history.

VOCABULARY

THE NEWS

6 A Match the headlines 1–8 with the explanations a)–h).

1 Actress survives **crash**
2 Politicians **attacked** by angry crowd
3 Student demonstration turns **violent**
4 Workers to **strike over pay**
5 Massive **earthquake** hits Italy
6 Most wanted **fugitive** arrested
7 Floods **destroy** crops
8 **Hostages** released after talks with rebels

a) Lots of angry people shout and throw things at some politicians.
b) People who were kept as prisoners are allowed to go free.
c) Police catch a man who they suspect committed a serious crime.
d) A natural disaster destroys part of a country.
e) A woman is involved in a car accident but doesn't die.
f) A lot of farmland is under water.
g) Many people might refuse to go to work.
h) People who are protesting begin to fight on the streets.

B Work in pairs. Describe some stories which have recently been in the news using the vocabulary in bold above.

speakout TIP

Headlines can be difficult. They contain incomplete sentences: articles and auxiliaries can be dropped, simple tenses are used instead of continuous or perfect tenses and the infinitive is used to talk about the future. Find examples in the headlines.

▷ page 79 VOCABULARYBANK

SPEAKING

7 A **Choose one of the news stories in the lesson or another important news story. Make notes to answer the questions below.**

1 What was the news story? Where were you when you heard the news?
2 What were you doing? Who were you with?
3 What did you think at first? How did you feel?
4 Did the news change things for you in any way?

B **Work with other students. Tell them about your story.**

WRITING

A NEWS REPORT; LEARN TO USE TIME LINKERS

8 A **Read the news report and answer the questions. Underline the parts of the news report which help you to answer.**

1 Who is the story about?
2 What happened?
3 Why did it happen?
4 Where did it happen?
5 When did it happen?
6 What is the situation now?

Fraud fugitive in Facebook trap

A man who was on the run from police in the US revealed where he was hiding through a series of Facebook updates.

Cameroon-born Maxi Sopo falsely obtained credit from banks while he was living in the US. By the time he had finished, he had stolen more than $200,000. He then escaped to Cancun in Mexico, where he was happily spending the money, until he made posts on his Facebook page telling the world that he was 'living in paradise'.

'He was making posts about how beautiful life is and how he was having a good time with his buddies,' said Assistant US Attorney Michael Scoville. 'He was definitely not living the way we wanted him to be living, given the charges he was facing,' he added.

However, during his time in Cancun, Mr Sopo also befriended a former justice department official on the networking site. This man, who had only met Mr Sopo a few times, was able to discover exactly where Mr Sopo was living. As soon as he had this information, he passed it to the Mexican authorities who arrested Sopo last month.

The twenty-six-year-old is currently in custody in Mexico City.

B **Read the news report again. Find examples of the following:**

1 quotes used to give someone's opinion
2 a concluding statement which gives us information about the current situation
3 an introductory statement which explains in one sentence what happened
4 more information about the background to the story

9 A **Look at the news report and find examples of the time linkers in the box.**

as soon as while during until by the time

B **Look at the words/phrases in the box above. Which time linker do we use to link an action that:**

1 happened previously? _*by the time*_
2 continues up to that point and then stops? ______
3 happens at the same time as another action? ______
4 happens at some point in a period of time? ______
5 happens immediately after something else has happened? ______

C **Complete the sentences with the correct time linker.**

1 I came ______ I heard the news.
2 They arrived ______ we were having dinner.
3 Her cat died ______ the night.
4 We waited ______ the lights had gone out.
5 ______ the fire engines arrived, the house was destroyed.

10 A **Work in pairs. Choose a headline and write six questions asking for information about the story.**

Actress survives crash

Politicians attacked by angry crowd

Man shot outside his house

B **Give your questions to another pair of students.**

C **Look at the questions and use them to write a short news report (100–150 words). Use the ideas in Exercise 8B to help you.**

D **Compare your stories with other students. Who has the best story?**

F telling a story
P intonation: sounding interested
V *say/tell*

VOCABULARY
SAY/TELL

1 A Work in pairs and discuss. How do you know when someone is lying? Do you think their behaviour changes?

B Read the text to check your answers.

How do you know if someone is lying?

From little white lies to lies which can destroy nations, people have lied for as long as they have told the truth. Some people are very good at it. So, how do we know if someone is lying?

Here are the things to look out for

1 The guilty hand: when someone is telling the truth they usually use more body language. They move their hands and their face more. When someone lies, their hands are still.

2 The lying eye: people find it very hard to tell you a lie if they're looking at you straight in the eyes. Normally, they look away just at the moment that they tell the lie.

3 The 'Me': when people tell a story about themselves, they tend to use a lot of 'me' words, like I, me, and my. When they tell a lie, they don't use the 'me' words as much.

2 A Match 1–6 with a)–f) to make sentences.

1 I'm terrible at telling
2 My brother told me
3 I think you should say
4 Sometimes it's better to tell
5 You should just say
6 I said

a) 'hello', but she didn't answer.
b) a white lie than to upset someone.
c) what you mean.
d) a funny story yesterday.
e) sorry.
f) jokes. I always forget the punch line!

B Add the phrases with *say* and *tell* from Exercise 2A to the table.

Say	Tell
'hello'	*a story*

C Work with other students. Do you agree/disagree with the statements? Why?

1 A lie can travel half way around the world while the truth is putting on its shoes.
2 A good storyteller should mix fiction with truth to make their stories interesting.
3 It's OK to tell lies sometimes.

A

FUNCTION
TELLING A STORY

3 A Look at the pictures above which tell a story. They are not in the correct order. What do you think is happening in each picture?

B 2.8 Listen to a woman telling her story. Number the pictures in the correct order.

4 A Look at the phrases we can use to help tell the sequence in a story. Add the sequencers from the box to the correct place in the table.

~~This happened when~~ The next thing I knew
Anyway, In the end, Before long,
And then, all of a sudden

beginning
In the beginning, … *This happened when*
describing what happened
Well, … So, …
ending
So, … Finally, …

B Listen to the story again, and tick the phrases you hear. Check your answers in the audio script on page 88.

▷ page 70 LANGUAGEBANK

5 A Work in pairs. Practise telling the story using the sequencers and the pictures to help you. Start like this:

This happened when the woman had an important interview and …

B 2.9 Do you think the woman was telling a true or false story? Listen to find out.

B

C

D

LEARN TO

SHOW INTEREST

6 A Look at phrases a)–j). Which phrases complete extracts 1–6?

a) what happened then?
b) What did you do?
c) Then what?
d) Oh no!
e) Oh dear.
f) How embarrassing!
g) That's really funny.
h) Really?
i) You're joking!
j) You're kidding!

1 W: So, anyway, erm … I then got on to the tube, um … to go for my interview.
M: Right, and ___*a*___
2 W: I've woken up shouting the word, 'Mum!'.
M: No! ______
3 W: At the top of my voice, in a packed, quiet tube.
M: ______
4 W: … they're looking at me in a rather strange way.
M: Right … ______
5 W: My face had swollen up! … And it was bright red, … and covered in blotches, spots …
M: Oh! ______
6 W: Yes, and the pills that my mother had given me were so out-of-date that they had caused an allergic reaction …
M: Oh! … ______

B 2.10 **INTONATION: sounding interested** Listen and check your answers. Notice how intonation is used to sound interested. Is it high or low?

C Listen again and repeat the phrases. Try to sound interested. Then repeat but try to sound bored. Can you hear the difference?

speakout TIP

When someone tells a story, try to use comments and questions to show that you are interested e.g. *How amazing!* Remember to check your intonation. Do you sound interested?

SPEAKING

7 A Prepare to tell a story. It can be a true story or a lie. Choose one of the situations below. Talk about when you:

- got stuck in a lift
- missed (or nearly missed) a flight
- lost something valuable
- spoke to someone famous
- got a tattoo
- went swimming at night
- were mistaken for someone else
- slept outside
- tried a very dangerous sport
- found something unusual

B Think about the details of your story. Think about the questions below and make some notes or practise telling your story. Try to use some of the sequencers from Exercise 4.

- Where were you?
- Why were you there?
- What were you doing?
- What happened?
- How did you feel?

C Work with other students. Take turns to tell your stories and listen and respond. Ask questions to decide if it is a true story or a lie.

A: *I once got stuck in a lift.*
B: *Really?*
A: *Yes. I was …*

D Tell the other students if it is a true story or a lie.

DVD PREVIEW

1 **Work in pairs. Discuss the questions.**

1 Which famous fictional thieves/investigators/detectives do you know about?
2 Which are famous in your country?
3 Do you watch any crime detective dramas? Which ones? What do you like/dislike about them?
4 What are the features of good detective dramas, e.g. interesting characters?

2 **Look at the pictures and read about the programme. What problems do you think Finch had when he stole the painting?**

Hustle

BBC

Hustle is a BBC drama series about a team of criminals who try to obtain and sell things in an illegal or dishonest way. In this programme we meet Finch, a burglar. He's in trouble with Customs, who believe that he has stolen a valuable piece of art. Unfortunately for Finch, when he stole the painting, things didn't go quite according to plan.

DVD VIEW

3 **A** **Watch the programme. What problems did Finch encounter?**

B **Match the words in the two columns to make common crime collocations. Work with your partner. What do these words mean?**

1 guard	a) thief
2 art	b) guard
3 valuable	c) weapon
4 burglar	d) officer
5 customs	e) dog
6 loaded	f) alarm
7 security	g) painting

C **Tick the things above which you see in the clip. Which of the above do you not see?**

4 **A** **Work in pairs and answer the questions.**

1 How does Finch get into the grounds of the mansion?
2 What is the security guard doing?
3 What does Finch do when he breaks into the house?
4 Why does Finch have to run with the artwork?
5 How does Finch escape?
6 What happens at the airport?
7 Why do customs officers search Finch? Do they find anything?
8 What do customs plan to do?

B **Watch the DVD again to check.**

C **Discuss what you think Finch does next. What do you think will happen?**

speakout a narrative

5 A Work in groups. Look at the pictures. What do you think happened?

B 2.11 Listen to someone telling the story. Do you think the story is true?

C Listen again and tick the key phrases you hear.

KEY PHRASES

This story is about …
The problem was that …
In fact, …
What he didn't realise/know was that …
However, …
Later, …
Because of this, …
In the end, …

6 A Work in pairs. Take turns to retell the story using the key phrases.

B Work in pairs. Student A: look at the picture story on page 84. Student B: look at the picture story on page 85. Use the phrases in Exercise 5C to tell your partner what happens in your story.

writeback a newspaper article

7 A Read about a famous art theft. Who stole the painting? Why did he steal it? What happened in the end?

Famous painting stolen

On 21st August, 1911, Leonardo da Vinci's Mona Lisa, one of the most famous paintings in the world, was stolen from the wall of the Louvre Museum, in Paris. At first, the police thought one of the guards might have stolen the painting, but seventeen days after the theft, they arrested poet Guillaume Apollinaire. However, he was released when police could find no evidence that he had committed the crime. Two years later, the real thief, Vincenzo Peruggia, was arrested in Italy. Peruggia had worked at the museum, and had stolen the painting because he was angry about how many Italian paintings were on display in France. He had planned to return the painting to the Italian Uffizi gallery, in Florence. The public was so excited at the news of finding the Mona Lisa that the painting was displayed throughout Italy before it was returned to France in 1913.

B Write up the story of Finch's art theft as a newspaper article, using the article above and the key phrases to help you.

V TYPES OF STORY

1 A Add the missing letters to complete the types of story.

1 One of my favourite a_ _ _ _ _ films of all time is *The Terminator*.
2 Jamie Foxx stars in *Ray*, a great b_ _ _ _ _ of Ray Charles.
3 *Pretty Woman*, starring Julia Roberts and Richard Gere, is my favourite r_ _ _ _ _ _ _ c_ _ _ _ _.
4 I'm not a great fan of p_ _ _ _ _ d_ _ _ _ _, but I thought this production of *Jane Eyre* was brilliant.
5 I loved the p_ _ _ _ _ _ _ _ _ _ _ - t_ _ _ _ _ _ _, *Silence of the Lambs*, but I found it very scary.
6 I still enjoy Agatha Christie's *Murder on the Orient Express*. It's one of the best ever d_ _ _ _ _ _ _ _ films.
7 I can't watch s_ _ _ _ _ _ f_ _ _ _ _ _ films, like *Star Wars* and *Alien*. I can't stand them.
8 I think d_ _ _ _ _ _ _ _ _ _ _, films like *Nixon*, are a great way to learn about what really happened during important events.

B Choose your three favourite film genres. Find other students who like the same genres and work together to make 'best ever' lists of the films in those genres.

G PRESENT PERFECT AND PAST SIMPLE

2 A Look at the phrases below. Have you done any of these things? Write sentences using *I've ...* , *I haven't ...* and *I have never ...* .

- see a famous band
- ride a horse
- visit another country
- run a marathon
- start a business
- travel on your own
- write a diary/blog
- organise a big family party
- play in a band/write a song
- walk in the mountains/go skiing
- swim with dolphins/go scuba diving
- meet someone famous
- go to university/change your job

B Choose one thing you have/haven't done and tell your partner more about it.

I've played in a band. When I was at university I played in a band called 'The Hooligans'.

G NARRATIVE TENSES

3 A Put the verbs in the correct tense to complete the story.

Sasha [1]____________ (wake) up late because she [2]____________ (forget) to set her alarm clock. She [3]____________ (have) breakfast when the telephone [4]____________ (ring). It was her boss. He wanted to know why she [5]____________ (not finish) the report that he [6]____________ (ask) her to do. She quickly [7]____________ (leave) the house to go to work. She [8]____________ (stand) on the train when she noticed that lots of people [9]____________ (look) at her feet. Then, she [10]____________ (realise) that she [11]____________ (forget) to put her shoes on. She [12]____________ (wear) her slippers.

B Can you remember a day when you woke up late? Why? What happened? Tell your partner.

V THE NEWS

4 A Underline the correct option to complete the headlines.

1 Postal *destroy/strike* causes huge delays
2 Police attacked during student *demonstration/crash*
3 *Fugitives/Hostages* released after negotiation with rebel leader
4 Hundreds homeless after *earthquake/violent* hits
5 *Fugitive/Flood* found hiding in forest
6 Train *strike/crash* kills sixty people
7 House *attacked/crashed* with petrol bomb

B Work in pairs. Choose two or three of the headlines in Exercise 3A. Write mini news stories giving more details about each story.

F TELLING A STORY

5 A Add a word to each speaker's part to correct the conversations.

1 **A:** This *happened* when I was living in Hong Kong.
B: Oh really? happened?
2 **A:** I was having a shower when all a sudden I saw a huge spider.
B: Oh no. What you do?
3 **A:** Anyway, before I knew it someone called the police.
B: Really? What next?
4 **A:** The next I knew, the man was running towards me and shouting.
B: don't believe it!
5 **A:** , anyway I was going up the ski-lift and I fell off.
B: embarrassing!
6 **A:** So, in end, I had to pay all the money back.
B: dear.

B Work in pairs. Choose three of the conversations above and expand the stories.

C Work in groups. Take turns to role-play your conversations.

3 future

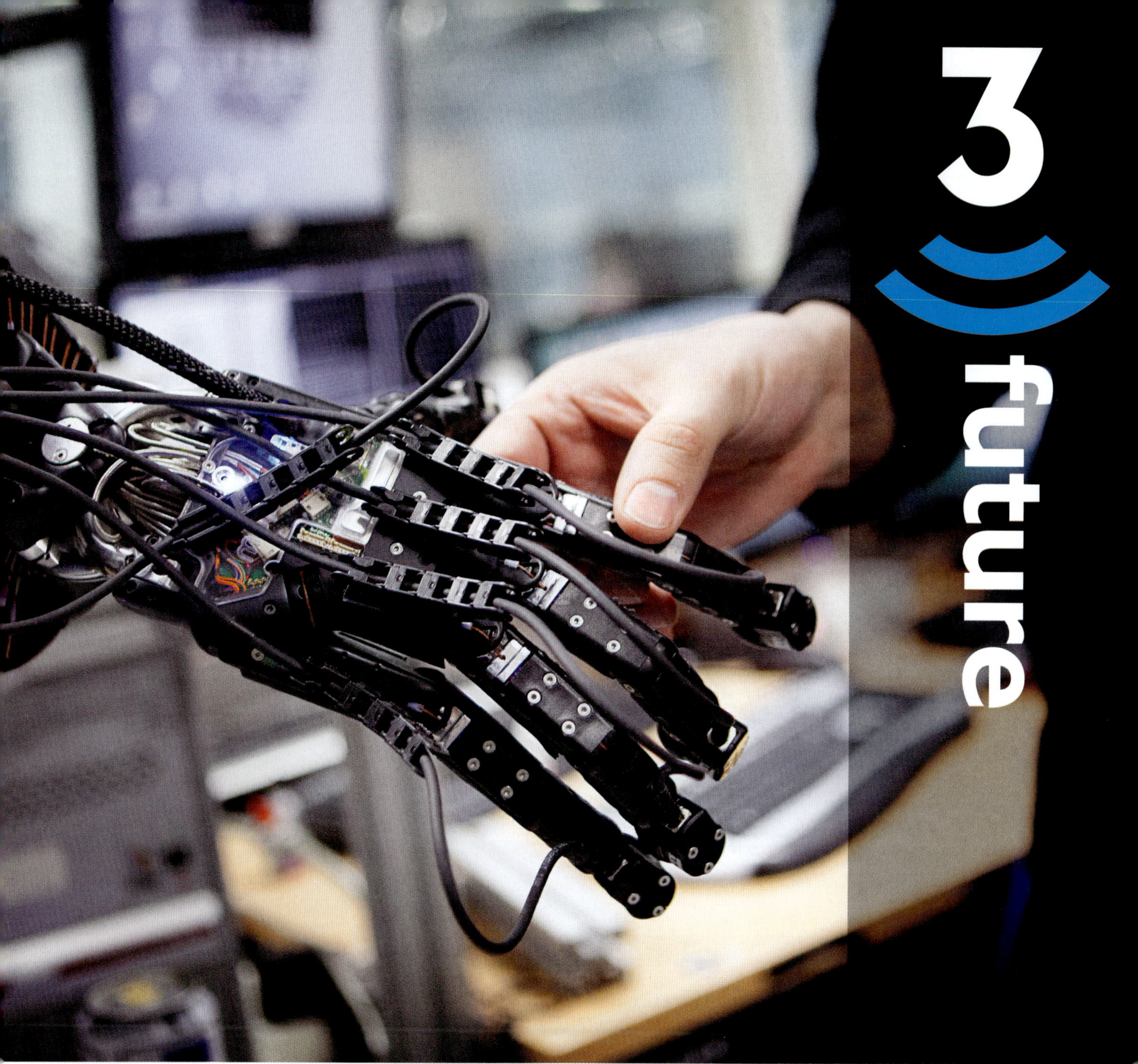

MAKING PLANS p32

TOMORROW'S WORLD p35

IN OTHER WORDS ... p38

YOUTUBE p40

SPEAKING **3.1** Discuss your plans and arrangements **3.2** Talk about predictions **3.3** Explain misunderstandings **3.4** Discuss how to create a video channel

LISTENING **3.1** Listen to people discussing making plans **3.3** Listen to a series of misunderstandings **3.4** Watch a BBC documentary about the rise of YouTube

READING **3.2** Read an article about the future

WRITING **3.1** Write a series of messages **3.4** Write a proposal

BBC INTERVIEWS

Can new technology help communication?

G the future (plans)
P fast speech: *going to*
V organisation

VOCABULARY
ORGANISATION

1 A **Work in pairs. Read the introduction to the questionnaire. Are you a planner or a procrastinator?**

B **In pairs ask and answer questions 1–4 in the questionnaire. Do you have similar answers?**

C **Find phrases in bold to match the definitions below.**

1 not pay attention to the things you are supposed to be doing
2 delay (a job)
3 spend time doing things that aren't important
4 put jobs in order of which is most important
5 do lots of different jobs at the same time
6 complete tasks
7 do jobs just before the time they need to be done
8 do things in advance
9 be careful with your time
10 begin a job

D **Work in groups. Answer the questions.**

1 When was the last time you left something until the last minute?
2 Can you think of a job that you have put off for a while? When do you plan to do it?
3 What do you get distracted by when you're working? How do you try to avoid distractions?
4 Do you think it's a good idea to write to-do lists?

▷ page 80 **VOCABULARYBANK**

LISTENING

2 ▶ 3.1 **Listen to three people discussing the questionnaire. Which of the following topics do they not talk about?**

making plans	holidays	writing lists	work
arrangements for tonight			

3 A **Work in pairs. Can you complete these sentences from the listening?**

1 You generally like to do things ahead of _______.
2 It's the only way to get _______ done.
3 You might need to change your _______, so why bother making plans in the first place?
4 I much prefer to _______ and see what happens.
5 This evening a _______ of mine's coming over.
6 I'm going to try out a new _______ recipe.
7 I'll see how I _______. I might go out, or I might just stay at home and _______.
8 I do get jobs done, but I never get started _______ away.

B **Listen again to check your answers.**

C **Discuss. Who would you prefer to work with, Laurie, Kenna or Javier? Why?**

Are you a planner or a procrastinator?

Do you plan your day or do you prefer to see what happens? A planner will spend the night before work making lists, prioritising, and making sure everything is under control. They arrive early and get started on their first task. A procrastinator, on the other hand, is more likely to arrive at work just in time, with a coffee and breakfast in their hand and a stressed look on their face.

When you have a job to do, or you need to **meet a deadline**, do you:

1 generally **do things ahead of time** or **leave things until the last minute**?
2 prefer to **get started** on a difficult job or **put off** doing difficult jobs until later?
3 tend to **get distracted** easily and **waste time** or do you **use your time wisely** and **get things done**?
4 write to-do lists and **prioritise tasks** or do you prefer to **multitask**?

GRAMMAR

THE FUTURE (PLANS)

4 **Read the conversation and find examples of the structures described below.**

Kenna: This evening a friend of mine's coming over. We're eating at my house – I'm going to try out a new pasta recipe. And then we're going to the cinema to see that new Argentinian film.

Laurie: Javier?

Javier: Uhhh … I don't really know. I'll see how I feel. I might go out, or I might just stay at home and relax. I told you, I really don't like to plan.

RULES

1 Use present continuous to talk about plans or arrangements which have already been made, e.g. *A friend of mine is coming over.*
2 Use *going to* + infinitive without *to* to talk about a plan or intention. You have decided that you want to do this, but you may not have made the arrangements, e.g. ____________
3 Use *might* + infinitive without *to* when you are undecided or not sure what the plan is, e.g. ____________
4 Use *will* + infinitive without *to*, to talk about the future when you have no specific plan, or you make the decision at the time of speaking, e.g. ____________

▷ page 72 **LANGUAGEBANK**

5 **A** 3.2 **Listen and complete the sentences.**

1 What ______ at the weekend?
2 We ______ my brother and his family.
3 Where ______ for them?
4 They ______ a party on Friday.
5 ______ with us tomorrow?
6 I'll ask Marion when she ______ .

B **FAST SPEECH: *going to*** **Listen again. Notice how the speakers sometimes pronounce *going to* /gənə/ in fast speech. Tick the sentences where *going to* is pronounced /gənə/.**

C **Listen again and practise saying the sentences fast.**

What are you going to do at the weekend?

6 **Underline the correct alternatives to complete the conversation.**

Pete: Hey Dax. What [1]*are you two doing/will you two do* on Saturday night?

Dax: I don't know. We [2]*might/will* go to the Death City Dread concert. What about you?

Pete: [3]*I'll have/I'm going to have* a bit of a party. My parents [4]*are going/will go* away for the weekend, so I've asked a few people to come over to my place. Kris [5]*will bring/is bringing* his DJ equipment round, so [6]*we're having/we'll have* music. And everyone [7]*is going to bring/might bring* some food and drink. Euan [8]*will come/is coming* with a few friends. Do you think you can make it?

Dax: It sounds great. [9]*I'm going to text/I'll text* Leyla to ask her what she thinks. Then [10]*I'm calling/I'll call* you back to let you know. Is that OK?

Pete: That's fine. [11]*I'll speak/I'm going to speak* to you later. Bye.

7 **A** **Write sentences for situations 1–6 below. Think about whether you have made arrangements already, then decide which tenses to use.**

1 something you plan to do at the weekend
Some friends are coming to stay. (I've already arranged this.)
I might go out for a pizza on Friday night. (I don't know yet.)
2 something you are going to do after the class
3 something you might buy in the near future
4 something that someone in your family is planning to do
5 a plan or ambition you have, related to your work/studies
6 something that you plan to do for your next holiday

B **Work in pairs. Compare your ideas. Ask and answer questions to find out more information.**

A: My sister's moving to Poland.
B: Really? That sounds exciting. Which city?

SPEAKING

8 A Think about two or three plans or arrangements with other people that you have made recently. Use the questions below to make some notes.

1 What is the plan?
2 Who is involved?
3 How did you communicate to make the arrangements?

B Work in groups. Tell the other students about your plans and how you made the arrangements. Do you have similar or different ways of organising yourselves?

WRITING

MESSAGES; LEARN TO USE NOTE FORM

9 Work in pairs. Look at messages 1–4 and answer the questions.

1 What do you think the relationship is between the writer and the person they're writing to?
2 Are the messages formal or informal?

Leyla
Gone to the dentist.
Be back at 4p.m.
Jen

Pete
Please call Tricia on
07679 437 562 asap
Lucy

Hope you enjoyed
the concert.
Dinner's in the oven.
F x

Can you pick us up
from football tonight?
See you later
Ben + Max

speakout TIP

Leave it out! When we write notes and messages we don't always write complete sentences. We often miss out small grammatical words to make the message shorter.

10 A Look at messages 1–4 in Exercise 9. The words in the box have been left out. Which message do they belong to?

I	We'll	Your	I've	Can you	I'll

B Rewrite messages 1–4 below using fewer words.

1
Are you feeling hungry?
Do you want to meet me
for lunch at Pavarotti's
1p.m.? Rx

2
We're going to see
Elton John in concert.
Would you like me
to book you a ticket?
Tonya

3
Pete called to say that
he won't be able to
come to dinner. Do you
think you could call him
back on 01954 627 823?
Thanks. Jayne

4
I'm really sorry but
I can't come to the
cinema tonight because
I've got too much work
to do. I hope you enjoy
the film.
Bess

11 Write short messages for the situations below.

1 You're going away for the weekend and would like your flatmate to water the plants.
2 You want to invite a classmate to the cinema.
3 You need to apologise to a work colleague for missing a meeting.

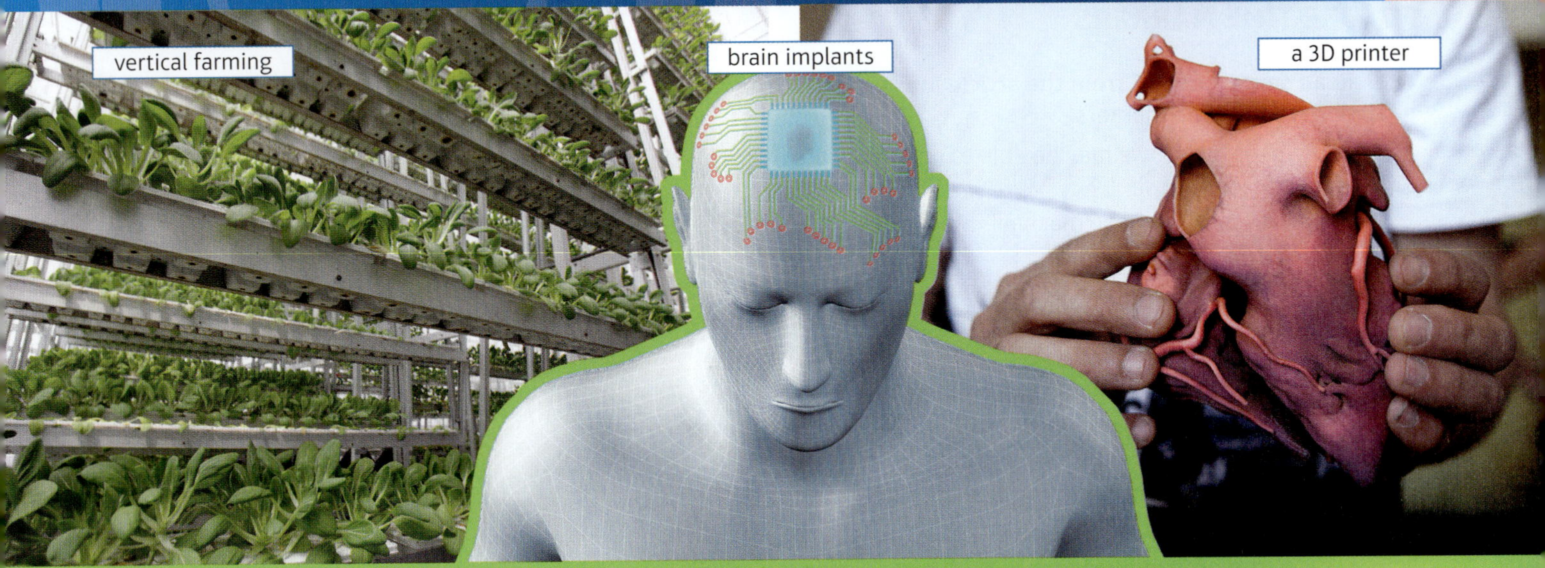

READING

1 Look at the photos and answer the questions.

1 What inventions or developments do the pictures show?
2 How do you think they can benefit people?

2 A Read the article. What does it tell us about the things shown in Exercise 1? What predictions does it make about translating machines and nano monitors?

B Complete the summary of the article with words from the text. Use one word in each gap.

The writer believes a machine will be able to [1]______ our words into different languages. She thinks we'll use monitors in our [2]______ to check our health, and 3D printers will make perfect [3]______ of human organs like the heart. We will entertain ourselves with virtual reality, as computers learn to interact with the [4]______. The problems caused by [5]______ change will mean vertical farming becomes popular.

C Discuss with other students.

1 Which ideas in the article do you like? Can you think of other uses for these inventions?
2 Which ideas don't you like? Why not?
3 Which ideas do you agree will probably come true?

A better world?

Communication

In the near future, we may be able to communicate in any language we choose. A number of companies are working on translating machines that use the voice frequencies of the speaker. This makes it sound as though the user is speaking the foreign language. We already have translating machines, but they are slow and inaccurate and they sound like robots. In only a year or two this new machine, which will be a headset, could come onto the market and allow us to speak every language under the sun.

Health

The future of health is going to be a tale of big and small. Tiny nano monitors will be placed inside our bodies, and these will produce Big Data – enormous amounts of information – that allow us to check our health and help us predict illnesses. Another big development probably won't be ready in the short term, but in the long term there is hope that 3D printers will make copies of body parts such as hearts, livers and kidneys. If it happens, this is likely to save millions of lives. Using 3D printers, we can already make copies of plastic and metal objects. The next step is to copy living tissue.

Entertainment

Full immersion virtual reality will be with us in perhaps ten to twenty years' time. We will be able to plant tiny microchips in the brain, allowing a person to experience games, movies, and virtual life as if they are real. As computers interact with the brain, we will have the sensation of touching, seeing, hearing, and smelling virtual objects in virtual worlds. Instead of just watching heroes in movies, signals to the brain will let us feel what our heroes feel, see what they see. Fortunately, if things get too terrifying, we will be able to switch it off with the push of a button!

Global problems

In the next thirty years, climate change is going to seriously affect traditional farming. Floods and droughts will disrupt farming patterns that have existed for thousands of years. Because of this, cities will have to start producing food, and vertical farming will become common. Tower blocks and skyscrapers will have gardens built into them. Each floor will grow different plants, fruits and vegetables, and the water will be recycled. Instead of stretching out for miles across the landscape, farmland will now rise hundreds of meters into the air.

VOCABULARY

FUTURE TIME MARKERS

3 A Read sentences 1–6 from the article in Exercise 2A and underline the time markers.

1 In the near future, we may be able to communicate in any language we choose.
2 In only a year or two the machine, which will be a headset, could come onto the market …
3 Another big development probably won't be ready in the short term,
4 … in the long term there is hope that 3D printers will make copies of body parts …
5 Full immersion virtual reality will be with us in perhaps ten to twenty years' time.
6 In the next thirty years, climate change is going to seriously affect traditional farming.

B Look at the time markers again. Which of them mean *soon*? Which mean *in a long time*? Which name a future date or time period? Group them.

C 3.3 STRESS IN TIME MARKERS Listen to the underlined expressions in 3A. Which words in these expressions are stressed? Which words are the most important to the meaning of each expression?

D Work in pairs. Ask and answer the questions using both the time markers given.

1 Will you still live in the same place: a) in the near future? b) in ten years' time?
2 What projects will you work on: a) in the short term? b) in the long term?
3 Will your working life/life as a student change: a) in the next five to ten years? b) in a year or two?

GRAMMAR

THE FUTURE (PREDICTIONS)

4 A Read the extracts from the article. Are the predictions certain (C) or possible (P)?

1 We may be able to communicate in any language we choose. *P*
2 In only a year or two, the headset could come onto the market.
3 This is likely to save millions of lives.
4 Climate change is going to seriously affect traditional farming.
5 Tower blocks and skyscrapers will have gardens.

B Look at the underlined words above. Complete the rules with *will*, *could*, *to* or *be*.

RULES

1 We use *will* + infinitive without *to* to make predictions about the future.
2 We use ______ *going to* + infinitive without *to* to make predictions when there is present evidence.
3 We use *may* or ______ + infinitive without *to* to say something is possible but not certain.
4 We use *likely* + infinitive with ______ to say something will probably happen.

page 72 **LANGUAGEBANK**

5 A Circle the correct alternative to complete the text.

Dr Michio Kaku is a physicist who makes TV programmes about the future. He believes we [1]*will be design/will design* new worlds that look like our own, and that virtual reality is [2]*become/going to become* more like our reality. In one programme, Kaku jumps into a remote controlled car, and tells us the car is so intelligent that the words 'traffic jam' and 'traffic accident' [3]*are going to diappear/going to disappear* from the language. He also says that in a few years' time microchips will be so cheap they [4]*are could be built/could be built* into every product we buy – our walls, our furniture, even our clothes. And they [5]*likely/are likely* to be so small we [6]*won't know/won't to know* they exist. Kaku also believes our sunglasses [7]*may become/may becoming* our future home entertainment centre. He then does a virtual dance using 3-D technology (his dance partner is hundreds of miles away) and explains that one day in the near future, 3-D technology [8]*is could replace/could replace* the telephone and [9]*reduce might/might reduce* air travel. Finally, he investigates robots and concludes that, in the long term, some of our closest friends [10]*might not be/might be not* people.

B Discuss. Which predictions, if they come true, will be good/bad for the world? Why?

SPEAKING

6 A Look at the pictures about the world in 2040. What information did you already know? Is there anything you find surprising or unlikely?

B Imagine you are a 'futurist' and it's your job to predict the future. Think about the topics in the box. What changes do you think will happen in these areas by 2040? Make some notes.

communication technology food
work habits cities the environment

C Work in pairs and discuss your ideas.

Communication: I think we will probably have video conference calls with people's holograms. There probably won't be …

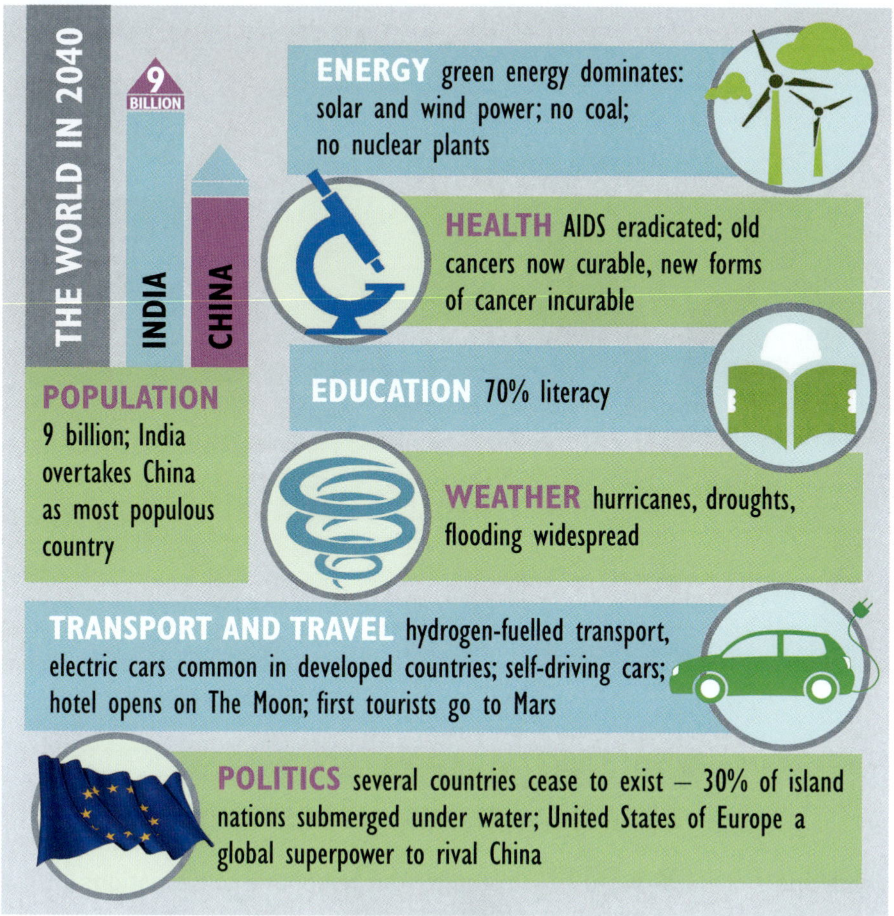

VOCABULARY *PLUS*

IDIOMS

7 A Read comments 1–4. Which of the topics in the images are they referring to?

1 'I like that statistic. I teach reading, so it's an issue that's close to my heart.'
2 'If that statistic is correct, then coastal countries like mine are running out of time.'
3 'This hits the nail on the head: we will eradicate old illnesses, but new ones will develop.'
4 'Let's face it: the world will be completely overcrowded.'

B Read the definition of an idiom and underline the idioms in sentences 1–4.

> **idiom** /ɪdɪəm/ *[C]* a group of words that have a special meaning when they are used together: *'On top of the world'* is an idiom meaning *'very happy'*

From Longman Active Study Dictionary.

C Look at the underlined idioms in Exercise 7A and decide if these statements about idioms are true (T) or false (F)?

1 Idioms are usually formal.
2 You cannot usually change the order of words in an idiom.
3 You can sometimes change the verb tense and the subject of an idiom.
4 You can usually guess the meaning from one word in the idiom.

D Work in pairs and compare your answers. Then turn to page 84 to check your answers.

speakout TIP

Write new idioms in a special place in your vocabulary notebook. Record them in context and add your own examples. Do this for the idioms in Exercises 7 and 8A. Then try them out. Make sure it's the right situation and you use the exact words.

8 Work in pairs. Look at the idioms organised by topic. What do the underlined idioms mean?

Problems
1 We forgot to pay our taxes. Now we're in hot water.
2 I said the wrong thing again. I always put my foot in it.

Time
3 We're working against the clock. We have two hours to finish the project.
4 I'm sure we can win this match but we're running out of time.

9 Look at the idioms organised by key words. Match idioms 1–6 with meanings a)–f).

Body parts
1 Keep an eye on him. *b*
2 Can you give me a hand?

Food and drink
3 It's not my cup of tea.
4 It was a piece of cake.

Animals
5 You're a dark horse!
6 I want to get out of the rat race.

a) I don't like it
b) watch
c) help me
d) the competitive world of work
e) you have a lot of secrets
f) easy

10 A Find and correct the mistakes. There is a mistake in each sentence.

1 When was the last time you gave someone the hand?
2 Which student do you think is a horse dark?
3 When's the last time you put your feet in it?
4 Which issues are close by your heart?
5 Do you often have to work against the clocks?
6 When were you last in warm water?

B Write an answer to each question. Then compare your answers.

▷ page 80 VOCABULARYBANK

3.3 IN OTHER WORDS ...

F dealing with misunderstandings
P linking in connected speech
V misunderstandings

VOCABULARY

MISUNDERSTANDINGS

1 Look at the photos. What is the situation in each one?

2 A Read sentences 1–8 and complete them with phrases a)–h). Which are about future arrangements?

1 When we meet later, make sure you go to the Judd Road in the town centre because ...
2 We mistakenly left home at 5.30 because ...
3 I was expecting to see Pete, my old school friend, but ...
4 I didn't do the homework because ...
5 I organised a party for tomorrow night! I thought her birthday was 6th May but ...
6 I ended up at the wrong house because ...
7 I called Deb to invite her over, but she thought I was a stranger because ...
8 I answered the phone, but ...

a) it was a **wrong number**.
b) I'd got the **wrong address**.
c) we **got the date wrong**.
d) **we thought** it started at 6.
e) **it was a different** Peter Smith.
f) there are two streets **with the same name**.
g) she **didn't recognise** my voice.
h) I **didn't realise** it was for today.

B Which expressions in bold show misunderstandings about: a) people b) places c) times d) someone on the phone?

C Can you remember a misunderstanding in your life about a time, person, place, etc? What happened? Tell other students.

FUNCTION

DEALING WITH MISUNDERSTANDINGS

3 A 3.4 Listen to four telephone conversations involving misunderstandings. What was the misunderstanding in each conversation?

B Listen again and answer the questions.

Conversation 1
1 Who did the woman want to speak to?
2 Who did she speak to?

Conversation 2
3 How did David make his hotel reservation?
4 What hotel does he want to stay in?

Conversation 3
5 What time does the show finish?
6 What time did the show start?

Conversation 4
7 What does the woman want to rent?
8 What is the date?

C Complete expressions 1–7 with the words in the box.

tell	that	me (x2)	saying	mean	name	again

1 I didn't catch any of _______.
2 You've lost _______.
3 Could you repeat the last _______?
4 Can you say that _______?
5 What exactly do you _______?
6 I don't get what you're _______.
7 Do you mean to _______ _______ ... ?

D 3.5 Listen and check. Then listen again and copy the intonation.

page 132 LANGUAGEBANK

4 A Put the underlined words in the correct order to complete B's responses. Use capital letters where necessary.

1 **A:** Oh no! I can't find the key.
B: do say mean to you we're going to be locked out all night?
Do you mean to say

2 **A:** And after Jimmy left Minnie, he married Millie, who used to be married to Billy.
B: lost me you've. Who are all these people?

3 **A:** There was a little accident with the spaghetti bolognese and your sofa.
B: mean exactly what you do?

4 **A:** The boss wants to see you. It's about the money that's missing from the accounts.
B: what don't saying get you're I.

5 **A:** Um, er, I think my new phone number is, um, 654 0987 6743.
B: catch I that any of didn't. What's the number?

6 **A:** My home address is 39 Kings Street, Manchester, Lancashire, M8 2TO.
B: that you say again can? I didn't hear.

7 **A:** We're leaving Los Angeles at 11p.m. OK? Then we arrive in Sydney at 5.50a.m.
B: part you the repeat could last? I didn't hear you.

B Work in pairs. What does speaker A say next? Continue the conversations with your own words.

LEARN TO REFORMULATE

5 A Read the extracts from audio 3.4. Underline five examples of how the speaker reformulates what he/she heard.

1 **A:** We've got no reservations in the name of Cullinan, and we're fully booked tonight.
B: So you're saying I can't stay here. This is the Sheldon Hotel, yes?

2 **C:** Didn't you say it starts at seven?
D: No, it starts at five and finishes at seven!
C: So what you mean is I've missed the whole show.

3 **E:** Yes, but today's a holiday and all the cars have been booked already.
F: Do you mean to tell me that there's nothing at all? No cars available?
E: There's nothing till tomorrow, I'm afraid.
F: But I definitely booked a car for today, the third of July.
E: It's the fourth of July today. In other words, your booking was for yesterday.

B 3.6 **LINKING IN CONNECTED SPEECH** Listen to the phrases. Notice how the words are linked together in fast speech.

So‿you're‿saying …

C Listen again and repeat the phrases.

SPEAKING

6 A Work in pairs and role-play the situation.

Student A

You are a guest at a hotel. Twenty minutes ago you called reception, asking for some soap to be sent to your room. Room service brought you some tomato soup. You want them to take the soup back and bring some soap. Call reception to make your complaint.

Student B

You are a receptionist at a hotel. A guest calls to make a complaint. Start the conversation by saying *'Reception. How can I help you?'*

Hello. Yes, I'm afraid I have a problem … Explain the problem.

Apologise for the misunderstanding and say you will send someone with soap.

Check details and thank the receptionist for their help.

Confirm details, apologise again and end the call.

B Change roles and turn to page 84.

C Work in pairs and take turns. Student A: ring reception and make a complaint. Student B: apologise and offer a solution. Use the flow charts to help and role-play the situations.

DVD PREVIEW

1 A Read six opinions about YouTube. What do the words in bold mean?

1 I love YouTube because the **creators** of the videos are often normal people like us, the **consumers**.
2 The thing I hate about YouTube is the **adverts**, especially when you can't skip them.
3 The **audience** for some YouTube videos may be bigger than for some TV programmes.
4 Most of the **content** on YouTube is terrible. The filming **techniques** are low quality.
5 I don't go on YouTube that much and I'd never **subscribe** to a YouTube channel.
6 Making good quality YouTube videos requires a big **investment** of time and money.

B Work in pairs and discuss statements 1–6 above. Which ones do you agree with?

2 Read the programme information. What is it about? Who does the presenter speak to?

BBC

The Culture Show YouTube: The Future of TV?

This BBC documentary looks at the rise of YouTube and finds out what the company is doing to improve its online content. Jacques Peretti goes into the YouTube office and talks to some of the young creators who are changing the entertainment industry.

DVD VIEW

3 Watch the DVD. What is YouTube doing to improve its online content?

4 A Watch the DVD again and complete the fact file.

VALUE:	$1,000,000,000
FOUNDED:	in [1] ______.
CREATORS:	for some, YouTube is a full-time job
MAKING MONEY:	YouTube invites popular creators to put [2] ______ on their videos.
STUDIO:	creators with 50,000 [3] ______ can use the studio.
BIGGEST STUDIO:	'Deep Focus'
CRITICISM OF BUSINESS MODEL:	[4] ______ think content should be free.

B Work in pairs. Answer the questions.

1 Who has 'some of the biggest audiences in Britain'?
2 Who makes more money: YouTube video creators or TV programme makers?
3 What kind of techniques do creators learn in the YouTube studios?
4 What will 'a better quality of content' bring for YouTube?
5 What does Andrew Keen say about the internet and 'the creative community'?

C Watch the DVD again to check your answers.

5 Discuss in groups.

1 Do you think the DVD clip is positive or negative about YouTube, or is it balanced?
2 What do you think of the type of short clips ('kids messing around in their bedrooms') in the programme?
3 Do you think that YouTube is 'the future of TV'? Do you think it will become more popular than mainstream TV or is it only aimed at young people?

speakout create a video channel

6 A You are going to create your own video channel. Think about the points below. Is there any other important information you should consider?

- name of channel
- type of video clips
- target audience
- what's special about the channel
- who will star in the videos
- competitors/rivals
- how frequently you will upload new videos

B 3.7 Listen to two people planning a new YouTube channel. What do they say about each of the points in Exercise 6A?

C Listen again and tick the key phrases you hear.

KEYPHRASES

The first thing [I think] is …
We came up with this idea.
It would be really [cool/interesting/fun] to …
What's the angle?
So the target audience is …
Who will be the presenters?
Who are our competitors or rivals?
How often will we upload new videos?
What about a name?

7 A Work in groups. Think of an idea for the task in Exercise 6A. Make sure you discuss all the points and take notes.

B Work with another group and take turns to present your ideas. What are the advantages and disadvantages of each idea?

writeback a proposal

8 A A new company is looking for funding to make videos. Read the company's proposal. Do you think it will get funding? Why?/Why not?

FUTURE SHOCK VIDEOS

We are looking for funding to make exciting and innovative videos about a topic that is close to everyone's heart: the environment. In the long term there will be big changes to the natural world including floods and major earthquakes. As a group of environmental scientists, we intend to predict the effects of these changes and, ultimately, to help prevent them.

We will combine straight reporting, docudrama and science fiction. The videos will be presented by some of the nation's leading scientists and thinkers, as well as actors. We will upload new videos once a month.

Our target audience is anyone interested in how the world will look in the next 30–100 years. It could be other scientists, students or anyone from the general public.

We thank you for your attention and look forward to hearing from you soon.

James Toffler

Please see the attachment for funding scales and further details of our financial plan.

B Use the sentence openers below to write a proposal for your idea from Exercise 7A. Invent any additional details you want to.

We are looking for …
We intend to …
The videos will be presented by …
We will upload new videos …
Our target audience is …
We thank you for …

C Work with a different group from the one you worked with in Exercise 7B and exchange proposals. Do you think the other group's proposal is worth funding? Why?/Why not?

3.5 ((LOOKBACK

Ⓥ ORGANISATION

1 A Complete the sentences with words from the box.

wisely ahead minute time prioritise multitask off distracted done started deadline

1 It's late. I really think we should get ______.
2 Why do you always have to leave things until the last ______?
3 Sorry, I got ______ by the football on the television.
4 You've got so many things to do. You'll have to ______ and start with the most important.
5 I worked hard and got a lot of things ______ this morning.
6 I'm afraid they're just wasting your ______.
7 I'd like to get this done ______ of time, so we can go on holiday.
8 I keep putting ______ writing my essay.
9 I'm going to have to stay up all night or I'll never meet the ______ for this work.
10 We won't be here for long, so use your time ______.
11 I think it's better not to ______ but to focus on doing one job at a time.

B Work in pairs. Choose two or three of the phrases from Exercise 1A and use them to make short dialogues.

A: We need to get a lot of things done, but we don't have much time.
B: Right. We'd better get started.

Ⓖ THE FUTURE (PLANS)

2 A Complete the paragraphs with phrases from the box.

'm going to have having 'm organising might 'm finishing are going I'll be are coming will going to

I [1]______ work at the end of the month. I've been a teacher here for nearly twenty years, so [2]______ sad when I leave the school for the last time. But in the future, I [3]______ more time to do some of the things I enjoy. My wife and I [4]______ travelling. We [5]______ visit Australia, which I've always wanted to do.

I'm [6]______ be forty next month, so I'm [7]______ a big party. Lots of people [8]______ that I don't see very often, so I'm really looking forward to it. I [9]______ a band, and lots of delicious food and drink, so everyone [10]______ have a good time.

B Write a short paragraph describing a plan you have for the future. Then compare your ideas with a partner.

Ⓥ FUTURE TIME MARKERS

3 A Choose the correct ending in each case, a) b) or c).

1 I might live in *a foreign country* in the long a) time b) term c) days.
2 I hope to *be retired* in twenty years' a) future b) ahead c) time.
3 I will finish *this course* in a month a) or two b) coming c) time.
4 I hope to *write my autobiography* a long time a) ago b) ahead c) from now.
5 I want to buy *a new car* in the near a) time b) future c) term.
6 I'm going to *go travelling* next a) year b) years c) future.

B Choose four of the sentences above. Change the words in italics so they are true for you.

Ⓖ THE FUTURE (PREDICTIONS)

4 A Find and correct the grammatical mistakes. One sentence is correct.

1 Man not will fly for fifty years. (1901)
2 There isn't going be any German reunification this century. (1984)
3 Democracy will to be dead by 1950. (1936)
4 By 1980 all power (electric, atomic, solar) is likely be almost free. (1956)
5 The Japanese car industry isn't likely to be successful in the US market. (1968)
6 Man will be never reach the Moon. (1957)
7 Television won't very matter in your lifetime or mine. (1936)
8 The internet may to become useful for business but never for the general public. (1989)

B Change the verbs so they mean the opposite and become intelligent predictions. You may need to change some other words.

Man will fly within fifty years

Ⓕ DEALING WITH MISUNDERSTANDINGS

5 A Complete B's responses using the words in the box.

lost mean to say saying don't do

1 **A:** I've heard that a lot of our employees like you.
B: I [1]______ get what you're [2]______.
A: And I'm looking for someone to take over the business when I retire.
B: What exactly [3]______ you [4]______?

2 **A:** David Johnson and Johnny Thomson are going to meet Tommy Davies tonight.
B: You've [5]______ me.
A: Johnson, Thomson and Davies are the company directors. They're meeting to discuss the company's future.
B: Do you mean [6]______ [7]______ they're meeting without me?

B Work in pairs. Write a dialogue that uses three of the phrases in Exercise 5A. Act out your dialogues.

4 Jobs

MILLIONAIRES p44

DREAM JOB p47

THAT'S A GOOD IDEA p50

GAVIN AND STACEY p52

SPEAKING **4.1** Discuss how important becoming a millionaire is for you **4.2** Talk about past habits **4.3** Participate in a meeting **4.4** Describe a day in your life

LISTENING **4.2** Listen to people describing dream jobs gone wrong **4.3** Listen to people making decisions in a meeting **4.4** Watch a BBC comedy about a man's first day in a new job

READING **4.1** Read an article about millionaires **4.2** Read a covering letter

WRITING **4.2** Write a covering letter **4.4** Write about your daily routine

BBC INTERVIEWS

Is your job a 'dream job'?

VOCABULARY

PERSONAL QUALITIES

1 A Read about the qualities people need to do their jobs. Which jobs do you think they are talking about?

"Winning is the most important thing for me. I've always been **competitive**, so I love my job. I think I'm **a good leader**. It's important that all the players know what they're doing and it's my job to tell them. The decisions I make are important for the whole team, so I can't be **indecisive**."

"I have classes of 80 to 100 children so I have to be **hard-working**. I do my best, because education is so important for the children. You need to be **a good communicator** in my job, so that you can get the children interested in what they have to learn. Often, we don't have very many resources, so we also need to be creative and be able to **think outside the box**."

"I'm **a risk taker**, so starting my own business wasn't difficult for me. I've always been very **motivated** and **ambitious**. I start work at 4.30a.m. every day. I don't enjoy sleep. You can't afford to be lazy if you want to make money."

B Match the words and phrases in bold above with the definitions 1–9.

1 work with a lot of effort ______
2 have problems making a decision ______
3 think differently or in a new way ______
4 want to be more successful than others ______
5 want to be successful or powerful ______
6 want to achieve somethng because it's interesting or exciting ______
7 person who does things which are dangerous ______
8 person who has the qualities to manage a group of people ______
9 person who can express ideas or feelings clearly to others ______

C Which qualities do you think you have? Work in pairs and compare your answers.

▷ page 81 VOCABULARYBANK

READING

2 A Which of the personal qualities discussed in Exercise 1 do you think are qualities you need to become a millionaire?

B Are the statements 1–6 about millionaires true (T) or false (F)?

1 Most millionaires are born rich.
2 Millionaires think that money is more important than love or marriage.
3 They work more than sixty hours a week.
4 They don't like to work when they're on holiday.
5 They do well at school and usually go to university.
6 They like spending money on designer goods.

C Read the article and check your answers.

D Work in pairs. Do you agree with the article? Do any of the facts surprise you? Why?

"You don't have to be born rich to be a millionaire"

1 So you want to be a millionaire, but have you got what it takes? To find out what millionaires are really like and what motivates them, the BBC programme *Mind of a Millionaire* did a survey. Psychologists looked at self-made millionaires to try and understand what qualities are needed to make a million. So, what is really important to a millionaire?

2 The answer, not surprisingly, is money, money and more money. Money is more important than love or marriage. And if you give a millionaire money, they won't spend it, they'll invest it to make more money. But you don't have to be born rich to be a millionaire. Most millionaires come from relatively poor backgrounds. And you don't have to work hard at school either. A lot of successful entrepreneurs were lazy at school and didn't get good results. However, you must have a clear idea of what you want to do (get rich) and you really ought to start early. A lot of millionaires left school early, to start their own businesses.

3 If you want to be a millionaire, not only do you have to work hard, but you should enjoy your work. And you shouldn't take too many holidays. Most millionaires work more than sixty hours a week. Half stay in contact with the office while they're on holiday and fourteen percent of them refuse to switch off. Having a good work-life balance is fine for people who only want to be moderately successful, but if you're really ambitious, you have to put in the hours.

4 What are millionaires like as people? The survey found that they are competitive, they like taking risks, and they are aggressive and self-confident. They'll do anything they can to get what they want.

5 Millionaires can break all sorts of rules. The only thing they mustn't do is break the law. Surprisingly, most millionaires are careful spenders. They prefer Gap to Gucci. Many of them choose not to spend money on expensive designer clothes – they would rather find a bargain on the high street. And they don't spend lots of money on expensive meals in restaurants either. They prefer to eat at home. However, they do like to drive Mercedes and go on at least three expensive holidays a year. One last thing: millionaires don't care what other people think of them. So, if you want to be a millionaire, you shouldn't worry about what other people think of you. Just do your own thing.

3 A **Underline words or phrases in the article that match meanings 1–6.**

1 their family didn't have much money (paragraph 2)
2 they never stop thinking about work (paragraph 3)
3 having enough time for work and for the things you enjoy (paragraph 3)
4 work long hours (paragraph 3)
5 find something for a good price (paragraph 5)
6 do what you want without worrying about what other people think (paragraph 5)

B **Work in pairs. Choose two or three of the expressions. Use them to make sentences about yourself, or people you know.**

GRAMMAR

MUST/HAVE TO/SHOULD (OBLIGATION)

4 A **Match the words in bold in sentences 1–6 with the meanings a)–e). One meaning matches with two sentences.**

1 You **don't have to** be born rich to be a millionaire.
2 If you want to be a millionaire, you **have to** work hard.
3 You **must** have a clear idea of what you want to do.
4 You **should** enjoy your work.
5 You **shouldn't** take too many holidays.
6 You **mustn't** worry about what other people think of you.

a) It's a good idea.
b) It's not necessary. You don't need to be/do this.
c) It's necessary. You have no choice.
d) It's important that you don't do this.
e) It's not a good idea.

B ▷ 4.1 **FAST SPEECH: *have to*** **Listen to the pronunciation of *have to* /hæftə/ in fast speech. Listen and repeat the sentences.**

▷ page 74 **LANGUAGEBANK**

5 A **Make sentences with the prompts. Use the positive or negative form of the word in brackets.**

1 postmen / get up early in the morning (have)
Postmen have to get up early in the morning.
2 window cleaners / be afraid of heights (must)
3 nurses / be patient and care about other people (should)
4 businessmen often / travel a lot (have)
5 politicians / do their job because they want fame (should)
6 teachers / enjoy working with children (must)
7 doctors / train for several years before they can work (have)
8 teachers / work in the school during the holidays (have)
9 police officers / good communicators / be (have)

▷ page 81 **VOCABULARYBANK**

B **Work in pairs. Think about three different jobs. Make sentences to describe what qualities are/aren't important for these jobs. Read your sentences to your partner. Can they guess which job it is?**

A: *These people have to be motivated. They should be good communicators, especially when talking to children. And they have to be very patient.*
B: *Teachers?*

SPEAKING

6 A Work in pairs. Do the quiz. Then check your score on page 85.

B Discuss. How many of the questions did you answer like a millionaire? Do you agree with the results on page 85? Is getting rich something which concerns you? Why?/Why not?

VOCABULARY *PLUS*

CONFUSING WORDS

7 Read the vocabulary notes and complete sentences 1 and 2.

> **job • work**
>
> **Work** is what you do to earn money:
> *What kind of **work** does he do?*
>
> A job is the particular type of work that you do:
> *Sam's got a **job** as a waiter.*
>
> **Job** can be plural, but **work** cannot.

1 I've finished my degree, so I'm looking for a ______.
2 It's not easy to find ______ when you're my age.

8 A Underline the correct alternative in the sentences below. What is the difference between these words?

1 He suddenly *remembered/reminded* that he had to go to the bank.
2 I have to call my boss later. Can you *remember/remind* me?
3 I've *forgotten/left* my keys in the car. I really should get them.
4 Did you *hear/listen* that noise?
5 Can you say that again? I'm sorry, I wasn't *listening/hearing*.
6 Being ill on holiday isn't much *fun/funny*.

B Turn to page 160 to check your answers.

▷ page 81 **VOCABULARYBANK**

speakout TIP

To help you remember confusing words and vocabulary, write them in personalised sentences in your notebook. Write sentences about your life using some of the words from Exercise 8.

9 A Complete questions 1–6 with a suitable word from Exercises 7 and 8.

1 What are the best paid ______ in your country?
2 Is there anything you often ______, like phone numbers or someone's name?
3 If you ______ carefully, what noises can you hear at the moment?
4 Do you write notes to ______ yourself about important things?
5 How much did you ______ for your first job? What did you buy?
6 What do you like doing for ______ ? Do you like playing games?

B Work in pairs. Take turns to ask and answer the questions above.

HAVE YOU GOT WHAT IT TAKES TO BE A MILLIONAIRE?

Do you answer these questions like a millionaire would?

1 Would you like to be …
- a) a bit richer
- b) a lot richer
- c) mega rich

2 If you wanted a pair of shoes that you couldn't afford, would you …
- a) buy them anyway
- b) wait until the sales and risk losing them
- c) walk away

3 How many credit cards do you carry with you?
- a) One or none
- b) Two
- c) More than two

4 If you could just afford to pay for it, would you splash out on …
- a) a heated swimming pool
- b) a racehorse
- c) a big party for all your friends

5 Do you most enjoy stories about …
- a) romance
- b) adventure
- c) mystery

6 Do you check that your bill is correct after a meal out?
- a) Yes
- b) No
- c) Only if I'm alone

7 What is 9 multiplied by 8?
- a) Did you get the answer right instantly?
- b) Or only after doing little sums in your head?
- c) Did you get the wrong answer?

8 If a favourite relative left you a watch that was not your style, would you …
- a) sell it
- b) keep it to sell on a rainy day
- c) keep it to help you remember them

DREAM JOB

G *used to, would*
P intonation: emphasis; linking: *used to*
V extreme adjectives

4.2

LISTENING

1 **Work in pairs. Look at the photos and answer the questions.**

1 What are these jobs? Would you like to do them? Why?/Why not?
2 What is your idea of a dream job?

2 A 4.2 **Listen to people talking about their dream jobs. Match the speaker to the photos.**

B **What problem does each speaker talk about?**

C **Listen again and answer questions 1–8. Write Nicola (N), Luca (L) or Amy (A).**

1 Who had a boss who worked in the media?
2 Who worked for a big company?
3 Who spent a lot of time by the sea as a child?
4 Who had to try and invent new ideas for the job?
5 Who decided to do this job because they saw someone else doing it?
6 Who had a different job in the summer and in the winter?
7 Who had a difficult relationship with their boss?
8 Who started to find their job boring?

D **Check your answers by reading audio script 4.2 on page 90.**

A Amy

B Nicola

C Luca

VOCABULARY

EXTREME ADJECTIVES

3 **Find the extreme adjectives in bold in audio script 4.2 on page 90. Match them to the gradable adjectives below.**

1 good: wonderful, amazing, ______
2 bad: awful, ______
3 big: enormous
4 small: tiny
5 tasty: ______
6 hot: ______
7 cold: freezing
8 tired: exhausted
9 angry: ______
10 interesting: ______
11 pretty: ______
12 difficult: ______

4 A **Complete conversations 1–6 with extreme adjectives.**

1 **A:** The food here tastes so good.
B: Yes, it's ______.
2 **A:** It's over thirty degrees outside today.
B: I know. It's absolutely ______.
3 **A:** Was your girlfriend angry about you being late?
B: Yes, she was really ______.
4 **A:** The view of the lake is really pretty.
B: Yes, it's ______, isn't it?
5 **A:** Do you find the job interesting?
B: I think it's absolutely ______.
6 **A:** It's hard to understand what he's saying.
B: I know. It's ______.

B 4.3 **INTONATION: emphasis** **Listen and mark the stress on the adjectives. Notice how speaker B emphasises the stressed syllable in their intonation.**

C **Listen again and shadow speaker B's response.**

GRAMMAR

USED TO, WOULD

5 A Read the texts. What did the children dream of doing? Have they achieved their dreams?

Childhood dreams

When I was young, I spent afternoons imagining that I had my own rocket ship. I would invite my cousins and my friends to join my crew, and we would lie on our backs inside a very large cardboard box and go through a countdown, blast off into space, spend the whole day exploring other planets, and be back in time for dinner. So that was sort of the beginning – my earliest memories of being fascinated by space.

Chang Diaz, rocket scientist

We used to live in France, and as a child, I always used to collect small insects that I found in the fields near my house. One day I found a butterfly. It couldn't fly, so I put it in a jar and looked after it. The next morning, when I opened the jar, the butterfly opened its wings and flew away. That was when I realised what I wanted to do with my life.

Lowri Davies, veterinary surgeon

B Look at the underlined words in sentences a)–d) and match them with rules 1–3.

a) I would invite my cousins and my friends to join my crew.

b) We used to live in France.

c) I always used to collect small insects.

d) One day I found a butterfly.

RULES

1 Use the past simple, not *used to* or *would*, to talk about specific events in the past. _______

2 Use *used to* or *would* to talk about a past habit. You can also use the past simple. _______ and _______

3 Use *used to* to talk about a past state. You cannot use *would* to talk about a past state. _______

▷ page 74 **LANGUAGEBANK**

6 A Complete the texts. Where possible, use *would*. Where neither *used to* or *would* are possible, use the past simple.

It's every young girl's dream to be an actress when she grows up. I [1]______ (love) watching beautiful actresses on television. I was so sure that was what I wanted to do that I [2]______ (practise) my Oscar speech in front of the mirror in the bathroom. I [3]______ (use) a shampoo bottle instead of a microphone, and I [4]______ (thank) all my family and friends, even my three cats, for helping me!

My family [5]______ (live) in Sheffield, just near the football stadium, so as a child, I [6]______ (go) to football matches most weekends. I remember the first match I went to, my granddad [7]______ (take) me. I was very young, and I had never seen so many people in one place at one time. It was quite frightening, and I don't think I [8]______ (watch) the game very much. But I remember that we won, and the crowd went crazy. After that, every week I [9]______ (ask) Granddad if he had tickets, and usually he did.

B ▶ 4.4 **LINKING: *used to*** Listen and repeat. Notice the pronunciation of *used to* /juːstə/. Practise saying the sentences.

1 I used to play football when I was a kid.
2 I used to practise every day.
3 We used to live in London.
4 I didn't use to like classical music.
5 My father used to take me fishing.
6 I used to ski, but now I snowboard.
7 We used to go to the cinema a lot.

C Did you use to do any of the things mentioned above? Tell your partner.

SPEAKING

7 Work in pairs and discuss.

1 What were your childhood dreams? Have you achieved them?
2 Did you have any interests or hobbies in the past which relate to your life (job/studies) now? What were they?
3 How have your ideas, opinions, hobbies, etc., changed? (Think about food you liked/hated as a child, television programmes you enjoyed etc.) Are there any things that you used to do, which you don't do now? Why did you stop? Would you do these things again?

As a child, I always used to dream about being an artist …

WRITING

A COVERING LETTER; LEARN TO ORGANISE YOUR IDEAS

8 **Read the text below and answer the questions.**

1 What kind of person would be good at this job?
2 Would you like to do this job? Why?/Why not?

Would you like to travel the world staying in some of the world's top holiday resorts for free? A luxury travel company is looking for a reviewer to try out top hotels and holiday resorts for one year. The lucky applicant will be expected to stay in a variety of locations that include Caribbean islands, waterside hotels in Venice, and some of the world's top ski destinations, as well as Las Vegas and Buenos Aires. They will be expected to write about their experiences on the company blog. No formal qualifications are needed. However, the successful applicant will be sociable, have great communication skills and, of course, a passion for travel.

9 **A** **Read the covering letter. Do you think this person would be good for the job? Why?/Why not?**

1 Dear Matthew Ray,

2 I'm writing to you regarding your advertisement for a professional travel reviewer which I saw on www.findajob.com. I would like to submit an application for the position. Please find my CV attached.

3 As an experienced travel blogger who has spent the last five years travelling around the world, I believe that I meet all the requirements you outline in your advertisement.

Good communicator with excellent language skills: As a regular travel blogger, over the last few years, I have built and maintained a wide audience of readers. I have also published newspaper and magazine articles and given radio interviews about my travel experiences. I am fluent in English and French, and also speak a little Russian.

Interest in travel and tourism: In addition to my own travels, I worked for six months for a tour bus company in Australia, where I had hands-on experience of tour guiding.

Proven ability in website management: As well as maintaining my own website, consisting of a journal and video weblog, with up-to-date photos and stories of my travels, I have helped to manage the website for a youth hostel in Ireland.

4 If you require any further information, or would like to arrange an interview, please call me on 07788658429 or email me at mjdaley@yahoo.com. I look forward to hearing from you at your earliest convenience.

5 Yours sincerely,

Megan Daley

B **Is the wording of the letter formal or informal? Find examples of expressions which tell you this.**

C **Underline phrases in the letter which match meanings 1–6.**

1 about (paragraph 2)
2 I want to apply for the job (paragraph 2)
3 I think I would be good for the job (paragraph 3)
4 practical experience of doing the job (paragraph 3)
5 I have shown that I am able to do this (paragraph 3)
6 as soon as you have the opportunity (paragraph 4)

D **Underline any other useful phrases.**

10 **Match the parts of the letter 1–5 with notes a)–e).**

Preparing a covering letter

A What qualities are they looking for? Write three to four points that show you have these qualities. Use the same words as they use in the advertisement.

B Address your letter to an individual. Only use 'Dear Sir/Madam' when you can't find out the recipient's name.

C Finish with a call to action. What is going to happen next? Are you going to call them or should they call you?

D Explain why you are contacting them. What is the job? Where have you seen it?

E Use 'Yours sincerely' if you know their name or 'Yours faithfully' if you don't

11 **Look at the job advertisements on page 86 and write a covering letter for one of the jobs. Use the sample letter and useful phrases to help you.**

4.3 THAT'S A GOOD IDEA

F reaching agreement
P sentence stress
V business

VOCABULARY

BUSINESS

1 A Work in pairs. Discuss. Would you consider starting your own business? What kind of business would you start? Is there anything stopping you from doing it?

B Complete the questions with words from the box.

fired salary work compete runs idea interview charge

1 Do you know anyone who ______ their own company?
2 Have you ever been in ______ of a team of people?
3 Have you ever been out of ______?
4 When did you last go for a job ______?
5 Have you ever had to ______ with others for a job?
6 Which jobs earn a high ______?
7 What kinds of things does someone have to do to get ______ from their job?
8 Can you think of reasons why a business ______ might fail?

C Take turns to ask and answer the questions above.

FUNCTION

REACHING AGREEMENT

2 4.5 Listen to a team having a meeting to decide how to set up a new café business. Write some notes about their decisions.

Setting up a new café:
Type of food? Name? Location?

3 A Look at the phrases in the table. Listen to the conversation again and tick any of the phrases you hear.

Giving opinions
I (really) feel that … The way I see things, … The way I see it, …
Commenting on other opinions
I (don't) see what you mean. Exactly! I'm not sure that I agree, actually. ✓ I'm not sure (that's a good idea). I'm not sure about that. I think that's a great idea. That's a good point. That sounds good. That's OK by me.
Suggestions
What about … ? / How about … ? Let's focus on … I suggest we think about … I think we should think about … How about if we (call it) … ? Why don't we (call it) … ?

B Check your answers in the audio script on page 90.

▷ page 74 **LANGUAGEBANK**

4 A Put the words in the correct order to make sentences and questions.

1 decide / I / on / name / we / think / a / should
2 good / a / that's / point
3 you / see / mean / what / I
4 suggest / location / the / on / I / focus / we
5 fine / that's / me / by
6 sure / I'm / that / agree / not / I
7 we / about / don't / it / why / think / ?
8 business / a / the / about / what / for / name / ?

B 4.6 **SENTENCE STRESS** Listen to the phrases. Which words are stressed?

C Listen again and repeat.

LEARN TO
MANAGE A DISCUSSION

5 A Complete the underlined phrases for managing a discussion.

1 First of ________ we need to decide on the location.
2 Let's ________ on the ideas we had for the location.
3 So, moving on to the next ________ , what kind of food are we going to serve?
4 ________ recap: a Portuguese café selling cakes and lunches, located near the station.
5 I think we need to come ________ to the type of café we're establishing.
6 Let's ________ up what we've decided.

B 4.7 Listen and check your answers.

C Cover up Exercise 5A. Which phrase would you use for these situations?

1 the end of a meeting to go over everything that has been discussed?
2 when you want to discuss the next issue?
3 to review what has been discussed so far?
4 to start a meeting and talk about the first point?
5 to get everybody to talk about the same thing?
6 to return to a point that was discussed previously?

SPEAKING

6 A Read the task and write down some ideas.

SET UP A COMPANY TO PROMOTE TOURISM

You are going to set up a tour company to promote tourism in your town/city/country (or the town/country where you are studying). You need to decide the following:

- the name and location of the company
- what type of tours you will organise (themed tours/language tours/sports tours, etc.) and where they will go
- how you will promote tourism
- how the company will be different from other tour companies

B Work in groups. Read your roles and come up with a plan for the business. You have five minutes.

Student A: It's your job to keep the meeting focused. Try to cover all the points.
Student B: Make sure you make notes about any decisions which are made. You will be the group's spokesperson and will have to sum up at the end of the meeting.
Student C: Try to come up with as many ideas as possible.

C When you are ready, start the discussion like this.

A: *Shall we start? First of all, …*

D Tell the other groups about your business plan. Which group do you think has the best plan?

DVD PREVIEW

1 **Work in pairs. Answer the questions.**

1 Do you enjoy watching comedy programmes? Why?/Why not?
2 Which ones are popular in your country?
3 Which comedy programmes do you enjoy watching?

2 **Read about the programme. What type of things do you think Gavin needs to learn on his first day at work? Who do you think he will meet?**

Gavin and Stacey

BBC

Gavin and Stacey is a BBC programme about a young couple. Gavin comes from Essex, near London, and Stacey comes from Cardiff, Wales. After a long-distance relationship conducted online and by telephone, they eventually get married and Gavin moves to Wales. In this episode, Gavin starts a new job. On his first day, his family want him to do well and be happy at work.

DVD VIEW

3 **A** **Watch the DVD. What is the main problem Gavin has during his first day at work?**

B **Match DVD extracts 1–5 to the correct responses a)–e).**

1 Mr Davies, good to see you again. *b*
2 Did you get your welcome pack?
3 Ready when you are.
4 Now here's somebody you've not met yet.
5 Parcel for you.

a) Oh, thanks.
b) Please, call me Huw.
c) Hi. Nice to meet you.
d) Yeah, I think so.
e) OK, let's show you around.

4 **A** **Answer the questions.**

1 What does Huw, the boss, give Gavin?
2 When does Gavin say he will call his mother?
3 How many phone calls does Gavin receive?
4 What does Uncle Bryn bring for Gavin?
5 What is the message on the balloon? Who do you think sent it to him?

B **Watch the DVD again to check.**

C **Discuss. How do you think Gavin will feel at the end of his first day at work?**

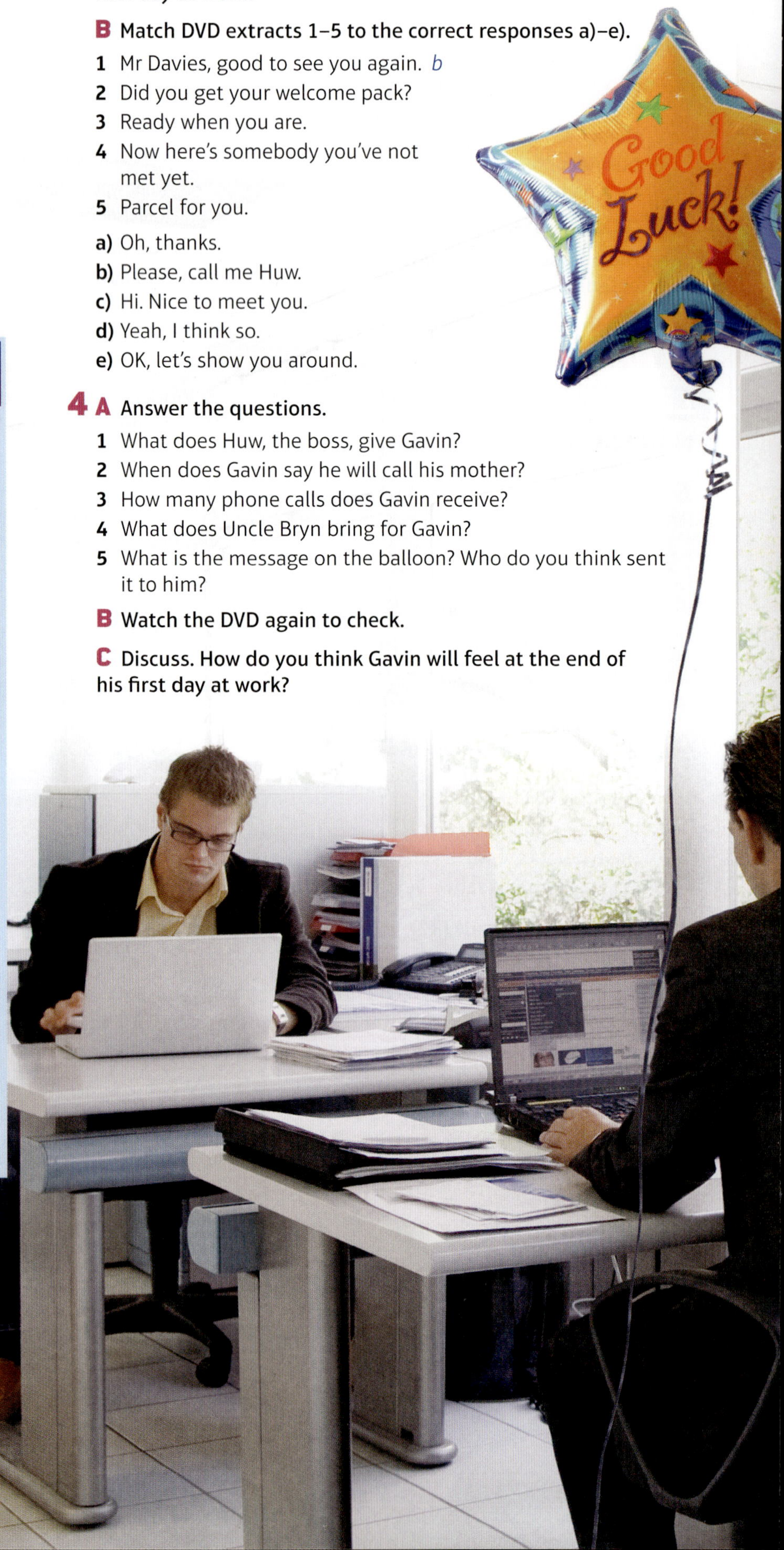

speakout a day in the life ...

5 A 4.8 **Listen to someone describing a typical day in her life. Do you think she likes her job?**

B Read the key phrases below. Complete each phrase by adding one word.

KEYPHRASES

I usually wake up ______ (about) 6.30.

I have to leave home by 8.30 at the ______.

The first ______ I do when I get to work/school is ...

In the afternoon I ______ to catch up on ...

I usually [make some deliveries/ do some shopping/ ...] on my ______ home.

I try to be ______ by (about) 7 o'clock.

I ______ just cook supper and watch some television.

C Listen again to check.

D Prepare to tell other students about a normal day in your life. Write notes about your typical day. What do you have in common?

- hours of work/studying
- tasks you have to do
- people you spend your day with
- problems and challenges
- how you relax
- the best parts of your day

writeback your daily routine

6 A Read about a day in the life of a gym instructor. Is his daily routine similar to yours? How is it different?

I work as a gym instructor in a sports centre. I **get up at** 5a.m. every morning and make a cup of coffee. I can't function until I've had my coffee! I drive to work – it takes about fifteen minutes on a good day – **usually getting there at about** 5.40. **The first thing I do is** switch on the lights and the air conditioning if it's summer (heating if it's winter), and then the radio. We have the radio on all day because our clients like listening to the news and the music. The sports centre opens at 6a.m.

I work in a team of four, although only two of us are ever in the gym at the same time. The instructors all wear sports clothes. **It's important to be** comfortable because we sometimes need to show new clients how to use the machines. Apart from this, **our other tasks are** quite simple: we check that everyone has their membership card when they come in, and we check that the machines are clean and safe.

I have a one-hour break for lunch, and I usually do two more hours after lunch. **I go home at about** 2.30.

The best part of the job is meeting people. Our clients range from eighteen-year-old body builders to eighty-year-olds who come to exercise and chat. I've never had any problems at the sports centre. It's a really nice job, though it doesn't pay very well. In the evenings **I relax by** reading a book and cooking for myself, and I'm usually in bed by 9.30p.m.

Frank Carduna

B Write about a typical day in your life using the sentence starters in bold in the text and the key phrases to help. Try to include two or three pieces of information that make your day different from everybody else's. Alternatively, look at the pictures on page 47. Imagine what a day in the life of this person would be like, and write about it.

PERSONAL QUALITIES

1 **Work in pairs. Student A: describe a word/phrase from the box in your own words, starting with *I am/like/enjoy*, etc. Don't say the word/phrase. Student B: listen and try to guess the word or phrase.**

hard-working indecisive a risk taker a good leader ambitious competitive think outside the box a good communicator

A: I enjoy working and want to succeed in what I do.
B: You're motivated?
A: Correct. Your turn to describe a word.

MUST/HAVE TO/SHOULD (OBLIGATION)

2 A Underline the correct alternative to complete the sentences.

1 I *have to/mustn't* call my mother today. It's her birthday.
2 I really *must/mustn't* do more exercise. I'm so unfit.
3 I'm lucky because I *don't have to/shouldn't* get up early in the morning. I'm a student.
4 I think you *should/shouldn't* study harder. Your exam results weren't very good.
5 You *mustn't/should* be afraid of taking risks, or you will never live your dreams.
6 I *shouldn't/don't have to* waste so much time on the computer. I'll never finish my work.

B Complete the sentences so that they are true for you.

1 I have to … this evening.
2 I really must do more …
3 I'm lucky because I don't have to …
4 I think you should … because …
5 You mustn't worry about …
6 I shouldn't waste so much time …

C Compare your ideas in pairs.

EXTREME ADJECTIVES

3 A Replace the underlined words in the sentences below with extreme adjectives in the box.

brilliant fascinating awful exhausted tiny boiling impossible delicious furious

1 I'm very tired. I didn't sleep well.
2 Shall we open a window? It's very hot in here.
3 My boss just called. He's very angry.
4 I find phrasal verbs very difficult to remember.
5 The holiday was very good, but the weather was very bad.
6 How can you work in this office? It's very small.
7 I find astronomy very interesting.
8 Did you cook this? It's very tasty.

B Work in pairs and take turns to test each other.

A: Very big.
B: Enormous.
A: Correct. Your turn.

USED TO, WOULD

4 A Replace the past simple with *used to* or *would* where possible. Where both are possible, choose *would*.

1 My family lived in Paris, but we moved when I was a teenager.
2 I spent a lot of time with my grandparents when I was younger.
3 For my first job, I washed dishes in a restaurant.
4 I didn't think money was important. Now I have lots of bills to pay.
5 We had a lot more free time before we had children.
6 My best friend at school lived just across the road from me.

B Change four of the sentences so that they are true for you.

C Compare with a partner. Find three things that you both used to do as children, but you don't do now.

REACHING AGREEMENT

5 A Complete the conversations.

1 **A:** The way I s_______ things, all cars should be banned from city centres.
B: E_______.
2 **A:** I really f_______ that we need to look at immigration.
B: That's a good p_______
3 **A:** The w_______ I see it, the company is making too much money.
B: I don't see what you m_______.
4 **A:** I th_______ we should ask for more money.
B: I'm not s_______ I agree, actually.
5 **A:** I s_______ we try to meet again next week.
B: T_______ fine by me.

B Work in pairs and practise the conversations.

6 **Work in groups. Look at the questions below and discuss. Try to reach agreement on each answer.**

1 Should there be a limit to the number of hours people can work in one week?

2 Should there be a minimum wage? What should it be?

3 How long should men/women be allowed to stay off work after they have children?

4 Should everyone be allowed to work from home at least once a week?

5 Should employees be allowed to wear to work whatever clothes they want?

5 solutions

LOW TECH SOLUTIONS p56

ASK THE EXPERTS p59

IT'S OUT OF ORDER p62

MAN VERSUS MACHINE p64

SPEAKING **5.1** Talk about inventions over the last 100 years **5.2** Present and answer questions on your area of expertise **5.3** Explain/Solve problems **5.4** Present a new machine

LISTENING **5.2** Listen to people answering difficult questions **5.3** Listen to conversations about technical problems **5.4** Watch a BBC programme about a race between a car and two people

READING **5.1** Read about some low technology solutions **5.2** Read a book review

WRITING **5.1** Write an advantages/disadvantages essay **5.4** Write an advertisement

BBC
INTERVIEWS

Are you good at solving problems?

5.1 LOW TECH SOLUTIONS

G comparatives/superlatives
P syllable stress
V technology

READING

1 **Work in pairs. Discuss the questions.**

1 In general, do you like or dislike new technology and gadgets like ebooks, tablets and phones?
2 Can you think of ways in which technology has made our lives better/worse?
3 Are there any problems which technology has helped to solve? Give examples.

2 A **Look at the prompts below. What information do you think could go in the gaps to describe the problems? Use the pictures to help you.**

1 New _______ tends to make things faster and more efficient.
2 Popular entertainment (theatre, cinema, music concerts, exhibitions) is often _______ and based in cities.
3 In many villages in Asia and Africa, access to _______ is still a huge problem.
4 The citizens of Bogotá, Colombia wanted young people to have more access to _______.

B **Read the text to check your answers.**

3 A **Work in pairs. Answer the questions.**

1 How is the Rural Academy (slow theatre) different from other theatre companies?
2 Why might people living in rural areas appreciate this type of theatre?
3 How does the Playpump help children to solve the problem of access to water?
4 How has the pump changed the lives of the young girls in particular?
5 How has the invention of the ebook changed how people read?
6 Where have they put the new libraries in Bogotá?

B **Discuss. What do you think of the solutions suggested? Which idea do you like best? Can you think of some other solutions to these problems?**

Why is it that people seem to think that the newest technology is always the best? From high-speed trains to high-speed internet, you could be forgiven for thinking that faster is always better (not to mention, more efficient and more economical). We decided to investigate a few simpler, more low-tech solutions to the world's problems.

Meet the slow theatre

Much of our popular entertainment these days is action-packed, expensive and based in cities. So, the Rural Academy decided they wanted to offer an alternative. Touring the United States, they take a horse-drawn theatre, and a bicycle-powered silent cinema on the road with them. They want to celebrate and call attention to life in more rural locations, in opposition to what they see as the global urbanisation of our culture, economy, media and art. By using a carriage pulled by horses, rather than a vehicle that runs on petrol, they offer a less expensive, low-tech alternative entertainment, which they hope will include more people and move at a slightly slower pace.

The roundabout water pump

Access to a clean water supply is still one of the biggest problems for people living in rural villages in Asia and Africa. To try and solve the problem, a company in South Africa has invented a way to use children's high energy levels to help pump water from underground. The Playpump is a water pump that is powered when the children use the roundabout. As they play, the water is pumped from below the ground into a storage tank. Before the pumps were installed, many young girls had to spend hours of their day walking to collect water, rather than going to school. With the new pumps, however, the girls don't need to miss school, so they get a much better education.

Bus stop libraries in Bogotá

The invention of the ebook has meant that books are now slightly cheaper and a lot lighter to carry. But in Bogotá, Colombia, they had a far better idea for helping people to read on the go. The city wanted to improve the access that young people had to books, but not by buying new tablets. They decided to install colourful book libraries around the city, in the parks and at bus stops. What could be better than to sit in the sunshine and read a book while waiting for your bus?

GRAMMAR

COMPARATIVES AND SUPERLATIVES

4 A Read the article again. Underline examples of comparatives and superlatives.

B Look at your examples and complete the rules. How do we form the comparatives and superlatives of common adjectives?

RULES

1 Adjectives with one syllable
comparatives: add ______
superlatives: add ______
2 Adjectives with two or more syllables
comparatives: add ______
superlatives: add ______

C Look at the sentences below and complete the rules with *small* or *big*.

a) Entertainment has become a lot/much/far more expensive.

b) Technology has made books a little/a little bit/slightly cheaper.

RULES

1 Use quantifiers *a lot/much/far* to talk about ______ differences.
2 Use quantifiers *a little/a little bit/slightly* to talk about ______ differences.

▷ page 76 **LANGUAGEBANK**

5 Complete the statements with the prompts in brackets.

1 The invention of the bicycle made it ______ (lot/easy) for people to travel from one village to another, to meet new people.

2 The world has become a ______ (much/safe) place to live since the invention of antibiotics. People are ______ (far/healthy) now than 100 years ago.

3 The invention of the washing machine has meant that it is ______ (lot/quick) for people to wash their clothes. I think it's ______ (good) invention of the last century.

4 Although we have computers, paper is still ______ (cheap) and ______ (flexible) way to record the written word.

5 Electricity is ______ (important) invention because without it many of the other things we have would not have been possible.

6 The invention of the telephone and the computer have meant that we are ______ (much/busy) now than we were in the past.

VOCABULARY

TECHNOLOGY

6 A Work in pairs. Put the words/phrases in the box into the correct word web.

~~electricity~~ nuclear power antibiotics vaccinations computer networks motorbikes genetic engineering washing machine vacuum cleaner space travel commercial aeroplanes solar power communications satellites

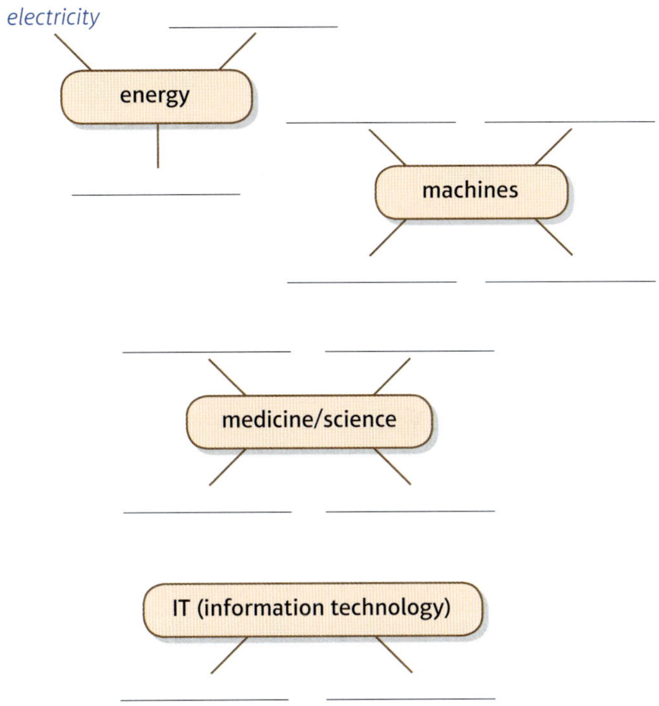

B Work in pairs. Can you add any more words to each word web?

C **SYLLABLE STRESS** Look at the words/phrases above and underline the main stress(es). Sometimes there can be more than one per word/phrase.

elec<u>tric</u>ity *<u>nu</u>clear <u>pow</u>er*

D ▶ 5.1 Listen and check. Then listen again and repeat.

▷ page 82 **VOCABULARYBANK**

SPEAKING

7 A Work in pairs. Choose an invention from the last 100 years. Write two or three sentences to describe how this invention has changed our lives. Don't say what the invention is.

This invention made it much easier to travel from one place to another. Even people in poor societies can use this invention because it does not need petrol.

B Read your sentences to other students. Can they guess the invention?

C Discuss which invention you think has been the best/worst? Why?

WRITING

AN ADVANTAGES/DISADVANTAGES ESSAY; LEARN TO USE DISCOURSE MARKERS

8 A What do you think are the main advantages and disadvantages of technology in everyday life? Write a list.

B Read the model essay. Does it mention any of your ideas?

The advantages and disadvantages of modern technology

1 It is easy to see the advantages of modern technology in our everyday lives. Technology has given us mobile phones, computers, televisions and many other useful things. However, most modern inventions come with a price – maybe social or environmental – so we need to look at both sides of the story.

2 One of the main advantages of modern technology can be seen in medical science. The discoveries of antibiotics and vaccinations have saved millions of lives around the world. In addition to this, modern technology has made industry more efficient.

3 On the other hand, modern technology is responsible for the development of weapons, which have caused a lot of destruction. Another disadvantage is that it makes us lazy. Nowadays, many people spend their lives sitting in front of computer screens. This is a development that surely has negative effects on our mental and physical health, making us more isolated and less active.

4 In my opinion, modern technology is a good thing. In general, the advantages outweigh the disadvantages. Of course there are drawbacks, but it is important to remember that technology itself is not the problem. The problem is that we use technology without always thinking about the harmful consequences.

C Match paragraphs 1–4 with descriptions a)–d).

a) discussion of disadvantages ______
b) conclusion ______
c) introduction 1
d) discussion of advantages ______

D Work in pairs. Complete the guidelines for writing an essay with the expressions in the box.

personal opinions	examples	notes	beginning	logical order

1 Sort out the facts – make ______ of all the relevant information you have on the subject.
2 Plan your argument – organise your notes and arrange the ideas in a ______.
3 Give your essay an appropriate ______. Describe what you are planning to say.
4 Decide how many paragraphs you need for your argument. Each paragraph should discuss one point. Use ______ to support your arguments.
5 Write a logical conclusion. Though the style of the essay is generally formal and impersonal, this might be the place to include some ______.

9 A Look at the underlined words and phrases in the essay. Put them in the correct place in the table.

introduce advantages The most important advantage is …
introduce disadvantages The main disadvantage is …
contrasting ideas Although, …
additional reasons As well as that, … And another thing, …
personal opinion/conclusion In general, … As far as I'm concerned, …

B Underline the correct alternatives.

Satellite TV: good or bad?
More and more people are watching satellite television. [1]*The main advantage / As well as that* is that you can choose exactly what you want to watch, and [2]*in addition to this / however* you can watch programmes in other languages.
[3]*However, / Although* this means that whereas people used to talk about programmes with colleagues and friends, now they usually don't watch the same programmes.
[4]*On the other hand / And another thing*, there is too much choice. There are so many programmes to choose from that people can't decide what to watch. [5]*This means that / As far as I'm concerned*, they watch too much television.
[6]*In my opinion / The problem is that*, satellite television is a good thing, as it gives people more choice. [7]*However, / In general*, people need to be careful that they choose their programmes carefully.

10 Choose one of the topics below and write an essay about the advantages and disadvantages of it. Look back at Exercises 8 and 9 to help you.

- modern technology in everyday life
- owning a car/bicycle
- playing computer games
- using a digital camera
- using email/text messages
- cheap flights

ASK THE EXPERTS

G question tags
P intonation: question tags
V information; word building: adjectives

5.2

SPEAKING

1 A Match photos A–F to the questions below.

1 Is it possible to surf a tidal wave?
2 Why is snow cold?
3 Is there an easy way to prove the Earth is round?
4 Why do onions make you cry?
5 Is a rainbow hot or cold?
6 Why are sumo wrestlers so fat?

B Work in pairs. How many questions above can you answer in two minutes?

C Turn to page 86 and check your answers.

VOCABULARY

INFORMATION

2 A Match the pairs of verbs in the box with situations 1–5.

~~question/wonder~~	discuss/debate	respond/reply
research/investigate	inquire/look into	argue/quarrel

1 Someone tells you something. You are not sure you agree.
question/wonder
2 Someone writes you a letter.
3 There is an interesting topic in class.
4 You disagree with someone and talk angrily with them.
5 You are writing a thesis for your Master's degree.
6 You need to find some information, e.g. about cinema times or to book a table.

B Read the sentences below. In which sentence is *wonder* a verb? In which sentence is it a noun?

a) I wonder if anyone has ever tried to surf a tidal wave.
b) I can name the seven wonders of the world.

C Underline the correct alternative to complete the sentences. Is the correct answer a noun or a verb?

1 The police officer continued his *investigation/wonder/inquire* into the robbery.
2 Didn't you get my email? You didn't *response/look into/reply*.
3 We had a very interesting *discuss/debate/wonder* about the death penalty.
4 I've nearly finished my *research/investigate/reply* into nuclear particles.
5 When I hear about all these social problems, I have to *inquire/question/respond* the education system.
6 You want a job here? No problem. My cousin is the boss. I'll *inquiry/debate/look into* it for you.
7 It was a silly *respond/quarrel/argue*. Now they are friends again.

LISTENING

3 A Work in groups and discuss.

1 How do you prefer to find information, on the internet, in books or by asking people? What does it depend on?

2 What type of questions do children ask? Think of some examples.

They sometimes ask difficult questions like: 'Why is snow cold?'

B Read a review of a book about questions children ask their parents. How did the author get the idea for the book? Are any of your questions included in the examples from the book?

Questions Daddy can't answer

It all began with a question asked by Dean, a four-year-old boy: 'Why do ships have round windows?' His father didn't know. And when his sister started behaving badly, Dean asked another question: 'Why can't we just cook her?' On a long drive the boy wondered why the road was so loud. His father replied, 'Because the people who live next to the road have their vacuum cleaners on.' The boy's inquiries kept coming: 'Why is the sky blue? Are rainbows hot or cold? What was it like living in the 1940s? What would hurt more – getting run over by a car or getting stung by a jellyfish? Why do police officers like doughnuts?'

Eventually, Jamieson decided to write down the questions. He thought it might be fun one day to show them to his son. Then he had a better idea: he'd research the answers. Some people might do their investigations on the internet. Not Mr Jamieson. He contacted experts ranging from astronomers to Buddhist monks, to scientists, to magicians, and asked lots of questions. He later turned these – and the experts' responses – into a book: *Father Knows Less.*

4 A Read five questions from the book *Father Knows Less*. Try to answer them. Compare your ideas with other students.

How many hairs are there on the human head?
Why are the windows on ships always round?
Why is there war?
Why did The Beatles break up?
What happens when your plane flies over a volcano?

B 5.2 Listen to some people trying to answer the questions in Exercise 4A. Are their answers the same as your ideas?

C Listen again and complete the notes.

1 Ships' round windows: _______
2 Number of hairs on a human head: _______
3 A plane flies over a volcano: _______
4 The Beatles broke up: _______
5 Reasons for war: different ideologies, a sense of honour, _______

GRAMMAR

QUESTION TAGS

5 A Complete questions 1–6. Then look at audio script 5.2 on page 91 to check.

1 Round windows are stronger, _______ they?
2 No, it's not that many, _______ it?
3 It depends whose head, _______ it?
4 Nothing happens, _______ it?
5 They got old, _______ they?
6 John Lennon went off with Yoko Ono, _______ he?

B Read the rules about question tags. Which rules are exemplified in 1–6 in Exercise 6A?

Rule 2 is shown in question number 3. It uses doesn't.

RULES

1 Use question tags to confirm information.
2 To form a question tag, repeat the auxiliary verb. For example, use *do* or *does* for the present. Use *will* or *won't* for the future.
3 After the auxiliary verb, use a pronoun (e.g. *he, she, it, they*).
4 If the sentence is positive, the question tag is negative.
5 If the sentence is negative, the question tag is positive.

page 76 LANGUAGEBANK

6 Look at the statements below and complete the question tags.

1 You're Italian, *aren't* you?
2 You aren't a doctor, *are* you?
3 You don't smoke, _______ you?
4 You play a musical instrument, _______ you?
5 You didn't know any of the other students before, _______ you?
6 Our teacher hasn't taught you before, _______ she?
7 You will be here tomorrow, _______ you?
8 You went to bed late last night, _______ you?
9 You've travelled a lot, _______ you?
10 You were good at sport when you were a child, _______ you?

7 A ▷ 5.3 **INTONATION: question tags** Listen to two questions. Notice how the intonation goes down when the speaker is sure of the answer. Notice how the intonation goes up when the speaker is not sure.

1 You're Italian, aren't you? (the speaker knows the answer)

2 You aren't a doctor, are you? (the speaker is not sure of the answer)

B ▷ 5.4 **Listen to the questions in Exercise 6. Which answers is the speaker sure about? Listen and repeat the questions, using the same intonation.**

C **Work in pairs. Choose six questions to ask your partner. Make sure your intonation is correct in the question tags.**

A: You play a guitar, don't you?
B: Yes, I do. I play bass in a band.

SPEAKING

8 **Work in groups and follow instructions 1–4 below.**

1 Think of one subject each that you know a lot about. Write your topics on a piece of paper.

tennis, Japanese cars, hip hop

2 Exchange papers with another group.

3 Think of statements about the subjects. Use question tags.

Rafael Nadal is the best tennis player in history, isn't he? The most popular Japanese car is the Toyota, isn't it?

4 Read your statements to the first group. Are they correct?

VOCABULARY *PLUS*

WORD BUILDING: ADJECTIVES

9 A **Read the text below. How was the ice cream cone invented?**

For over a hundred years ice cream was sold mainly in dishes. Then one day, a creative ice cream seller turned a hopeless situation into a profitable one. In 1904, at a festival, he ran out of spoons and dishes. He bought some wafers from a vendor next to him and put the ice cream into them. The customers loved them and the idea spread quickly. The world has been thankful ever since!

B **Underline four adjectives in the text and add them to the word web below. Can you think of other examples of adjectives that fit these patterns?**

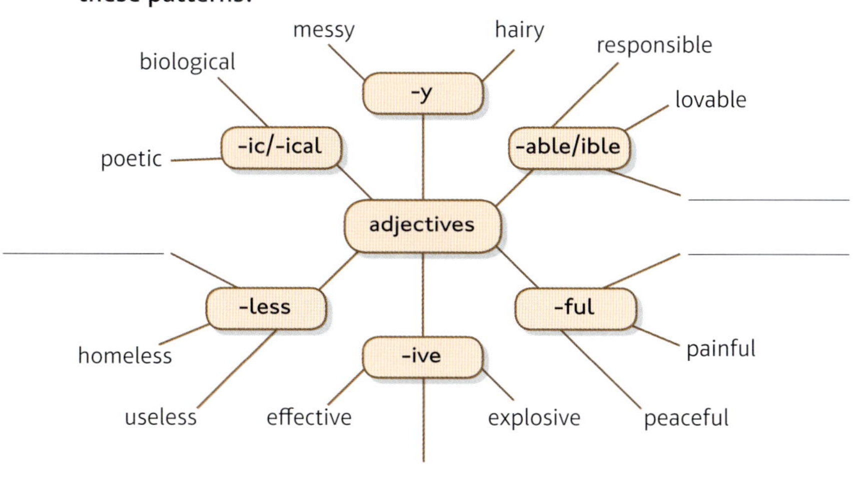

speakout TIP

Use L1. L1 is your First Language. Some suffixes in your L1 might have similar meanings to suffixes in English. For example, the Italian *-ivo/a* means the same as the English *-ive*. Can you think of any examples from your language?

10 **Complete the text. Add suffixes to the words in brackets.**

The city of Detroit, USA was famous for its [1]______ (value) car industry. In the early days, the city was [2]______ (response) for the majority of cars in the USA, and Detroit's streets were full of cars. A police officer called William Potts saw that the organisation of the traffic was [3]______ (hope) and the traffic was very slow. So, in 1920, he developed an [4]______ (effect) system of lights to regulate the flow of cars. He used the same colours as the railway system and put the lights in a tower so that it would be [5]______ (ease) for drivers to see them even on [6]______ (rain) days. Potts's system was very [7]______ (success). When other countries realised how [8]______ (use) it was, the system spread all over the world.

11 A **Complete the words by adding suffixes.**

Find someone who:

1 has a peace*ful* hobby.
2 is hope______ at maths.
3 is a good, care______ driver.
4 is quite mess______ at home.
5 thinks he/she is quite creat______.
6 is quite knowledge______ about politics.

B **Work in groups. Ask and answer questions about the information above.**

You've got a peaceful hobby, haven't you?

▷ page 82 **VOCABULARYBANK**

5.3 IT'S OUT OF ORDER

F polite requests
P intonation: polite requests
V problems and solutions

VOCABULARY

PROBLEMS AND SOLUTIONS

1 A Think of two pieces of technology you have used in the last twenty-four hours. Did you have any problems with them? What problems can you have with them?

B Work in pairs. Look at the photos. What is the problem in each case?

C Look at the phrases in bold. Are they problems (P) or solutions (S)? Which phrases can you use to talk about the problems in pictures A–E above?

1 It's **broken down**.
2 It **needs recharging**.
3 It's **out of order**.
4 It **needs fixing**.
5 There is no **reception** (for my phone).
6 **Try switching it off** (and on again).
7 It **keeps making this strange noise**.
8 **It's crashed/frozen**.
9 It **doesn't work** (any more).
10 We have to **sort it out**.
11 **Save it onto a memory stick**.
12 Shall I **print it for you**?

D Work in pairs and answer the questions.

1 Have any of these problems happened to you or anyone you know recently?
2 How did you feel when it happened?
3 How did you try to solve the problem?

FUNCTION

POLITE REQUESTS

2 A 5.5 Listen to four conversations. What is the problem in each case?

B Read questions 1–8. Which can you answer? Listen again to check.

1 In conversation 1, what question does the man ask?
2 Where does the woman suggest that he goes?
3 In conversation 2, what does the woman 'keep losing'?
4 What does the man suggest?
5 In conversation 3, what does the vacuum cleaner 'keep making'?
6 Does the woman give the man instructions about what to do to fix his vacuum cleaner?
7 In conversation 4, what does the man ask for?
8 Who does the man need to speak to?

C Complete the extracts in the table with the correct words.

Could you	1 ______ the line, please? 2 ______ me a refund?
Could you tell me	who I should 3 ______ to? what the 4 ______ is?
Do you know	what the problem is? if there's another 5 ______ somewhere?
Would you mind	6 ______ at it for me? 7 ______ him for me?

C 5.6 Listen and repeat the requests.

page 76 LANGUAGEBANK

LEARN TO
RESPOND TO REQUESTS

3 A Read some conversation extracts from Exercise 2. Complete the responses with the phrases in the box.

Yes, I can   I'm not sure   I'm afraid I can't Yes, of course (x2)   Of course not   Sure/OK Let me have a look

1 **M:** Do you know if there's another machine somewhere? I really need to get some money.
W: Hmm … _______. There might be one in the shopping centre.

2 **W:** Would you mind looking at it for me?
M: _______.

3 **W:** Do you know what the problem is?
M: _______.

4 **W:** Could you tell me what the problem is, sir?
M: _______. It keeps making a funny noise. And it's just not working properly.

5 **W:** Could you hold the line, please?
M: _______.

6 **M:** Could you give me a refund?
W: _______ do that.
M: Well, could you tell me who I should speak to?
W: _______. You need to speak to the manager.
M: OK. Would you mind calling him for me?
W: _______. I'll just call him.

B Read audio script 5.5 on page 91 to check.

4 A Make polite requests and responses with the prompts in brackets.

1 **A:** I can't concentrate. (Would / mind / turn / music down)?
B: Sure. Sorry about that.

2 **A:** I need to speak to the manager. (Do / know / if / anyone in the office)?
B: Let me have a look.

3 **A:** I'm afraid Mr Soul isn't here at the moment.
B: (Do / know / when / coming back)?
A: (not / sure). Do you want me to check?
B: Thank you.

4 **A:** (Could / tell / how / machine works)? I don't know how to turn it on.
B: (Yes / course).

5 **A:** I need to take this machine to the repair service. (Would / mind / help / me)?
B: (course / not). Leave it here.

6 **A:** My computer has frozen. (Could / tell / who / I / speak / to)?
B: OK. (Let / have / look).

B 5.7 Listen to check your answers.

C **INTONATION: polite requests** Does the speaker's voice start high or low? Listen again and repeat the requests copying the polite intonation.

SPEAKING

5 A Work in pairs. Read your role and think about the phrases you are going to use. Then role-play the situation below.

Student B
You need to call your sister but you can't get any reception on your phone. Ask Student A if he/she knows where you can get reception.

Student A
Tell Student B that you have reception on your phone. Suggest that he/she tries standing outside.

Student B
You still can't get any reception. Ask Student A if you can borrow his/her phone to send a text message.

Student A
Tell Student B he/she can borrow your phone to make the phone call.

Student B
Thank Student A for his/her help.

B Change roles and role-play the situation below.

Student A
You can't get the printer to work. Ask Student B if he/she can help you.

Student B
Suggest Student A tries turning it off and then on again. Ask if that has worked.

Student A
It still doesn't work. Ask Student B if he/she knows of other printers in the building.

Student B
Tell Student A he/she can use your printer.

Student A
Thank Student B for his/her help.

C Choose one or two situations from Exercises 4 and 5. Write a conversation using the flow charts above to help. Then role-play it with a partner.

5.4 MAN VERSUS MACHINE

DVD PREVIEW

1 Work in pairs and answer the questions.

1 Look at the person on page 65. What type of sport is he doing?

2 Would you like to try this sport? Why?/Why not?

2 Read about the programme. Who do you think will win the race? Why?

Top Gear

Top Gear is the BBC's international award-winning television series about motor vehicles, mainly cars. More than 350 million viewers worldwide enjoy watching the presenters with their quirky, humorous style. On the show they compare and test-drive cars, and organise all kinds of crazy races. In this programme, James May, possibly the slowest driver in Great Britain, challenges two freerunners to a race in Liverpool city centre. James has to drive six miles towards the Liver building in the city centre in a Peugeot 207. The two teenagers who try to beat him will run and jump over buildings, taking a much more direct route. Who do you think will get there first?

3 Watch the DVD to see if you were right. Number the events in the correct order.

a) The men jump over James's car. ______

b) James arrives at the Liver building. ______

c) James checks his speed. ______

d) The men jump over people eating at a restaurant. ______

e) James stops at a red traffic light. ______

4 Watch the DVD again. What does James May say? Complete the phrases.

1 As we can see, it's a very pretty car, but is it any ______?

2 I'm going to have a race, and it's against the latest French development in urban transport solutions: a couple of young men in silly ______.

3 Parkour: that's a French invention, and involves that sort of thing. Running around the ______ leaping across buildings and benches.

4 Come on – we're not all ______!

5 I must have averaged ten or twelve miles an hour. I should ______.

6 They are not here. No sign of combat trousers man. I've ______!

speakout present a new machine

5 A **Work in pairs. Answer the questions and complete the tasks.**

1 Write a list of things you have to do every day.
2 Are there any things on this list which you don't enjoy? Could a machine do them for you?
3 Invent a machine which would help you do one of the things. Draw a picture of your machine.

B ▶ 5.8 **Listen to someone talking about a new machine. What is the invention? What does it do?**

C **Listen again and tick the key phrases he uses.**

> **KEYPHRASES**
>
> I'm going to tell you about …
> Basically, …
> The way it works is this.
> It works like this …
> First of all, ….
> Then/Also, you can …
> All you have to do is …
> Make sure you …
> The best thing about it is that …

D **Prepare and practise a short presentation about your new machine. Use your picture and the useful phrases to explain how it works.**

E **Present your ideas to the class. Which invention do you think is the best?**

writeback an advertisement

6 A **Read the advertisement and answer the questions. What is the musical shower? How does it work?**

> ### The musical shower
>
> If you like listening to music when you have a shower, then you might already have a stereo in your bathroom. But imagine how much better it would be if your shower-head also had an MP3 player attached to it.
>
> It will download your favourite tunes, or radio programmes at night. Then in the morning, your shower will automatically play your favourite tunes for you. Try our musical shower.
>
> There's no better way to start the day.

B **Write an advertisement (advert) for your invention (120–180 words). Use the advert above and the key phrases to help.**

5.5 LOOKBACK

G COMPARATIVES/ SUPERLATIVES

1 A Look at the information and complete sentences (1–4) using the prompts in brackets.

100 years ago in the US: the average life expectancy was forty-seven years, only eight percent of homes had a phone, the maximum speed limit in most cities was ten miles per hour, the average wage was twenty-two cents per hour, and ninety percent of all doctors had no college education.

1 100 years ago, people didn't live ______ as they do today. (long)
2 It used to be ______ to communicate with people on the other side of the world. (far, difficult)
3 It is ______ for modern businesses to pay their employees. (far, expensive)
4 Nowadays, doctors are ______ than they were in the past. (much, educated)

B Write sentences about a hundred years ago. Compare them with your partner.

V TECHNOLOGY

2 A Complete the words in sentences 1–6.

1 I don't agree with nu______ po______. I think it's a dangerous way of making el______.
2 Sp______ tr______ is a waste of money. Why do we need to send people to the Moon?
3 I couldn't live without my wa______ ma______. I hate dirty clothes.
4 I had to have loads of va______ when I went to Malawi. I didn't want to get ill.
5 I think ge______ en______ is a bit worrying. People might start to only want babies which are beautiful.
6 Doctors give people too many an______. So now, some medicines don't work any more.

B Work in pairs. Choose three sentences you disagree with. Tell your partner why.

G INFORMATION

3 A Put the letters in italics in the correct order to find words related to questions.

1 In class last week, we *used discs* …

In class last week, we discussed …

2 I can't answer *nose quits* about …
3 I try to *pen rods* quickly to …
4 In the next few months I'm going to *took lion* … (2 words)
5 I recently *quid rein* about …
6 I *own red* what happened to …
7 I enjoy a good *tea bed* especially about …
8 It would be interesting to *sit negative* a crime like …

B Complete the sentences so that they are true for you.

G QUESTION TAGS

4 A Complete the sentences with the correct question tag.

1 She wrote the first *Harry Potter* book in a café, *didn't she*?
2 This man, who is U2's singer, does a lot of humanitarian work, ______?
3 This actor has won an Oscar for *Forrest Gump*, ______?
4 He was probably the greatest basketball player in history, ______?
5 She lived in Calcutta, where she helped street children, but she wasn't from India, ______?
6 He became Cuba's leader in 1959 and he didn't transfer power to his brother until 2006, ______?
7 Her full name is Madonna Louise Ciccone, ______?
8 Her husband was US President. She's very popular but she probably won't be as famous as him, ______?

B Who are these sentences about?

1 J K Rowling

C Work in groups. One student thinks of a famous person. The others ask tag questions to find out who it is.

A: You're a man, aren't you?
B: Yes.

F POLITE REQUESTS

5 A Match requests 1–5 with responses a)–e).

1 Excuse me, could you tell me where I can find the bathroom?
2 Could you call me a taxi?
3 Would you mind helping me with my bags? They're very heavy.
4 Would you mind opening the window?
5 Could you tell me what time the restaurant opens?

a) Sure. It's very hot in here, isn't it?
b) Yes, of course. It's just over there, down the stairs and on the left.
c) Yes, of course. Where do you want to go to?
d) I'm not sure. Let me have a look. Yes, it opens at 11a.m.
e) Of course not. Let me take your suitcase.

B Work in pairs. Take turns to practise the conversations using the prompts below.

Student A:
- where/bathroom?
- call/taxi?
- shop/close?
- get/door?

Student B
- open/window?
- restaurant/open?
- help/shopping?
- tell/platform the train leaves from?

IRREGULAR VERBS

Verb	Past simple	Past participle
be	was	been
beat	beat	beaten
become	became	become
begin	began	begun
bend	bent	bent
bet	bet	bet
bite	bit	bitten
bleed	bled	bled
blow	blew	blown
break	broke	broken
bring	brought	brought
broadcast	broadcast	broadcast
build	built	built
burn	burned/burnt	burned/burnt
burst	burst	burst
buy	bought	bought
catch	caught	caught
choose	chose	chosen
come	came	come
cost	cost	cost
cut	cut	cut
deal	dealt	dealt
dig	dig	dug
do	did	done
draw	drew	drawn
dream	dreamed/dreamt	dreamed/dreamt
drink	drank	drunk
drive	drove	driven
eat	ate	eaten
fall	fell	fallen
feel	felt	felt
feed	fed	fed
fight	fought	fought
find	found	found
fly	flew	flown
forbid	forbade	forbidden
forget	forgot	forgotten
forgive	forgave	forgiven
freeze	froze	frozen
get	got	got
give	gave	given
go	went	gone
grow	grew	grown
hang	hung	hung
have	had	had
hear	heard	heard
hide	hid	hidden
hit	hit	hit
hold	held	held
hurt	hurt	hurt
keep	kept	kept
know	knew	known
lay	laid	laid
lead	led	led
leap	leapt	leapt
learn	learned/learnt	learned/learnt

Verb	Past simple	Past participle
leave	left	left
lend	lent	lent
let	let	let
lie	lay	lain
light	lit	lit
lose	lost	lost
make	made	made
mean	meant	meant
meet	met	met
mistake	mistook	mistaken
pay	paid	paid
put	put	put
read /ri:d/	read /red/	read /red/
ride	rode	ridden
ring	rang	rung
rise	rose	risen
run	ran	run
say	said	said
see	saw	seen
sell	sold	sold
send	sent	sent
set	set	set
shake	shook	shaken
shine	shone	shone
shoot	shot	shot
show	showed	shown
shrink	shrank	shrunk
shut	shut	shut
sing	sang	sung
sink	sank	sunk
sit	sat	sat
sleep	slept	slept
slide	slid	slid
smell	smelled/smelt	smelled/smelt
speak	spoke	spoken
spell	spelt	spelt
spend	spent	spent
spill	spilled/spilt	spilled/spilt
split	split	split
spread	spread	spread
stand	stood	stood
steal	stole	stolen
stick	stuck	stuck
sting	stung	stung
swim	swam	swum
take	took	taken
teach	taught	taught
tear	tore	torn
tell	told	told
think	thought	thought
throw	threw	thrown
understand	understood	understood
wake	woke	woken
wear	wore	worn
win	won	won
write	wrote	written

GRAMMAR

1.1 question forms

object questions

Object questions use the word order: question word + auxiliary verb + subject + infinitive.

question word	auxiliary verb	subject	verb
Where	do	you	work?
What	did	she	say?
When	are	they	coming?

***yes/no* questions**

Yes/No questions don't use a question word. The answer to the question is *Yes or No*.

auxiliary verb	subject	verb
Does	he	smoke?
Did	we	win?
Have	they	arrived?

subject questions

When the *wh-* question word is the subject of the question:

- we don't use an auxiliary verb (*do*, *did*, etc.).
- we use the same word order as in an affirmative sentence.

question word	verb	object
Who	wants	ice cream?
What	happened?	
Who	ate	the cheese?

questions with prepositions

When we use a verb + preposition expression (but not multi-word verbs) such as *look for*, *depend on*, *write about*, etc., we usually keep the verb and preposition together:

*What did you **talk about**?* *Who are you **looking for**?*

In very formal English we sometimes move the preposition to the front of the sentence. Compare:

*What does it **depend on**?* *On what does it **depend**?*

1.2 review of verb tenses

present simple

+	He **looks** happy.
–	He **doesn't look** happy.
?	**Does** he **look** happy?

Use the present simple to talk about something that is always or generally true, habits, routines, with *be* and other state verbs (see below).

present continuous

+	We**'re staying** here.
–	We **aren't staying** here.
?	**Are** we **staying** here?

Use the present continuous to talk about an activity happening at the time of speaking or a temporary activity happening around now. It may be happening at the moment, but maybe not.

past simple

+	They **worked** hard.
–	They **didn't work** hard.
?	**Did** they **work** hard?

Use the past simple to talk about finished actions, events or situations in the past.

past continuous

+	I **was living** there during the 90s.
–	I **wasn't living** there during the 90s.
?	**Were** you **living** there?

Use the past continuous to talk about an action or situation in progress at a particular time in the past. This action was not finished at that time.

state verbs and dynamic verbs

State verbs are not usually used in the continuous form. The most common state verbs are:

- attitude verbs: *love, hate, like, want, prefer*
- thinking verbs: *believe, know, remember, understand, mean, imagine*
- sense verbs: *see, hear, sound, appear, seem*
- belonging verbs: *own, possess, belong to, have, contain, include*

Some state verbs can be used in the continuous form when they describe actions, e.g. *see, have, think*:

*I'**m seeing** Phil tonight.* (see = meet)
*We'**re having** a party.* (have = organise)
*I'**m thinking** of going to university.* (think = consider)

1.3 talking about yourself

introducing a question
Could I ask a question? There are a couple of things I'd like to ask about. Can I ask you about that? I have a query.

introducing an opinion
For me (the most important thing is) … I'd have to say … In my opinion, … One thing I'd like to say is that …

PRACTICE

1.1

A Write questions for the answers in italics.

1 Where ______________________________?
I live *in Madrid*.
2 Who ______________________________?
Nick won the game.
3 Does ______________________________?
No, he doesn't eat meat.
4 What ______________________________?
They are *sleeping*.
5 What ______________________________?
I'm writing about *my first holiday*.
6 When ______________________________?
We arrived *yesterday*.
7 Who ______________________________?
We ate the chocolate.
8 Did ______________________________?
Yes, we liked the film.

B Put the words in brackets in the correct places to make questions.

1 the President? (killed, who)
____
2 were you thinking? (what, about)
____
3 to the old theatre? (happened, what)
____
4 Where your great-grandparents come? (from, did)
____
5 your ancestors from here? (come, did)
____
6 she here for a long time? (worked, has)
____
7 is all that noise? (who, making)
____
8 house you looking for? (are, which)
____

1.2

A Underline the correct alternatives.

'Like most translators, I [1]*'m speaking/speak* several languages. At the moment, I [2]*'m attending/attend* a conference. I [3]*was doing/did* some work for an internet company when I [4]*was hearing/heard* about this conference. I [5]*was arriving/arrived* three days ago and I'm going to stay until Monday, when it ends.'

My best friend is called Gina. We [6]*aren't speaking/don't speak* to each other every day, but we're very close. I [7]*was meeting/met* her on my first morning at university. I [8]*was looking/looked* for the library when she came up to me and asked, 'Excuse me, [9]*do you know/are you knowing* where the library is?' We [10]*were finding/found* it together!

B Put the verbs in brackets into the correct tense.

1 Sit down and watch the game! We __________ (win) 2–1. Ronaldo scored two minutes ago.
2 John wasn't here last summer. He __________ (travel) around Africa.
3 Fifty years ago, my favourite writer __________ (die).
4 I didn't do the homework because I __________ (not listen) when the teacher told us what to do.
5 DVDs __________ (not work) very well on my laptop, so I use the TV and DVD player.
6 What's that smell? Can you turn off the oven? I think the food __________ (burn).
7 __________ (see) that film last night? What did you think?
8 Everyone knows that smoking __________ (cause) cancer.

1.3

A Find and correct the mistakes in the conversation below. There are six mistakes.

A: There are a couple of things I'd like ask about.
B: Go ahead.
A: Firstly, which of your films do you think is the best?
B: I'd having to say *Millennium Dreamer*. For me, it's my best film and it was my first comedy.
A: Can I ask you around that? You've never done comedy before. Why not?
B: I don't know. I suppose people think I'm a serious actor.
A: Could I ask question about your image? Is it accurate? Are you really the strong silent type in real life?
B: No. One of thing I'd like to say is that these images are invented by the media. By my opinion, good actors are never just one thing. That's why they're actors.

GRAMMAR

2.1 present perfect and past simple

Present perfect simple: *have/has* + past participle (*lived, worked, seen* etc.)

+	I**'ve been** to Poland a few times.
–	He **hasn't worked** here before.
?	**Have** you **bought** a new car?

For irregular past participles see the list of irregular verbs on page 67.

time up to now

Use the present perfect for actions which have happened in your life before now. These are often general experiences. It isn't important exactly when these things happened. Conversations which begin like this in the present perfect usually continue in the past simple as the speaker adds details:

*I**'ve been** to Colombia. Really? Where **did** you **go**?*
*He**'s played** in an Indie band. What **were they called**?*

We often use the adverbs *ever* and *never* with the present perfect:

*We**'ve never** been to China.* *Have you **ever** been to the Opera?*

recent events

Use the present perfect to talk about events which happened a short time ago. We often use the adverbs *just, yet* and *already*:

*I've **just** finished his book. It was brilliant.*
*We've **already** eaten.*
*Have you done your homework **yet**?*
*We've seen a lot of Jude **recently**.*

present perfect or past simple?

Use the past simple to talk about a specific event which happened at a specific time:

*I**'ve been** to Sweden.*
(At some time in my life up to now. We don't know when.)
*We **went** to Stockholm in 2002.*
NOT ~~*We've been to Stockholm in 2002.*~~
(This is a specific occasion and date, so we use the past simple.)

2.2 narrative tenses

past simple

Use the past simple for states and actions in the past. We often specify the time when they happened:

*I **left** university **in 1996**.* *He **didn't know** the way to Sal's house.*

past continuous

Use the past continuous to talk about the background information for a story. Use the past simple to talk about the main events.

BACKGROUND INFORMATION past continuous		MAIN EVENT past simple
*I **was walking** through the park …* *The sun **was shining** …* *The birds **were singing** …*	*WHEN*	*… I **heard** a noise*

past ∼∼∼∼∼∼∼∼∼∼∼∼∼∼| now

*As I **was walking** through the park, the sun **was shining** and the birds **were singing**. Suddenly, I **heard** a loud noise.*

Often the past continuous action is interrupted by another action (in the past simple):

*I **was having** a bath when the phone **rang**.*

We can use conjunctions like *as* and *while* to talk about two actions which were happening at the same time:

***While** I was reading the paper, I watched the women buying vegetables in the market.*

For more information on state and dynamic verbs section 1.2, page 68.

past perfect

+	I **had finished** my work.
–	They **hadn't had** time.
?	**Had** they **been** there before?

Use the past perfect to make it clear that one action happened before the other.

past perfect	past simple	present
I lost my wallet.	*I didn't have any money.*	

past |————|————| now

I didn't have any money because I had lost my wallet.

When *before* or *after* is used in the sentence, it's already clear which action comes before the other, so we can use the past simple instead of the past perfect:

*She **had lived** in London for five years **before** she moved to New York.*
*She **lived** in London for five years **before** she moved to New York.*

We often use the past perfect with 'thinking' verbs like *remember, realise, think, discover, find out*, etc.:

*When I got to the school, I **realised** I'd left my books at home.*

2.3 telling a story

beginning the story	This happened when … In the beginning, …
describing what happened	Well, … Anyway, … Before long, … So, … And then, all of a sudden … The next thing I knew, …
ending the story	In the end, … Finally, …

questions to keep a story going	So, what happened? What did you do? What happened next? Really?
responses to show interest	I don't believe it! Oh no. / Oh dear. How embarrassing! That's really funny. You must be joking. Yes, I know.

PRACTICE

2.1

A Tick the correct sentences, a) or b).

1 a) I've been to India last year.
b) I went to India last year.
2 a) I finished my studies in 2005.
b) I've finished my studies in 2005.
3 a) Did you have lunch yet?
b) Have you had lunch yet?
4 a) Did you ever see *Metallica* play live?
b) Have you ever seen *Metallica* play live?
5 a) Is this the first time you've tried judo?
b) Is this the first time you tried judo?
6 a) It's the most beautiful place I've ever been to.
b) It's the most beautiful place I ever went to.

B Use the prompts to make short conversations.

1 A: you / be / here / before? (ever)
B: no / not
2 A: you / see / the film *The Reader*?
B: no / not / see (yet)
3 A: he / be / to Budapest?
B: yes / go / last summer
4 A: you / finish / that book? (yet)
B: yes / start / the next one (already)
5 A: you / see / Maria?
B: yes, she / leave / a message for you
6 A: he / decide / what job / want to do? (yet)
B: no / have / not

2.2

A Underline the correct alternatives to complete the story.

I remember when Marvin Gaye [1]*died/had died*. I [2]*had been/was going* to one of his concerts a few months before. In fact, he [3]*hadn't played/wasn't playing* very well and I was disappointed. I also remember when JFK was shot. I [4]*had lived/was living* with my parents in New York and I [5]*studied/was studying* at the time. I remember the cleaning lady [6]*came/was coming* into the room, and said to me, 'Hey, President Lincoln has been shot.' I [7]*replied/was replying*, 'I know that.' 'No,' she said. 'President Lincoln has been shot!' So I said, 'What do you mean?' And she said, 'Oh no, I mean … President, you know, what's his name, the one now. President Kennedy's been shot.' So then I [8]*was turning/turned* on the radio.

B Find and correct the mistakes. One sentence is correct.

1 I was leaving the room when I had heard someone shouting.
2 I couldn't open the door because I left my keys at home.
3 We drove through the tunnel when the car broke down.
4 As soon as the film started I realised I seen it before.
5 I never been to Egypt before, so I was really excited to see the pyramids.
6 By the time we arrived at the party, everybody else is leaving.
7 We had waited for nearly an hour before the waiter took our order.
8 I looked through some old photographs when I found this one of you.

2.3

A Complete the conversation with the words and phrases in the box.

In the end	don't believe it	The next thing I knew	this happened when
So, what happened	Well	really funny	Anyway
You must be joking	So		

A: Well, [1] ________________ I was working in a photographic store.
B: [2] ________________?
A: [3] ________________, one day a woman came in and asked if we could fix the problem she had with a photograph. [4] ________________ I asked her what the problem was.
B: OK.
A: [5] ________________, she had taken this old photo out of her bag which showed an old man sitting behind a cow, milking it. [6] ________________, when I asked her what she wanted us to do to the photo, she said, 'Can you move the cow?' 'Move the cow?' I asked. 'Yes,' she replied. 'I want to see what my grandfather looked like.' She pointed to the feet sticking out from under the cow.
B: Oh no. [7] ________________.
A: No, seriously. She wanted us to move the cow, so that she could see her grandfather's face.
B: I [8] ________________! So, what happened next?
A: [9] ________________, when I told her we couldn't do it, she got quite angry, and left the shop saying, 'Then I'll have to take it to someone else.'
B: That's [10] ________________.

GRAMMAR

3.1 the future (plans)

be going to

+	I'**m going to** start university next year.
–	He **isn't going to** get a job this year.
?	Where **are** you **going to** stay?

When using be going to use the word order: subject + *am/are/is* + *going to* + infinitive without *to*. Use *be going to* to talk about future plans or intentions. When the verb is *go* or *come*, we often use the present continuous:

*We'**re going** to (go to) Spain. We'**re going** to Spain.*
*I'**m going** to come and see you later. I'**m coming** to see you later.*

present continuous

+	I'**m starting** my course in September.
–	We'**re** not **going** away for very long.
?	What time **are** you **leaving** in the morning?

The present continuous is formed: subject + *am/are/is* (*not*) + verb + *-ing*. Use the present continuous to talk about future plans, when arrangements have already been made. We usually specify a future time such as *next week*, *on Friday*, etc., unless it is already clear that we are talking about the future:

*We'**re flying** to Greece **on Friday**.* (We've already bought the tickets.)
*She'**s staying** in a hotel **near the airport**.* (The hotel is already booked.)

In some cases it doesn't matter if it's the present continuous or *be going to*:

*I'**m playing** football on Saturday.*
*I'**m going to** play football on Saturday.*

will

+	We'**ll meet** you at the station.
–	I **won't see** you tomorrow.
?	**Will** you **want** a taxi?

When there is no plan or arrangement (when we make a decision at the time of speaking), we often use *will*: *I'm tired. I think I'**ll go** to bed.* (subject + *will* + infinitive)

For use of *be going to* and *will* for prediction, see section 3.2 below.

might

+	I **might go** out later.
–	We **might not be able** to finish all this work tomorrow.

Use *might* + infinitive without to to talk about plans, when we are unsure what the plan is:

*I **might stay** at home and watch a DVD.*
(But I'm not sure. I might go out.)

spoken grammar

We do not usually use *might* + infinitive without *to* in the question form. It seems old-fashioned and formal:

Do you think you might see Evelyn?
NOT ~~*Might you see Evelyn?*~~

3.2 the future (predictions)

will

Use *will* to make predictions:

*Smartphones **will organise** our lives.*
*She's so talented that I'm sure she'**ll become** famous.*

We often use *I think* and *I hope* with *will*:

*I **think** John **will** become a doctor.*
*She **hopes** she **will** work in the theatre.*

be going to

Use *be going to* to make predictions when there is present evidence:

*We only have two cars. It'**s going to be** difficult to take eleven people tomorrow.*

We use *probably* to make the prediction less certain. *Probably* usually comes after *will*:

*The dollar **will probably get** stronger this year.*

Probably comes after *to be* when we use it with *be going to*:

*E-readers **are probably going to** become cheaper.*

may* and *might

Use *may* or *might* to make predictions which are less certain. The negative forms are *may not* and *might not*:

*Some of our workers **may lose** their jobs because of the restructuring.*
*We **might not go** away this year because we don't have any money.*

could

Use *could* to make predictions which are less certain:

*Global warming **could destroy** large parts of Asia in the next thirty years.*

be likely to

Use *be likely to* to make predictions when something is probable. The negative is *be unlikely to* or *not be likely to*:

*Regina **is likely to be** late because she works until seven.*
*We'**re unlikely to reach** Paris before lunch because of all the traffic.*
***Are** you **likely to be** hungry later?*

Likely/Unlikely are adjectives:

*Will we start at 5.00? It's **unlikely**.*

spoken grammar

Might is more common than may in spoken English.
May is a little bit more formal.

3.3 dealing with misunderstandings

saying you didn't hear something	I didn't catch any of that.
saying you don't understand someone's opinion	You've lost me. I don't get what you're saying.
asking someone to explain something more clearly	What exactly do you mean? Do you mean to say …?
asking someone to repeat something	Can you say that again? Could you repeat the last part/name/thing you said?

PRACTICE

3.1

A Complete the conversation. Use the prompts in brackets where necessary.

A: Where [1] ____________ you going?

B: I'm [2] ____________ to Paul's house. We' [3] ____________ going to watch the football.

A: OK. Who [4] ____________? (play)

B: Real Madrid versus Barcelona.

A: I see. And what time are you [5] ____________ home? (come)

B: I don't know.

A: How [6] ____________ getting home?

B: I'm not sure. I [7] ____________ his dad to drive me home, or I [8] ____________ catch the bus. (ask/might)

B Find and correct the mistakes. There is one mistake in each sentence.

1 Will you going out this weekend?
2 I'm sorry I can't come. I playing tennis after work.
3 I don't feel very well. I think I stay at home.
4 What you going to do?
5 We go for a picnic, so I hope it doesn't rain.
6 Is that the phone? Don't worry – I'm going to get it.
7 They might going to a concert.
8 I'm sorry we can't come, but we going to visit my mother this weekend.

3.2

A Rewrite the sentences below using the words in brackets.

1 We probably won't win the cup this year. (might)
We ____________
2 I may be late. (likely)
I'm ____________
3 That company will close in July. (going)
That company ____________
4 He probably won't call after 10.00. (unlikely)
He ____________
5 I'm not going to give up exercise. (won't)
I ____________
6 We might have a problem with the flight. (may)
There ____________
7 She'll get angry when she sees this. (going)
She ____________
8 Are you going to visit us? (will)
____
9 I would love it if he comes to the party. (hope)
____
10 It is thought prices will rise if they complete the development. (could)
Prices ____________

B Put the pairs of words in the box into the correct place to complete the sentences.

will be	aren't going	won't know	might not
likely to	may arrive	is going	not likely

1 Jenny be able to meet us tonight because she has to work late.
2 Several of our workers are lose their jobs this year because of the economic recession.
3 In twenty years' time, cars able to fly.
4 The predicted storm at any moment.
5 The children to stay with me because I'm busy.
6 I my exam results until August.
7 It's that we'll arrive before 6.00 because there are train delays.
8 Watch out! That painting to fall off the wall!

3.3

A Match 1–7 with a)–g) to make sentences and questions.

1 I didn't catch	a) you're saying.
2 You've lost	b) you mean?
3 I don't get what	c) that again?
4 What exactly do	d) to say …?
5 Could you repeat the	e) any of that.
6 Do you mean	f) last name?
7 Can you say	g) me.

GRAMMAR

4.1 *must, have to, should* (obligation)

must, have to

+	I **must** get up at 5 tomorrow. They **have to** start work early. We **must** start on time. She **has to** get there early.
–	You **mustn't** do that! We **don't have to** worry. They **mustn't** be late. He **doesn't have to** bring anything.
?	Do I/we/you **have to** bring …? (**Must** you go so early?)* **Does** he/she/it **have to** go?

*Question forms with *must* are not very common, and sound quite formal. We usually use *Do I have to …?* instead.

Use *must* and *have to* to talk about obligations. These things are necessary or important. *Must* is often used for a personal obligation (something we have decided for ourselves that we must do):

*I **must** give up eating chocolate.*

Must is also used in written rules:

*All applicants **must** provide proof of identity.*

Have to is used for external obligation:

*We **have to** wear a uniform.* (It's a company rule.)

Often you can use *must* or *have to* with the same meaning, but in spoken English *have to* is more common.

Don't have to and *mustn't* have different meanings.

Mustn't means 'it is not allowed'. *Don't/Doesn't have to* means it is not necessary, but you can do it if you want:

*You **mustn't** smoke cigarettes anywhere in the building.* (It is not permitted and it's dangerous.)

*You **don't have to** work after 6.* (It's not necessary.)

Must can only be used to talk about present or future obligation. To talk about a past obligation, use *had to*:

*We **had to** get up early to catch the plane.*

spoken grammar

Have/Has got to means the same as *have/has to* in the context of obligation and is used a lot in spoken English:

*I've **got to** get some money from the bank.*
*She's **got to** get another job.*

should/shouldn't

+	I/You/He/She/It/We/They	**should** see this film.
–		**shouldn't** smoke in the house.
?	Do you think we **should** …?*	

**Should we …* is more formal, and not very common.

Use *should* to talk about weak obligations (not as strong as *must* or *have to*). Often it is used for things which you think are a good idea (advice):

*You **should** come to work in smart clothes.*

Use *shouldn't to* talk about things which are not a good idea:

*You **shouldn't** go to bed so late.*

Ought to has the same meaning as *should*, but is not usually used in the negative or questions:

*You **ought to** call her.* = You should call her.

4.2 *used to, would*

used to

+	I/You/He/She/It/We/They	**used to** live in France.
–		**didn't use** to see my parents.
?	Did they **use to** visit?	

Use *used to* to talk about past habits/states, which have often changed or are not true now. You can also use the past simple.

*As a child, I **used to** love eating sweets.*
*As a child I **ate** a lot of sweets.*

We can also use *would* to talk about past habits, but not to talk about past states.

*I **would** go to the sweet shop every day.* (habit)
*As a child, I **was** very happy.*
*As a child I **used to be** very happy.* (state)
NOT ~~*As a child, I would be very happy.*~~ (state)

Do not use *used to* to talk about things that happened only once, or for a specific number of times/length of time. Use the past simple for this:

*My family **moved** to America last year.*
NOT ~~*My family used to move to America last year.*~~
*We **went** to Italy twice on holiday.*
NOT ~~*We used to go to Italy twice on holiday.*~~
*I **studied** at university for three years.*
NOT ~~*I used to study at university for three years.*~~

spoken grammar

Never used to is more common in spoken English than *didn't use to*.

*We **never used to** see them, except for during August.*

In short answers in spoken English, we often leave out the verb or phrase after *used to*.

*Do you smoke? No, **I used to**, but I don't any more.*

4.3 reaching agreement

giving opinions
I (really) feel that …
The way I see things, …
The way I see it, …

suggestions
What about …?
I suggest we focus on …
I think we should think about …
I suggest we think about …
How about if / Why don't we (call it)…?

commenting on other opinions	
That's a good idea.	I (don't) see what you mean.
That's a good point.	I'm not sure that I agree, actually.
That's fine by me.	I'm not sure that … is a good idea.
That's OK by me.	
Exactly!	

PRACTICE

4.1 **A** Underline the correct alternative to complete the text.

The worst jobs in the world?

If you like travelling to exotic places, perhaps you [1]*should/shouldn't* try this job. Helge Zieler is a mosquito researcher. In order to study the biting habits of the mosquito which spreads malaria in Brazil, Helge [2]*has to/doesn't have to* sit inside a mosquito net while hundreds of mosquitoes bite him. Every time he sees a mosquito land on his body, he [3]*must/have to* suck it into a tube in his mouth, and then blow it into a container. On a good evening, Helge can catch 500 mosquitoes in three hours. But to do this, he receives 3,000 bites (an average of seventeen bites per minute for 180 minutes). He [4]*mustn't/must* forget his anti-malaria tablets. Once he caught malaria and it took him two years to recover.

You [5]*shouldn't/don't have to* drive too fast on the roads, especially when you're driving in the countryside. Why? Because more than 400 million animals are killed on the roads every year. Joanne Keene knows, because she [6]*has to/shouldn't* remove them. Car drivers [7]*don't have to/must* pick the animals up, so Joanne drives around in a huge truck full of dead cats and raccoons. 'It's a hard job,' she says, 'because we work very long hours. We [8]*mustn't/must* be on call 24 hours a day.'

B Match 1–8 with a)–h) to make sentences.

1 It's a good job but we …
2 I love Saturday mornings, because I don't have to
3 I think you should
4 The doctor told me that I
5 You mustn't
6 You don't have to
7 Francois is very lucky. His father is very rich, so he
8 I really must

a) have to work hard.
b) should do more exercise.
c) come to work dressed in jeans. You have to look smart.
d) doesn't have to work at all.
e) give up smoking. It's not good for my health.
f) get up for work. I can stay in bed until 10a.m.
g) send the forms in until September, but it's a good idea to send them early.
h) think about whether you really want to apply for the job.

4.2 **A** Cross out the alternative which is not possible.

1 I *used to play/played/play* a lot of tennis when I was younger.
2 After school I *would take/used to take/take* the bus home.
3 He *never used to play/would play/played* the guitar, but he doesn't play any more.
4 I *didn't use to enjoy/didn't enjoy/wouldn't enjoy* school, but I worked hard anyway.
5 Tim *used to have/would have/had* long hair.
6 I *studied/used to study/didn't use to study* French for five years.

B Make sentences with used to or would using the words in brackets. Sometimes both may be possible.

1 In Ancient Greece, people ______________ (think) the world was flat, but Aristotle thought it was round.
2 In the olden days, people ______________ (not have) cars, so they rode horses.
3 ______________ people really ______________ (enjoy) watching gladiator fights in Ancient Rome?
4 In the sixteenth century, ladies ______________ (put) a white powder containing lead on their faces. It was poisonous.
5 Two hundred years ago, they ______________ (not use) anaesthetics to perform operations.
6 Before iron was invented, soldiers ______________ (fight) using bronze swords, but they weren't very strong and often changed shape in battle.
7 The Romans ______________ (make) themselves sick, so that they could eat more during their huge banquets.
8 Why ______________ people ______________ (eat) garlic in Ancient Egypt? It was to cure toothache.

4.3 **A** Using the words in italics, rewrite the second sentence so it has the same meaning as the first.

1 Let's begin.
I think we ___should begin___.
2 I suggest we look at the emails first.
Why ______________ ?
3 I don't understand.
I ______________ *you mean.*
4 I agree with that idea.
It's ______________ *me.*
5 From my point of view, it works very well.
The way ______________ *things, it works very well.*
6 I agree with what you have just said.
That's ______________ *point.*

GRAMMAR

5.1 comparatives and superlatives

one-syllable adjectives and two-syllable adjectives ending in *-y*

adjective	comparative	superlative	notes
cheap fast	cheaper faster	the cheapest the fastest	+*-er*/*the* +*-est*
easy friendly	easier friendlier	the easiest the friendliest	*-y* changes to *-i* + *-er* / *the* +*-est*
big	bigger	the biggest	adjective ending in *CVC double final consonant
large	larger	the largest	adjective ending in *-e*, add *-r* / *the* + *-st*

*CVC – consonant, vowel, consonant

two-syllable and longer adjectives

adjective	comparative	superlative	notes
important	more/less important than	the most/least important	+ *more/less … than*, or *the most/the least … in the …*

irregular adjectives

adjective	comparative	superlative
good	better	the best
bad	worse	the worst
Far	further/farther	the furthest/farthest

ways of comparing

Here are some common expressions used for making comparisons: *It's exactly/about the same as …, It's very similar to …, It's not as … as*:

*It's **exactly the same as** the one we had.*
*It's **very similar** to somewhere I stayed.*
*He's **not as tall as** I expected.*

It's a lot/much/far more + adjective:
*It's **far more beautiful** than I imagined.*

It's a little/a little bit/slightly:
*It's **slightly smaller** than the last flat I lived in.*

using superlatives

Here are some common expressions used with superlatives: *by far the most …, one of the most …, the second (third/fourth) most …*

*It's **by far the most** delicious meal I've ever eaten.*
*It's **one of the most** beautiful places in the world.*

We often use superlatives with a phrase beginning *in the …*:

*She's by far the best student **in the class**.*
*It's one of the tallest buildings **in the world**.*

5.2 question tags

To make question tags, add auxiliary verb + pronoun at the end of the question. For a positive sentence, use a negative tag: *You **play** tennis, **don't you**?* For a negative sentence use a positive tag: *They **weren't** here, **were they**?*

Use contractions in the tag, not the full verb: *He's nice, isn't he?* NOT ~~*He's nice, is not he?*~~ N.B. Use a comma before the question tag and a question mark after it.

	positive verb + negative tag	negative verb + positive tag
present	You're twenty, aren't you?	She doesn't swim, does she?
past	They came back, didn't they?	You didn't see Tim, did you?
present perfect	You've lost it, haven't you?	He hasn't seen us, has he?
future	I'll be back by 10.00, won't I?	We won't lose, will we?

Use question tags to check information that you think is true. Also use question tags to sound less direct (a way to sound polite).

If we are sure of the information, the intonation falls on the question tag:

You're coming tomorrow, aren't you?
(expect the answer 'yes'.)

If we are really not sure, the intonation rises on the question tag:

She's from Europe, isn't she?
(maybe she isn't)

5.3 polite requests

request	responses
Could you carry this bag **for me**? **Could you** bring your laptop with you?	Yes, of course. I'm afraid I can't/ I'm sorry, I can't.
Could you tell me the way to the hotel? **Could you tell me** what time it is?	Yes, I can. It's … Let me have a look.
Do you know what time the shops open? **Do you know** how to get there?	I'm not sure.
Would you mind coming a little bit earlier? **Would you mind** booking us a table?	Of course not. OK/Sure.

watch out!

Could you tell me …? and *Do you know …?* are not direct questions; the word order is the same as for statements:

Could you tell me what time it is?
NOT ~~*Could you tell me what time is it?*~~
Do you know what time the shops open?
NOT ~~*Do you know what time do the shops open?*~~

Would you mind … + *-ing*:
Would you mind watering my plants when I go away?
NOT ~~*Would you mind to water …?*~~

Would you mind …? is followed by a negative response:
Would you mind helping me? No, of course not.
(I'm happy to help you) NOT ~~*Yes, of course.*~~
(I would mind helping you = I'm not happy to help you)

PRACTICE

5.1

A Complete the sentences with the comparative or superlative form of the adjectives in brackets.

1 We usually fly to Italy instead of going in the car, because it's ____________. (quick)
2 They had to travel ____________ than they wanted to find a hotel. (far)
3 When I was a teenager, I was much ____________ than I am now. (not confident)
4 He's one of ____________ children in the class. (naughty)
5 Exams are much ____________ now than they were when I was at school. (easy)
6 Sweden is ____________ than Norway. (big)
7 K2 is the second ____________ mountain in the world. (high)
8 This book is slightly ____________ to understand than his last book. The plot is very complicated. (difficult)
9 He used to be a teacher, but he's decided to become a firefighter. It's a much ____________ job. (dangerous)
10 It's by far ____________ film I've ever seen. (good)

B Rewrite the sentences using the words in bold, so that they have the same meaning.

1 My brother is slightly taller than I am. **bit**
____
2 The journey to the coast took much longer than we had expected. **far**
____
3 It's easily the most expensive restaurant I've ever been to. **by**
____
4 Your shoes and my shoes are almost the same. **similar**
____
5 People here are much healthier now that they have clean water. **lot**
____

5.2

A Match 1–8 with a)–h) to make tag questions.

1 Clive was an engineer,
2 You're from Ethiopia,
3 Shania isn't an actress,
4 They haven't been here before,
5 He'll be home soon,
6 You work here,
7 She hasn't met you,
8 They won't finish on time,

a) have they?
b) won't he?
c) has she?
d) aren't you?
e) is she?
f) will they?
g) wasn't he?
h) don't you?

B Find and correct the mistakes. There is one mistake in each question.

1 You weren't happy, weren't you?
2 It'll probably rain, doesn't it?
3 She researched her roots, didn't her?
4 They always ask tricky questions, they don't?
5 I take after my dad, doesn't he?
6 You've met Kevin's fiancée, have not you?
7 I put my foot in it yesterday, haven't I?
8 My mentor will give me a hand, he won't?
9 You had a lot on your mind, doesn't you?
10 Phil and Luke are on holiday, are not they?

5.3

A Find the mistakes and correct them. There is an extra word or two in each line.

1 **A:** Excuse me, could you is hold the door for me?
B: Yes, I do of course.
2 **A:** Do you know when the next train does to leaves?
B: I'm not OK sure.
3 **A:** Would you to mind staying behind after the meeting?
B: It's sure. That's fine.
4 **A:** Could is possible you tell me what Tim's phone number is?
B: Let me have a to look.
5 **A:** Would you mind to looking after my bag while I go to the bathroom?
B: No, of course not mind.
6 **A:** Could you tell for me the way to the station?
B: Yes, so I can.

Lesson 1.2 RELATIONSHIPS

1 A Complete the family tree with the words in the box.

~~in-laws~~ sister-in-law niece nephew grandparents on my mother's side ex-husband stepfather stepdaughter

B Tell your partner about one or two people in your family.

Lesson 1.2 COLLOCATIONS with *take*, *get*, *do* and *go*

1 Write the words and phrases in italics in the correct places in the word webs below.

1 *your best, exercise, nothing for you, the cleaning*

do
- *hobby* ______ (action)
- *well* ______ (good effort)
- *the washing up* ______ (something at home)
- *you good* ______ (be affected)

2 *fired, a prize, excited, food poisoning*

get
- *a good salary* ______ (earn)
- *a job* ______ (change your work situation)
- *flu/a cold* ______ (become ill)
- *depressed* ______ (become)

3 *a look, the blame, sugar, ages*

take
- *medicine* ______ (swallow)
- *ten minutes* ______ (use time)
- *a photo* ______ (action)
- *responsibility* ______ (accepting something)

4 *on holiday, crazy, together, badly*

go
- *blind* ______ (become)
- *well* ______ (happen)
- *by bus* ______ (travel)
- *with* ______ (fit)

Lesson 2.1 PREPOSITIONS of place

1 Match descriptions 1–5 with pictures A–E.

1 They drove along the motorway, and over the bridge.
2 They went around the city.
3 They drove through the main square, past the post office and turned left by the station.
4 The hotel is near the city centre, between the National Museum and the cathedral.
5 The house is next to the supermarket, opposite the cinema.

A
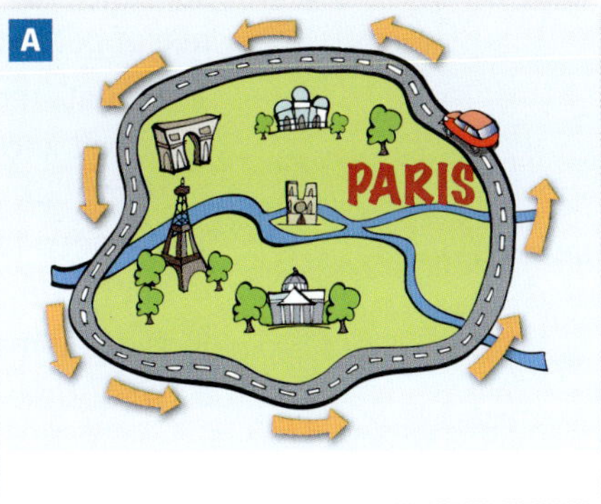

B

C

D

E

Lesson 2.2 THE NEWS

1 A Read the text and match the words and phrases in bold with definitions 1–10 below.

1 a group of criminals who work together ____________
2 thieves carrying weapons ____________ ____________
3 an attack by criminals on a bank, shop, etc., to steal money or valuable things ____________
4 (doing something) while threatening to shoot someone ____________ ____________
5 people whose job it is to protect people or a place, or to make sure that a person does not escape ____________ ____________
6 leave a place or dangerous situation when someone is trying to catch you ____________
7 people who saw the crime ____________ ____________
8 took people who were involved in a crime away (to a police station) ____________
9 warn people that something bad is happening ____________ ____________ ____________
10 made someone do this ____________

Two **security guards** were kidnapped and held hostage for twelve hours by a **gang** of **armed robbers**, who attempted to **raid** a security depot. The robbers held the guards **at gunpoint** and **forced** them to hand over keys and security information. They then proceeded to fill a lorry with more than £53 million in notes. Another £150 million was left behind because there was no more room in the getaway vehicle. Luckily, one of the guards managed to **raise the alarm**, and the police arrived and **arrested** the gang before they could **escape**. **Eye witnesses** said that they saw at least eight men being arrested.

B Divide the words and phrases into two groups: people and actions. Which words do not fit in either group?

C Tell your partner about a crime you've heard about. It can be from the news, a film or your own experience.

Lesson 3.1 EXPRESSIONS with *get*

1 A Look at the examples for the different uses of *get*.

get + noun = obtain
*Sophie **got a new job** yesterday.*
get + noun = receive
*He **got a letter** from the company.*
get + noun = buy
*Can you remember to **get some milk** on the way home?*
get somewhere
*What time did you **get here**?*
get + adjective
*I'm **getting bored** of this.*
get in phrasal verbs
*I really need to **get on with** my work.*

B Underline the expressions with *get* in sentences 1–6. Match each sentence with the correct use of *get* in Exercise 1A

1 He gets money by selling furniture on the internet.
2 I don't know when I'll get around to finishing that book.
3 We need to get permission to use the room.
4 I'm getting tired. Shall we finish there?
5 Did you manage to get some new trousers?
6 What time does the train get to Budapest?

Lesson 3.2 IDIOMS

1 A Match pictures A–F with the idioms in the box.

be in two minds	let your hair down	break the ice	travel light	learn (something) by heart	go window shopping

A

B

C

D

E

F

B Complete the sentences with the idioms above.

1 Tomorrow there's a test on this poem. I have to ____________ it ____________ ____________.
2 I'm ____________ ____________ ____________. I don't know if I want the black one or the red one.
3 Everyone was nervous, so Jackie told a few jokes to ____________ ____________ ____________.
4 He always ____________ ____________. He only takes one suitcase even for long trips.
5 I've got no money at the moment but we can go ____________ ____________ if you want.
6 You've been working non-stop. Why don't you go out and ____________ ____________ ____________ ____________?

C What do you think the idioms mean? Use a dictionary to help you.

Lesson 4.1 PERSONAL QUALITIES

1 A Complete the sentences with the adjectives in the box.

reliable sensible easy-going aggressive bright honest keen punctual moody independent

1 She is very ______________ . She works well by herself.
2 You never know what to expect. She's very ______________ , so one minute she's happy, and the next minute, she's shouting at you.
3 She's very ______________ . I'm sure she will know what to do if there's a difficult situation.
4 He's extremely ______________ . He is never late for appointments.
5 My new manager is very ______________ . She doesn't mind what time we get to work, what we wear. She never looks stressed.
6 He always tells the truth. He's very ______________ .
7 She's always looking for extra jobs to do. She's very ______________ .
8 He's very ______________ . He learns very quickly.
9 You know that you can trust and depend on him. He's hard-working and very ______________ .
10 He nearly attacked one of his employees when he arrived late for the meeting. He's very ______________ .

B **Look at the adjectives in the box again. Do they describe positive or negative characteristics? Do you have any of these characteristics?**

Lesson 4.1 WORKING LIFE

1 A Match descriptions 1–3 with jobs A–C.

1 I work as a ______________ for a large corporation. I usually **work nine-to-five**, but sometimes I have to work late. My job involves checking and responding to emails, **answering phone enquiries** and **organising** my boss's diary.

2 I'm an ______________ . I tend to **work long hours. I'm responsible for** a small team of people. I spend a lot of my time attending meetings, and **dealing with problems**. I **advise clients** on their accounts and **write updates and reports** for the website.

3 I'm a ______________ . Lots of people wouldn't like what I do, because it's **an outdoor job**, and it's a **physical job**, but I love it. I **work for myself**, so I can be very independent, and I **work flexible hours**, which is good for me. It's a very sociable job, too. I talk to people all day long. I couldn't do **an office job**. I would die of boredom!

A Window cleaner

B Personal assistant

C Accountant

B **Work in pairs. What do the phrases in bold mean?**

Lesson 4.1 CONFUSING WORDS

1 A Choose the correct option from the words in bold to complete the pairs of sentences.

1 **actually • currently**
a) I expected the first week in my new job to be awful, but ______________ it was fine.
b) I am ______________ working in London, but before I was working in Paris.

2 **career • course**
a) She's doing a Spanish ______________ at the moment, and she's really enjoying it.
b) Ted spent most of his ______________ as a teacher.

3 **borrow • lend**
a) Do you think you could ______________ me a pen?
b) I had to ______________ some money from a friend.

4 **argument • discussion**
a) We had an interesting ______________ about the Prime Minister and we all agreed he should resign.
b) I had an ______________ with my mother. She's always telling me what to do!

5 **miss • lose**
a) Hurry up, or we'll ______________ the bus.
b) Why do I always ______________ my car keys?

B **Check your answers in a dictionary.**

Lesson 5.1 TECHNOLOGY

1 Match words and phrases 1–10 with pictures A–J.

1 plug it in
2 press the button
3 have an injection
4 have an operation
5 run out of petrol
6 break down
7 (not) get a connection
8 restart/reboot the computer
9 do an experiment
10 switch it on/off

A

B

C

D

E

F

G

H

I
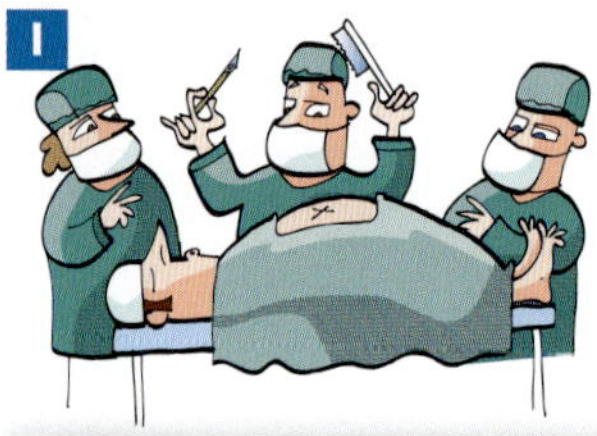

J

Lesson 5.2 WORD BUILDING noun (suffixes)

1 A Look at the table in Exercise B. It shows six different suffixes used to form nouns from verbs and adjectives.

B Underline the stressed part of each word in the table. What patterns do you notice about where the stress occurs?

In -ation words, the stress always comes on the a of -ation.

-ation	education relaxation imagination immigration
-ion	pollution instruction depression competition
-ment	entertainment improvement employment agreement
-ing	running smoking laughing eating
-ness	weakness loneliness happiness kindness
-ity	creativity stupidity sensitivity responsibility

C Cover the table and complete sentences 1–10 with the correct form of the verbs and adjectives in brackets.

1 I think a bit of ____________ (compete) in schools is a good thing.
2 There has been a great ____________ (improve) in his work recently.
3 Dealing with problem clients is not my ____________ (responsible).
4 ____________ (lonely) is one of the worst aspects of getting old.
5 He suffers from ____________ (depress).
6 Try to use your ____________ (imagine).
7 I couldn't believe my own ____________ (stupid)!
8 There is live ____________ (entertain) from 8p.m.
9 I was amazed by his ____________ (kind).
10 I didn't hear the last ____________ (instruct).

pay
imitate
heavy
skate
informal
direct
achieve
quote
dance
fit
promote
secure

2 Change the words above to the correct noun form and add them to the table.

Lesson 1.2

3 C Look at your drawing. Does it include these things?

Lesson 1.2

7 B Read the text and check your answers.

Stella magazine commissioned YouGov, a research agency, to interview over 1,000 women in the UK about everything from their eating habits to their relationships and family values, to find out what they really think. Here are some of the results.

Eighty percent of women say that losing their health is their greatest concern, followed by putting on weight (52%) and losing their jobs (24%). It seems that British women aren't too happy with their bodies: twenty-three percent of women are on a diet now and fifty-eight percent have **gone on a diet** in the past. Only four percent of women **do** more than seven hours' **exercise** per week, while twenty-one percent do no exercise at all.

The biggest challenge for modern women is balancing home and work life (82%), followed by bringing up happy children (56%) and finding time for themselves (52%).

As for their love lives, nine percent of women aged 45–54 met their husbands through the internet, and forty-nine percent of women believe that the best age to **get married** is between 25 and 29.

And what about the relationships between men and women? Fifty-nine percent think fathers should **take more responsibility** for their children. These women are also less than content with their husbands' efforts at home: fifty-one percent say they currently **do** over seventy-five percent of the **housework**. Despite this, over seventy percent of women would prefer to have a male boss than a female.

And their heroes? The woman they most admire is ex-Prime Minister Margaret Thatcher (7%), followed by the Queen (5%).

Lesson 1.3

8 A Student A: read your instructions below.

You work for a famous business school. Student B wants to do a course at the school. Interview him/her. Use the following prompts and ask about:

- his/her reason for doing the course
- his/her work experience
- his/her expectations of the course
- his/her plans for the future

Prepare the questions. Remember to ask your partner why he/she is a good candidate for the school and, at the end, if he/she has any queries about the business school.

B Change roles and role-play the interview again.

Lesson 2.1

1 B Read and check your answers.

HOLLYWOOD versus history

Fact or fiction:

1 **Fiction:** the film *The Last Samurai* does tell the story of the samurai rebellion, but the character Nathan Algren did not exist.

2 **Fiction:** in truth, we know very little about William Shakespeare's personal life, or what provided his inspiration.

3 **Partly true:** the film *Braveheart* does tell the story of how William Wallace fought to free Scotland, but kilts were not worn in Scotland until 300 years later. And there are many other historical inaccuracies.

4 **Partly true:** the film *Apollo 13* was praised for its accuracy. Much of the dialogue was taken directly from recordings. However, the pilot's exact words were, 'OK, Houston, we've had a problem here'.

Lesson 2.1

8 A Student B: write *Have you ever …?* questions using the prompts in the box below.

win a competition/some money
eat something very unusual
break a bone in your body
lock yourself out of the house
ride a horse/motorbike
climb a mountain/run more than two kilometres

Lesson 2.4

6 B Student A: Look at the picture story. What happened? Why was the robbery attempt a failure? Prepare to tell your story to your partner using the phrases in Exercise 5C.

Lesson 3.3

6 B Change roles and role-play the situation.

Student B

You are a guest at a hotel. Your room is too small. Ten minutes ago you called reception to ask if there are any suites available. Then room service arrived with a trolley of sweets (cakes, ice cream, etc.). Call reception to make your complaint.

Student A

You are a receptionist at a hotel. A guest calls to make a complaint. Start the conversation by saying '*Reception. How can I help you?*'

Hello. Yes, I'm afraid I have a problem … Explain the problem again and ask if there is a suite available.

Apologise for the misunderstanding. Explain that there are no suites available at the moment, but there will be tomorrow.

Check details and thank the receptionist for their help.

Confirm details, apologise again and end the call.

Lesson 3.2

7 D Check your answers.

1 False. Compare: *This is absolutely correct.* (formal) *This hits the nail on the head.* (informal)

2 True. The order of the words in *hit the nail on the head, let's face it, close to my heart,* etc. cannot be changed.

3 True. They don't have much time. *They're running out of time.* (present continuous) *We didn't finish. We ran out of time.* (past simple)

4 True. *It's close to my heart* = I feel passionate about it.

Lesson 4.1

6 A Work out your score. Add up the number of points (0, 1 or 2) for each answer. Use your total to find out if you work like a millionaire.

Question 1	**a) 0**	**b) 1**	**c) 2**
Question 2	**a) 1**	**b) 2**	**c) 0**
Question 3	**a) 0**	**b) 1**	**c) 2**
Question 4	**a) 1**	**b) 2**	**c) 0**
Question 5	**a) 0**	**b) 1**	**c) 2**

Key:

Score 8–10 You work like a millionaire!
You are very ambitious and enjoy your work. Keep going. Sooner or later all your hard work will pay off and you can live like a millionaire, too.

Score 6–7 You have millionaire potential!
You understand hard work, and if you make it your top priority, you could be a millionaire, too. Keep focused on your goal.

Score 0–5 You don't work like a millionaire!
The clearest characteristics of self-made millionaires is that they work hard and they enjoy their work. You seem to prefer a work–life balance, where work and money are not your top priorities.

Lesson 4.1

8 B Read the vocabulary notes and check your answers.

remember • remind

If you **remember** something, a fact or event from the past, or something you earlier decided to do, comes back into your mind:
He suddenly remembered he had to go to the bank.
If someone **reminds** you to do something, or something reminds you of something, they make you remember it:
Can you remind me?

forget • leave

If you want to talk about the place where you have left something, use the verb **leave**, not the verb **forget**. Compare:
I've forgotten my book and I've forgotten my keys.
I've left my keys in the car.
Don't say: *I've forgotten my keys in the car.*

listen • hear

If you **hear** something, you know that sound has been made, and can often recognise what it is:
Did you hear that noise?
If you **listen** to something or someone, you pay attention to the words, sounds and music that they are making:
Can you say that again? I'm sorry, I wasn't listening.

fun • funny

Use **fun** to talk about events and activities that are enjoyable, such as games and parties. We can also use it to talk about events that aren't enjoyable.
Being ill on holiday isn't much fun.
Funny is an adjective that describes someone or something that makes you laugh:
Bob's jokes are really funny.

Lesson 2.4

6 B Student B: Look at the picture story. What happened? Why was the burglary attempt a failure? Prepare to tell your story to your partner using the phrases in Exercise 5C.

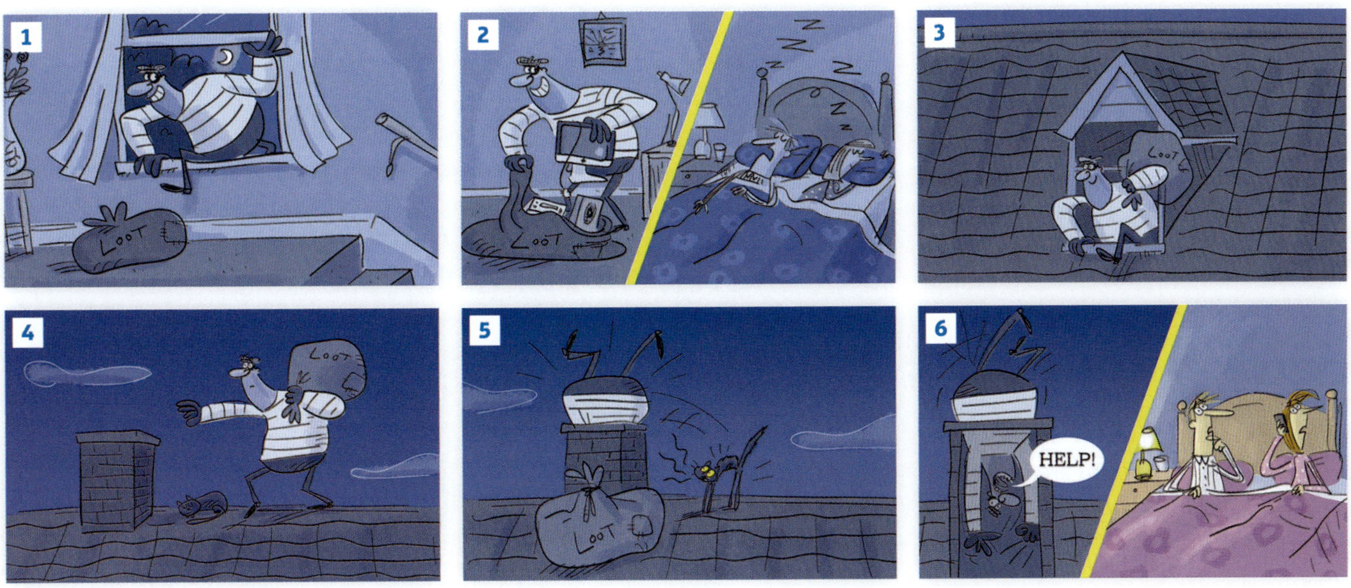

Lesson 4.2

11 **Choose one of the job advertisements below and write your covering letter.**

JOB OPPORTUNITIES

FASHION DESIGNER WANTED:

We are looking for a graphic designer with a background in the fashion trade. You should have relevant experience and be up-to-date with fashion trends. Strong hand illustration as well as computer design is essential.

Please submit a copy of your CV with relevant samples of work.

TEACHING ASSISTANT, BAHAMAS

Primary school is looking for a teaching assistant to start ASAP. The school is a short walk from the beach. No formal qualifications are necessary; however, a genuine love for the job is required.

Please forward CVs or contact me for further information.

TRAVEL WRITER REQUIRED.

Travel writer wanted to join our small team. The successful applicant will travel around the world, staying in luxury hotels, and dining in fine restaurants. He/She will need to send a weekly update, including a short review. No previous experience required, but good communication skills and a love of travel essential.

Lesson 5.2

1 **C** **Check your answers.**

1 Nobody has ever done it, but in theory, yes it is possible.

2 Because it is made of frozen water. It must be below zero degrees Celsius to freeze.

3 Yes. If you travel, you'll notice that you can see different constellations of stars. This is because the surface of the Earth is curved.

4 When we cut an onion, it releases a substance called lachrymatory-factor synthase. When a very small amount goes in your eye it irritates the eye. We then produce tears (we cry) to wash the substance away.

5 Neither hot nor cold. A rainbow is an optical phenomenon caused by the refraction and reflection of sunlight by water. It is the same temperature as the air around it.

6 Because the heavier you are, the more difficult it is to push you out of the ring (which is how you win a sumo wrestling match).

Lesson 1.3

8 **A** **Student B: read your instructions below.**

You want to do a course at a famous business school which is well-known for its practical courses. It will give you contacts in the business world. Think about these things:

- the business you want to start
- relevant work experience you have with another company

Student A will interview you for the course. He/She will ask about your:

- reason for doing the course
- work experience
- expectations of the course
- plans for the future

Prepare your answers and think of some questions to ask about the school.

B **Change roles and role-play the interview again.**

Unit 1 Recording 3

Part one

Is your brain male or female? Well, you might think it's a strange question but some researchers have found that men and women's brains are actually wired differently. So, let's do a test to see if your brain is male or female. In a moment, we're going to ask you to draw a picture of a bicycle. So, make sure you have a pen or pencil ready.

Part two

OK, so I want you to draw a picture of a bicycle. You have exactly one minute, starting now ... Make it as beautiful or normal as you like. Include as much detail as you can. You've got forty-five seconds left ... You've got another fifteen seconds ...
You've got five seconds left ... four, three, two, one, zero, stop. Right, stop drawing please. Now, write down on your piece of paper, whether you, the artist, are male or female. That's all we need to know for the experiment. Now turn to page a hundred and fifty-eight to see what a real bike looks like.

(For this edition, turn to page eighty three.)

Unit 1 Recording 4

Part three

Now, count up the parts on your drawing. Did you include wheels? A handlebar? A saddle? A chain? A crossbar? Pedals? Did your bike have at least five parts? And could it work? Now for the difference between the men's drawings of a bicycle and the women's: female drawings often include a person riding the bike; men's drawings don't usually include a person. This is a clear indication that women think people are important. Men, on the other hand, are more interested in getting the machine right. So, how did you do? Is your brain male or female?

Unit 1 Recording 5

Conversation 1

S = student T = teacher

T: And what about your expectations of the course?
S: Well, as I said, I've studied English for many years and spent time in Britain, but that was a few years ago. So for me the most important thing is to just refresh ... and try to remember my English and practise speaking and listening.
T: OK. You've got a very good level of English so we'd put you in the advanced class. Is there anything else?
S: Could I ask a question?
T: Of course.
S: I can take the morning class from nine to twelve. Is that right?
T: Yes, that's right.
S: And in the afternoon there are options? Optional classes?
T: Yes, these are special classes with a special focus like English idioms, conversation, pronunciation. We have the full list here.
S: I see. Thank you.
T: No problem. OK, well, thank you very much.

Conversation 2

I = Interviewer A = Applicant

I: There are a couple of things I'd like to ask about, Jade. Your CV says you have some experience of looking after children?
A: Yes, I was a tutor on a summer camp last year.
I: Can I ask you about that? What type of things did you do?
A: Um, well, I organised games.
I: Games for?
A: The children.
I: OK. And what age were the children?
A: Um ... seven to ten.
I: OK. And you enjoyed it?
A: Yes.
I: What aspect, what part did you enjoy, would you say?
A: I suppose I'd have to say I liked the games best.
I: And any problems?
A: Um, no.
I: What about the different ages? We often find that different ages together can be difficult.
A: It depends. In my opinion, you can usually get the older children to help the younger ones.

Conversation 3

I = Interviewer S = Student

I: I think that's about it. Do you have any questions? Any queries?
S: Um, yes, actually I do have a query.
I: Yes, go ahead.
S: It's about online classes at the university.
I: Right.
S: If I'm accepted, I saw that there are ... urm, that it's possible to take some courses online.
I: That's right.
S: So I wouldn't need to attend classes?
I: Not for the online courses. But, erm ... well, one thing I'd like to say is that the online courses are, in many ways, more difficult than face-to-face courses. Certainly in terms of reading and writing, they're really quite demanding.

Unit 1 Recording 7

OK so I'm going to tell you something about myself. My name is Monica Nielson and I live in a small town near Bologna, in Italy. I think three words that describe me would be happy, talkative and hard-working. One of the things I love about my lifestyle is that I love the house where I live. I live in an apartment with my boyfriend, and it's an old apartment in the historical part of town, so it's very beautiful. It's quite small, so I suppose that's one thing I don't like. My favourite smell is the smell of the sea. We live quite far from the sea here, but in the summer, I love to drive to the coast, and breathe the sea air. It makes me feel good. And, finally ... if I could change one thing about the past, I would bring my grandmother back. She was a lovely lady and I miss her a lot.

Unit 2 Recording 3

P1 = Presenter 1 P2 = Presenter 2 R = Rosie (a film historian)

P1: Hi and welcome to The Film Show, where today we're looking at the Hollywood biopic and why it's become so popular. Now, Hollywood has always used true stories in its films. In fact, they began making successful films in the 1920s, and since then there have been thousands of films based on true stories.
P2: That's right, but in recent years, there've been more and more biopics. Directors have turned to the lives of famous people as a source of material. So, why is it that some of the best films in recent years have been based on real events, or inspired by real people?
P1: Today, we're talking to Rosie Truman, an actor and a film historian. Rosie, why do you think Hollywood is doing so many biopics?
R: Well, one reason is that audiences really enjoy films about people that they already know something about, but they want to know more. So, from these films we've learnt something. We've learnt about the difficult lives of some of the biggest music legends, like Ray Charles and Johnny Cash. And we've learnt about the lives of politicians, like George Bush, or sporting heroes, like Muhammad Ali. It's a way in which Hollywood can actually teach us about history in an entertaining way. And it's interesting.
P2: Yes, I think that's right.
P2: But what about the actors, Rosie? I mean, many of the actors have won Oscars for their roles in these films. What's it like for them?

R: Well, I think actors just love these roles. It's very exciting to be asked to play a character who everyone already knows. Look at Helen Mirren. She won an Oscar for her role playing the Queen, and it's probably one of her greatest successes.
P1: Oh, absolutely! So, how do they do it? How does an actor prepare for a role like this? Do they meet the person that they're going to play?
R: Well, yes, obviously, if that person is still alive, then that's a great way for the actor to study the character, to see how they move and how they talk. In fact, I know that Helen Mirren met the Queen for tea, you know, very English. And that really helped her to understand her character. And Will Smith, who played Muhammad Ali … well, when they met, they got on really well, and … and they became friends.
P2: But what about playing a character that everyone knows, like George Bush, for example?
R: Yes, it's funny actually, when you're playing a character that people recognise, you have to work really hard at getting the voice right. Josh Brolin played George Bush. And when he was preparing for the film, he talked to himself all day in a Texan accent. He even phoned hotels in Texas, just so he could listen to their accent.
P1: Really? That's funny. What about actors who can't meet the character in person? What do they do?
R: Well, there are other ways to prepare. Audrey Tautou, for example. She played Coco Chanel. So she couldn't meet her in person, but she watched hours and hours of film footage. She watched her in interviews, and she looked at the photographs. Tautou wanted to look like Coco Chanel when she was on screen, so that we would recognise the image.
P2: That's right. And it was a beautiful film.
R: It was, and you know one of the things …

Unit 2 Recording 6

P = Presenter N1 = 1st news clip N2 = 2nd news clip
N3 = 3rd news clip N4 = 4th news clip

P: Hello. I know what I was doing. Do you?
N1: Buckingham Palace has announced the death of Diana, Princess of Wales. The Princess, who was thirty-six, died late last night in a car crash in central Paris.
N2: It's one small step for man, one giant leap for mankind.
N3: Breaking news in here at five live. There are reports that a plane has crashed into the World Trade Center in New York. That's a plane is reportedly crashed into the World Trade Center in New York, setting it on fire …
N4: President Kennedy and Governor John Connally of Texas were shot today from an ambush as President Kennedy's motorcade left the centre of Dallas …

Unit 2 Recording 8

W = Woman M = Man

M: OK, so, tell me all about it …
W: Well, in the beginning, I was at home, and … um … this was just one morning before a very important interview …
M: Uh-huh.
W: And … um … I didn't feel well, so my mother had given me some pills, and um … then I didn't think anything more about it. So, anyway, erm … I then got on to the tube, um … to go for my interview.
M: Right, and what happened then?
W: Well, um … clearly I must have fallen asleep, because I wasn't feeling great by this time. And um, I'm starting to feel sleepy, so I'm thinking I must have fallen asleep. Anyway, erm … I was getting some funny looks, even before I fell asleep, but anyway. I fell asleep, and then I realised, before long, um … I must have been having a dream, I suppose, about my mother. And all of a sudden, I've woken up, but I haven't just woken up, I've woken up shouting the word, 'Mum!'.
M: No! You're joking!
W: At the top of my voice, in a packed, quiet tube.
M: Oh no!
W: Yes, and everybody's staring at me, and that did not help, er, matters. Anyway, I've got off the tube, and I've then arrived at my interview, put all that behind me, I'm not, I'm still not feeling a hundred per cent perfect, but nevertheless arrived at my interview on time, and go in, and think, actually 'This is going rather well. They're not saying an awful lot, and come to think of it, they're looking at me in a rather strange way.'
M: Right …Then what?
W: Well, the next thing I knew, I have left the interview, and said 'thank you very much for seeing me, blah-di-blah … and gone to the ladies' room. And there in the mirror, I could see what everyone was looking at, and why they couldn't say anything,
M: What was it?
W: My face had swollen up!
M: Ah! No way!
W: It was bright red, and …
M: No!
W: and covered in blotches, spots …
M: Oh! You're kidding!
W: Yes, and the pills that my mother had given me were so out-of-date that they had caused an allergic reaction …
M: Oh! How embarrassing!
W: I know.

Unit 2 Recording 9

M = Man W2 = 2nd woman W = Woman

M: OK. What do we reckon? True or false?
W2: Erm … I don't know. I think it might be false because … I don't know …
M: Yeah, she was a little bit slow in telling the story …
W2: I don't know if your mum would give you out-of-date pills …
M: Yeah, would a mother giver her daughter out-of-date pills?
W2: I think false.
M: It sounded like she was trying to think of what to say next, so … you t think false, I think false.
W: Yes, it was false!

Unit 2 Recording 11

OK. This story is about a man called Radu Dogaru, who stole famous paintings from a museum in Rotterdam. In fact, he stole paintings by Picasso, Matisse and Monet. The paintings were worth millions of pounds. What Radu didn't realise was that because the paintings were so famous, he had difficulty selling them. So, he tried to hide them at home. Later, the police thought they had caught Radu. However, the problem was that when they went to search for the paintings, they couldn't find them. It seems that when Radu's mother, Olga, found out what Radu had done, she destroyed the paintings by burning them in her oven in order to protect her son. In the end, Radu was arrested for the theft.

Unit 3 Recording 1

L = Laurie K = Kenna J = Javier

L: OK, so what do you think, Kenna? Are you a planner or a procrastinator?
K: Me? Oh a planner, definitely.
L: Yes, I think so. You generally like to do things ahead of time.
K: Absolutely. Yeah. I like to be organised, and know when everything is happening.
I have to be like that, actually. It's the only way to get everything done.

J: Really? I hate planning. I like to leave things until the last minute. I mean, you never know what's going to happen. You might need to change your plans, so why bother making plans in the first place? No, I like not knowing what I'm going to be doing.
K: But that's impossible. What about holidays, for example? You must know what you're doing for your next holiday. I mean, you need to decide where you're going, how you're going to travel, book the dates, get the tickets ... There's so much do organise. Surely you have to plan for holidays? You can't just put that off until later.
J: Not really. I don't mind where I go.
K: No, I don't believe, ... you're just saying that. I think you do make plans, you just don't like to admit it.
J: No, really. I much prefer to wait and see what happens. I might get invited somewhere.
L: OK, so maybe for holidays. But what about tonight? Have you made any plans for tonight?
K: Yes. Of course. I can tell you exactly what I'm doing tonight. This evening a friend of mine's coming over. We're eating at my house – I'm going to try out a new pasta recipe. And then we're going to the cinema to see that new Argentinian film.
L: Javier?
J: Uhhh ... I don't really know. I'll see how I feel. I might go out, or I might just stay at home and relax. I told you. I really don't like to plan.
L: How about at about work? Are you more organised at work? Do you multitask? I mean, how do you make sure you get everything done?
J: ... actually, I think I am a procrastinator. I do get jobs done, but I never get started straight away. I tend to waste time and get distracted and leave the job for ages. And then just before the deadline, I work really hard, sometimes all night. And then I don't stop until the job is done. It's quite stressful, but everything gets done in the end.
K: You don't use your time very wisely then? Oh no, I'd hate that. I don't think I could work with you.

Unit 3 Recording 4

Conversation 1

W = Woman M = Man

W: Hi. Me again. I've sent an attachment with all the figures for the last six months. That should be all you need.
M: Sorry – I didn't catch any of that.
W: I've sent the figures in an attachment. Is that Tom?
M: You've lost me. Who is this?
W: This is Ana Lucia. Is that Tom?
M: No, this is Willy's Burger Bar. What number are you trying to get?
W: 845 6795.
M: I think you've got the wrong number.
W: Oh I'm sorry.

Conversation 2

W = Woman M = Man

M: I've got a reservation in the name of David Cullinan.
W: Just one moment. Umm, could you repeat the last name?
M: Cullinan. C-u-l-l-i-n-a-n.
W: Cullinan. I can't find the name. Did you make the reservation over the phone?
M: Yes, just yesterday.
W: Sorry, let me just see if there are any messages here. I won't be a moment. I'm sorry. We've got no reservations in the name of Cullinan, and we're fully booked tonight.
M: So you're saying I can't stay here. This is the Sheldon Hotel, yes?
W: No, this is The Felton. With an 'f'.
M: Really? So I'm in the wrong hotel.
W: The Sheldon is on Queen's Road, just around the corner.
M: Oh no. Sorry, can you say that again – where is it?
W: On Queen's Road, just around the corner.

Conversation 3

F = Father G = Girl

G: You've missed the best bits. You're late.
F: What exactly do you mean? The show starts at 7.00, doesn't it?
G: No, it finishes at 7.00!
F: Didn't you say it starts at 7.00?
G: No, it starts at 5.00 and finishes at 7.00!
F: So what you mean is I've missed the whole show.
G: Yes.

Conversation 4

M = Man W = Woman

M: We've got nothing for you, I'm afraid.
W: I don't get what you're saying. You're a car rental company, right?
M: Yes, but today's a holiday and all the cars have been booked already.
W: Do you mean to tell me that there's nothing at all? No cars available?
M: There's nothing till tomorrow, I'm afraid.
W: But I definitely booked a car for today, the third of July.
M: It's the fourth of July today. In other words, your booking was for yesterday.
W: It can't be. Is it?
M: It's the fourth today, madam.
W: Oh no, I've got the date wrong.

Unit 3 Recording 7

W = Woman M = Man

W: OK, so we're looking at creating a video channel.
M: Yep. The first thing, I think, is what's our target audience?
W: Yeah, what's our aim?
M: Well, we came up with this idea.
W: Go on.
M: That it would be really cool to do a series of videos about local places, but with a special angle.
W: Oh that sounds good. What's the angle?
M: An hour to kill. So, say you're in Sydney or Istanbul or anywhere really, and you have an hour to kill, we have a video of someone describing something to do in that place in an hour or less.
W: Oh I see. So the target audience is tourists.
M: It could be tourists or local people. Say you find yourself in a part of the city that you don't know very well.
W: OK.
M: And you have a bit of spare time, by going onto our video channel you get all kinds of suggestions of what to do or where to visit in under an hour. And the clips are filmed on location so you get to see the places, too.
W: I like it. So who will be the presenters? Will you have any star names?
M: No, we don't have any money! We'd get local people to host each video clip, with just one camera, kind of cheap and cheerful, low production values, but really cool content.
W: Who are our competitors or rivals? It must have been done before.
M: Oh I'm sure, but I don't know if it's been done with the angle of an hour to kill.
W: OK. Um, what else? How often will we upload videos?
M: Well we'll try to get coverage of as many cities and towns around the world as possible. So, I don't know, one a day? So in a year we'll have three-hundred-and-sixty-five. Then we just carry on from there.
W: Wow. Very ambitious. What about a name?
M: We thought of One Hour Wonders.
W: One Hour Wonders. I like it!

Unit 4 Recording 2

Luca

Well, I've always loved sport and swimming. As a kid I used to spend all my free time in the summer on the beach with my friends. We would swim or surf, or just play about in the water. And there was always a lifeguard there on the beach, and I used to think, 'What a **brilliant** job!'. So, when I left school, I trained to be a lifeguard. I really enjoyed the job for a few years. In the summer I would work on the beach, and then in the winter I would go skiing. It was my dream job. I loved it. But after a while, I started to get bored. I was just on this **boiling** beach all day, watching all the **beautiful** people, but I couldn't really enjoy myself, you know. I just had to stand there and watch. So I knew it was time to find something else to do.

Nicola

I used to be an ice-cream taster and for a while it was definitely my dream job. I mean can you imagine anything better than sitting at work eating **delicious** ice cream all day? I was in heaven. I was working for a big company, with a team of food scientists, and our job was to come up with new ideas for ice cream flavours. So, I suppose that was the problem, because a lot of the time, we had to try new flavours, like curry and lime ice cream, or cheese and sausage, and we would have to taste it, and usually it was **terrible**, really disgusting. Now most people would just say, 'Yuck, I'm not eating that again'. But unfortunately, when it's your job, you have to keep tasting it to see if they have made it any better. Sometimes we would taste thirty different ice cream flavours before lunch. So, it wasn't all good.

Amy

I was a professional shopper for a while. It was good fun at first. The lady I worked for was a television presenter, and she needed outfits to wear on television, but she didn't have time to go shopping. So I would go out and buy clothes for her, then she would try them on at home, and I would take back anything that was no good. It was a **fascinating** insight into how some people live. But as time went on I realised she was **impossible** to please. One time I had to buy her an outfit for a special event she was going to, and I bought her a few different things to try on, but she didn't like any of them, and she was really **furious** that I hadn't found her something different. It wasn't really my fault, but I lost my job soon after that.

Unit 4 Recording 5

W1 = Woman 1 W2 = Woman 2 M1 = Man 1 M2 = Man 2

W1: OK, so we're looking at plans for the new café. First of all, we need to decide on the location. Then we'll look at what kind of food we're going to offer, and possible names for the café.
M1: Yes, that sounds good.
W2: OK.
W1: Right. Let's focus on the ideas we had for the location. We looked at some options last time, but we need to make a decision.
M1: I liked the one near the station. It would be really busy during the week when everyone comes in for work. But what does everyone else think?
M2: Yes, I think the station idea is good.
W2: I think we need to decide on the kind of atmosphere we're looking for. The location near the shopping centre would be a really nice place to visit at the weekend.
W1: Hmm.
M1: I'm not sure that I agree, actually. The way I see things, we need to choose the location which will give us the most custom. And I think that will be the café near the station.
M2: And it's cheaper.
W2: That's a good point. I suppose so.
W1: So, shall we say we'll look at the location near the station?
All: Yes. Good idea. Yes, OK.
W1: Good. So, moving on to the next point, what kind of food are we going to serve? What do you think?
M1: Hmm … how about an Italian café?
W2: Mmm … I'm not sure …We talked about Italian, but there are lots of other Italian cafes around. I really feel that it would be hard to make ours different.
W1: OK – good point. I think we should think about something different then. Any ideas?
M2: Well, I was thinking about a Portuguese café, you know, with delicious cakes and pastries. There are quite a lot of Portuguese people in this area, and tourists too. I think that style of café would be really popular.
W2: Yeah, a Portuguese café. I think that's a great idea. What do you think?
All: That's OK. Yeah. Nice.
M1: That's a nice idea. We could do Portuguese-style lunches too, for office workers.
W1: Yes, maybe. So, are we all agreed? A Portuguese café?
All: Yes. That's fine by me.
W1: OK. Let's recap. A Portuguese café selling cakes and lunches, located near the station. Right. So, what would we call it? Café Express?
M1: I'm not sure about that. I think we need to come back to the type of café we're establishing. So Café Portugal? Or something like that …
W2: Why don't we call it Café do Sol? Or Café Lisboa? Café … umm … Café Fado …
W1: I like Café Lisboa. I think it sounds really good and Lisbon's a beautiful city.
M1: Café Lisboa. I like it.
M2: Yes, that sounds good.
W1: OK, we're running out of time. Let's sum up what we've decided. It's going to be a Portuguese café. We think the station location might be good. And we like the name Café Lisboa. Is that right?
All: Yes, I think so. That's right.
W1: OK, so we'll need to decide on …

Unit 4 Recording 8

I'm a pharmacist so I work six days a week. The pharmacy opens at nine a.m., but I need to be at work before then so I can get everything ready. I usually wake up at about six thirty, so I can get the kids up and ready for school, and then go for a run before work. I have to leave home by eight-thirty at the latest. The morning is the busiest time in the pharmacy, so the first thing I do when I get to work is start preparing prescriptions so they're ready for customers to collect. It's a community pharmacy, so I know a lot of the patients quite well. As well as giving out medicines, we try to give advice on healthy living. I think people really appreciate being able to talk to someone in the pharmacy and get advice or treatments without having to see a doctor. I usually have lunch at about one p.m. Sometimes I bring my own lunch, and on other days I like to leave the shop and wander around. I might buy something to eat or even try out a new café. The area near where I work is really nice, and I often bump into people I know. In the afternoon I try to catch up on all the admin tasks that need doing. I check my emails and upload information to our website. I often take phone calls from receptionists, nurses and even doctors from the local surgery, checking information about medication.
I leave the shop at about five thirty p.m. but I usually make some deliveries on my way home. Some of our older patients can't travel to the pharmacy themselves, so they rely on this service. I try to be home by about seven o'clock so that I have time to read to the children and put them to bed. I'm usually too exhausted to do very much in the evening, so I generally just cook supper and watch some television. And then I like to plan my next day in my head before going to bed. It's a long day, but I love my job.

Unit 5 Recording 2

W1 = Woman 1 W2 = Woman 2 M = Man

W1: Why are the windows round on ships?
M: Round windows are stronger, aren't they?
W2: Are they? I've no idea.
W1: That's right. According to the book, they're less likely to break.
W2: Ah.
M: There you go.
W1: What about this second one? How many hairs are there on the human head?
W2: Erm … A million?
M: No, it's not that many, is it?
W2: It depends whose head, doesn't it? On my dad's there are about three.
W1: The answer is about ten thousand.
M: Oh, really?
W2: I think that's a bit of a stupid question because it depends, doesn't it?
M: Well, it was a four-year-old who asked the question.
W2: Oh yeah, that's true.
W1: Next question: What happens when your plane flies over a volcano?
W2: Ummm.
M: Nothing happens, does it? Well, it depends on whether the volcano is erupting? Or whether it's active.
W2: Yeah.
W1: Well, according to the book, Jamieson asked a pilot. And the pilot said as he was flying over the volcano, his engines shut down, stopped working completely.
W2: Scary. Did he get hot?
W1: Hmm, it doesn't say. But he obviously survived. So there you go. Anyway, what about this one? Why did The Beatles break up?
W2: Dunno. They got old, didn't they?
M: No, John Lennon went off with Yoko Ono, didn't he?
W1: Well, Jamieson wrote to Yoko Ono and she replied, 'Because they all grew up, wanted to do things their own way, and they did.'
W2: Oh that's interesting.
M: I'm amazed she replied.
W1: Me, too. OK, last one. After watching a violent video game, the little boy asked why is there war?
W2: Great question.
M: That's a really good question.
W2: Hmm, because men like fighting?
M: Political reasons. One country wants the land or the oil or the gold.
W1: Well, Jamieson asked lots of experts. Most of them didn't or couldn't answer. Then he asked an American army colonel, who said there are four big reasons: different ideologies, a sense of honour, economic reasons, and fear.
M: Uh-huh.
W2: Good question for a four-year-old.
M: And a good answer.

Unit 5 Recording 5

Conversation 1

M = Man W = Woman

M: Arggh. Oh no.
W: What's the matter?
M: Oh. This cash machine's not working. Do you know if there's another machine somewhere? I really need to get some money.
W: Hmm … I'm not sure. There might be one in the shopping centre.
M: Thanks.

Conversation 2

M = Man W = Woman

W: Argh!
M: What's the matter?
W: My laptop's just crashed, again. That's the third time it's happened. Would you mind looking at it for me?
M: Sure.
W: Thanks. It's so annoying. I keep losing my documents. Do you know what the problem is?
M: Let me have a look. There's a lot of stuff on here. Why don't you save the documents onto a memory stick?
W: That's a good idea.
M: And then do you want me to try …

Conversation 3

M = Man W = Woman

W: Customer services. Good morning.
M: Um, yes. I've got a problem with my vacuum cleaner.
W: Could you tell me what the problem is, sir?
M: Yes, I can. It keeps making a funny noise. And it's just not working properly.
W: You say it keeps making a funny noise …
M: Yes, that's right.
W: OK. Let's see if I can find someone who can help you. Could you hold the line, please?
M: Yes, of course.

Conversation 4

M = Man W = Woman

M: Oh. I don't believe it! Excuse me, this machine's not working. It's just taken my money. Could you give me a refund?
W: I'm afraid I can't do that.
M: Why not?
W: Well, I'm not allowed to give refunds.
M: But I've just lost my money. And I still need a ticket.
W: I can sell you a ticket, but I can't give you a refund.
M: Well, could you tell me who I should speak to?
W: Yes, of course. You need to speak to the manager.
M: OK. Would you mind calling him for me?
W: Of course not. I'll just call him.

Unit 5 Recording 8

I'm going to tell you about Robo-Chef. Basically, Robo-Chef can prepare and cook all your favourite recipes. It works like this. First of all, it washes and prepares all the vegetables, then it prepares your dish, and cooks it for you on your cooker. Robo-Chef comes complete with hundreds of menus already programmed. But you can also programme Robo-Chef with your own recipes, or, if you want to try something new, you can download new recipes whenever you like. All you have to do is choose the dish you want, decide how many people you want Robo-Chef to cook for, and what time you want the meal to be ready. So, let's say you would like a vegetable lasagne for six people, ready by eight o'clock. Then, just make sure you have all the ingredients in the kitchen, press the button, and that's it. You can go out to work, and when you come home in the evening, your delicious supper will be ready. What could be easier? Robo-Chef is the chef of the future.

speakout 2ND EDITION

Intermediate Workbook

with key

Antonia Clare • JJ Wilson
Stephanie Dimond-Bayir

BBC

Pearson Education Limited
Edinburgh Gate
Harlow
Essex CM20 2JE
England
and Associated Companies throughout the world.

www.pearsonelt.com

First published 2015
This edition published 2016
ISBN: 978-1-292-14931-8

Set in Aptifer sans 10/12 pt
Printed in China by Golden Cup

Illustration acknowledgements
195 Eric (kja-artists.com): pp13, 24, 38; 087 Sean (kla-artists.com): pp8, 11, 22, 36, 40, 41, 49, 55, 61

Photo acknowledgements
The publisher would like to thank the following for their kind permission to reproduce their photographs:

(Key: b-bottom; c-centre; l-left; r-right; t-top)

123RF.com: 24 (A), Antonio Abrignani 66, Dmitry Rukhlenko 4; **Alamy Images:** Cultura Creative 46c, Danita Delimont 24 (B), Image Source 7, Juice Images 18br, moodboard 24 (C), Radius Images 24 (D), Alan Wrigley 51b; **Corbis:** Bettmann 10, Fancy / Randy Faris 23, Retna Ltd / Armando Gallo 64tr, Stew Slavin / Bettmann 34; **Fotolia.com:** Alliance 46r; **Getty Images:** Ableimages / Photodisc 39bl, AFP / Kazuhiro Nogi 64tc, AFP / Torsten Blackwood 25tr, Antony Giblin / Lonely Planet Images 13, Blend Images / Brand X Pictures 54, Graham Chadwick 64tl, E+ / Isitsharp 18bc, Glow Images 69t, Hemera / Erwin Purnomosidi 24 (F), Jupiterimages / Creatas 27, Jupiterimages / Photolibrary 69b, Jupiterimages / Stockbyte 39tr, Photodisc / Nick Daly 39tl, Stock4B 69c, Stockbyte / Jack Hollingsworth 24 (E); **Pearson Education Ltd:** Studio 8 39br; **Press Association Images:** AP / Brian Cassey 25tl; **Rex Features:** David Hartley 48tl, Sharok Hatami 48tc, Vitra Haus building, Vitra Design Museum, architects Herzog & de Meuron, Weil am Rhein, Baden-Wuerttemberg, Germany, Europe, 2010 20br; **Shutterstock.com:** Everydaysunshine 67 (A), Joe Gough 67 (C), Stuart Jenner 46l, Maridav 18bl, Michaeljung 50b, Dinesh Picholiya 67 (D), Anna Shepulova 67 (E), Szefei 67 (B); **The Kobal Collection:** No Trace Camping / Caramel Film / Fastnet Films 9tr, Paramount 9tl, United Artists 48tr

Every effort has been made to trace the copyright holders and we apologise in advance for any unintentional omissions. We would be pleased to insert the appropriate acknowledgement in any subsequent edition of this publication.

CONTENTS

VOCABULARY

LANGUAGE

1 A Read the information about Shin. Rearrange the letters in italics to complete the sentences.

1 My family is British Chinese so I grew up *uginblial*, speaking Chinese and English. ___bilingual___
2 Actually, I have a high level of *yucenfl* in Spanish, too. ____________
3 Of course, many of my friends are British so their *rethom goetun* is English. ____________
4 However London is very cosmopolitan – it is easy to meet *ginerof* people here. ____________
5 My best friend Sylvie is from Poland but she sounds like a *vetina preeska*. ____________
6 Sometimes I teach her *glans* as she didn't learn informal words in school. ____________
7 And she teaches me computer *gronja* – I find it difficult but she works in IT! ____________
8 In some ways Sylvie has better *gleranin stetsgerai* than me. ____________
9 I think her strongest *kills* is writing – she is amazing. ____________
10 I am quite careless in comparison and my *cccaaury* can be weak. ____________

B Use the words from Exercise 1A to complete the sentences. You may need to change the form of the word.

1 ___Bilingualism___ is an advantage in today's world.
2 My mother is ____________ in several languages – she's really clever.
3 I wish I could use language more ____________. I make a lot of mistakes.
4 What is your ____________? You sound German.
5 He always feels like a ____________ in his own country because he hasn't lived there for years.
6 I don't like ____________; I prefer it when people use standard English.
7 Do you have good listening ____________?
8 Dan is a ____________ so he checks all the English in the business documents.

GRAMMAR

QUESTION FORMS

2 A Circle the question with the correct form.

1 **a)** What kind of activity you helps learn new vocabulary?
b) What kind of activity helps you learn new vocabulary?
2 **a)** Which language you wanted to learn when you were younger?
b) Which language did you want to learn when you were younger?
3 **a)** You ever wish you had a different mother tongue?
b) Do you ever wish you had a different mother tongue?
4 **a)** What type of thing you do read in English?
b) What type of thing do you read in English?
5 **a)** As a child, did you like finding out about different countries?
b) As a child, did you to like finding out about different countries?
6 **a)** When did you first speak to a foreign person?
b) When you first speak to a foreign person?
7 **a)** If you have to speak in English, what do you always worry?
b) If you have to speak in English, what do you always worry about?

B Match questions 1–7 in Exercise 2A with answers a)–g).

a) Oh, English of course because it is international. 2
b) Yes. I was always interested in different cultures.
c) Mostly my pronunciation – I don't feel confident about it.
d) I review a few words every day and write example sentences.
e) A few years ago on my first trip abroad.
f) Not really. But I wish I had learnt English earlier.
g) Websites mostly, for online news. And sometimes magazines about films.

3 A 1.1 Listen and write the questions you hear.

1 ______________________________
2 ______________________________
3 ______________________________
4 ______________________________
5 ______________________________
6 ______________________________

B Listen again and repeat, paying attention to the intonation.

LISTENING

4 A 1.2 Listen to three people answering the questions below. Write their answers.

Which language did you learn?

How did you learn it?

	Which?	How?
Maria	______	______
Ahmed	______	______
Jessie	______	______

B Listen again and answer the questions.

1 Which country outside Europe did Maria visit?

______

2 What is her job now?

______

3 Where did Ahmed move to?

______

4 How did he communicate to start with?

______

5 Why does Jessie think British people don't learn other languages?

______

6 Which country did she live in for a while?

______

C Read the extracts from the recording. What do you think the words and phrases in bold mean? Match them with meanings a)–f).

1 … they were really **keen** for me to learn English …
2 It was a **culture shock** …
3 … living in Beirut always felt very **cosmopolitan**.
4 But I did some **part-time** Dutch lessons …
5 … we aren't **brilliant** at learning new languages.
6 I **picked** it **up** in my day-to-day life.

a) a feeling of confusion when in a new and different country
b) extremely intelligent or skilled
c) for only part of a day or a week
d) very interested, wanting to do something very much
e) to learn informally without lessons by exposure
f) having people from different parts of the world

WRITING

EMAILS OF INTRODUCTION; LEARN TO WRITE FORMAL AND INFORMAL EMAILS

5 A Read the purposes of two emails. Which email needs to be formal?

1 Introduce myself to a member of my host family in Spain before I visit.
2 Introduce myself as the new chairperson of the Teachers' Association.

B Read the emails and underline the correct alternatives.

To: psanchez@yoohoo.es
Subject: hi!
From: danielagjones@hitmail.com
[1]*Hi Pilar/Dear Madam Pilar,*

[2]*I am writing to greet you./How are you?* As you know, I'm going to stay with you this summer. I [3]*have decided to/thought I'd* send an email to introduce myself. My name's Daniela, but my friends call me Danny, and I hope you will, too.

I'm eighteen years old and at university here in Manchester, studying Business and Economics. I've got lots of hobbies. I love horse-riding, swimming, listening to music, and I also play the flute. My favourite hobby, though, is dancing. I [4]*am particularly keen on/really like* samba and salsa.

I [5]*can't wait to stay/look forward to staying* with you in Spain, though my Spanish isn't very good!
[6]*Hope/I do hope* to hear from you soon.
Danny

To: membership@taas.com
Subject: Introductions
From: hatquistj@ltsu.edu
[7]*Dear members/Hello everybody,*

[8]*I'm writing to say hi/I am writing to introduce myself.* As many of you know, I will begin in the role of chairperson of the Teachers' Association of Amlen State at the end of this month. [9]*I would like to take this opportunity/I really want* to outline my major plans for the Association over the coming year.

I am a maths and physics teacher. I have been in the profession for over forty years in a variety of roles: teacher, administrative assistant, head teacher and school inspector.

My first priority is to increase membership. In the last six years we have seen a decrease of almost 30% in our numbers. I have various proposals for achieving this, which [10]*I'll tell you about/I will explain* during our first meeting next month.

[11]*I look forward to working with you all/See you all soon.*
[12]*All the best/Yours sincerely,*
Jacqueline Hatquist

C Read the instructions and write an email (120–150 words).

You are going on an adventure trip for students of English. You will join ten other students from all over the world on a one-month tour of India. The tour will include cultural visits and two hours of English lessons every day. Write an email of introduction to the other students.

VOCABULARY

RELATIONSHIPS

1 A Put the words in the box into categories 1–4.

employee fiancée fiancé classmate pupil boss team-mate godfather godmother member

1 Person you work with:
____

2 Person who studies with you:
____

3 Person you are close to (almost family):
____

4 Person you do a hobby with:
____

B Complete the sentences with the words in Exercise 1A.

1 This is Marianna, my ___________. We're getting married next year.
2 Dave is my ___________. We're both in Year 12 at Cokethorpe High School.
3 She asked her ___________ for some time off work, but he said no.
4 I'm a ___________ of a swimming club. We meet twice a week at the sports centre.
5 Luisa got 100% in her exam. She's the best ___________ in my class.
6 He's an ___________ of GEO Foods. He's been there for six years.
7 When I was born, my father asked John, his best friend, to be my ___________.
8 Leticia is my ___________. We play in the same basketball team.

2 A Underline the stressed syllable in the words in italics.

1 He was an *employee* here.
2 I had a wonderful *mentor*.
3 All *pupils* wear a uniform.
4 We were *team-mates* for years.
5 Have you met my *fiancée*?
6 Talk to your *partner*.
7 She's my *godmother*.
8 That club is for *members* only.

B 1.3 Listen and check. Then listen and shadow the sentences (say them at the same time).

GRAMMAR

REVIEW OF VERB TENSES

3 Complete the conversations with the correct form of the verbs in brackets.

1 A: I need a holiday, but flights ___________ (be) always expensive at this time of year.
B: That's true, but I ___________ (find) a cheap flight to Mexico on the net yesterday.

2 A: Grace ___________ (win) the lottery last week!
B: That's right. She ___________ (sleep) when her brother called to tell her.

3 A: I ___________ (not like) football.
B: Why ___________ you ___________ (not tell) me earlier? The tickets cost £70 each!

4 A: ___________ you ___________ (hear) about the accident last week?
B: Yes, the boys ___________ (drive) along Court Street when a motorbike hit the car.

5 A: ___________ you ___________ (need) somewhere to stay? I have a spare room.
B: No, it's OK. I ___________ (stay) with my sister.

6 A: I ___________ (read) a novel called *The Luminaries* at the moment.
B: Oh yes. I found it so boring that I ___________ (not finish) it.

7 A: I like an early start, so I ___________ (get up) at six every morning.
B: Me too. I always ___________ (leave) the house by seven.

8 A: John! Are you ready? We ___________ (wait) for you!
B: OK, here I am! Sorry about that. I ___________ (look) for my hat! I couldn't find it anywhere.

4 Match beginnings a) and b) with endings i) and ii).

1 **a)** Do you use the computer? *ii*
b) Are you using the computer? *i*
i) I need it for a few minutes.
ii) Or is everything done by phone?

2 **a)** She tries to work
b) She's trying to work
i) , so please be quiet.
ii) on her book for two hours every day.

3 **a)** It doesn't snow
b) It isn't snowing,
i) much in New Mexico.
ii) so we can go out now.

4 **a)** What are you doing
b) What do you do
i) for a living?
ii) now? Do you want to go for a coffee?

5 **a)** He was playing squash
b) He played squash
i) for the team last year.
ii) when he broke his ankle.

READING

5 A Do you think statements 1–4 are about men or women? Who said them: men or women?

1 They do things first, and think about the risks later.
2 They remember useless information.
3 They notice when something is dirty or needs replacing.
4 They always remember birthdays and anniversaries.

B Read the text below and check.

C Write the name of the person who makes similar statements to the ones below.

1 Men hate to say, 'I don't know'. *Aisha*
2 Men cannot 'multitask'; they can only concentrate on one thing at a time. ______
3 Men are very direct when they need something. ______
4 Women are more fluent than men when they speak. ______
5 Women are more maternal; they understand what is good for young children. ______
6 Women have better memories for dates than men. ______

D Find words in the text to match definitions 1–5.

1 the ability to see the position, size or shape of things (paragraph 2) ______
2 give you the tools or abilities that you need (paragraph 2) ______
3 more or to a greater degree (paragraph 3) ______
4 not closely (paragraph 5) ______
5 natural abilities or feelings that make people and animals know something (paragraph 7) ______

VOCABULARY PLUS

COLLOCATIONS

6 Complete the phrases with *go*, *take*, *get* or *do*. Use each verb three times.

1	*get* a job	7	______ grey
2	______ off coffee	8	______ her a favour
3	______ part in a quiz	9	______ responsibility
4	______ some research	10	______ angry
5	______ my homework	11	______ up the guitar
6	______ on with people	12	______ for a walk

chatzone1

Men and Women – What They Say About Each Other

1 The battle of the sexes has probably been going on since the first caveman left his dirty dishes on the floor of the cave. A subject of endless discussion, it has inspired a million jokes and articles and almost as many books.

2 However, a recent study tells us that men and women really do think differently. Our brains are built in a different way. The results of the study suggest that men have better spatial perception (driving, ball sports), while women's brains equip them better for remembering words and speaking fluently.

3 The scientists examined only a small part of the brain, and they say that further research needs to be done. Here at *chatzone1* we have done some less scientific research. We asked people, 'What are the differences between the sexes?' Here are their answers.

What women say about men

4 Men remember useless information, like how fast an aeroplane can go, even if they'll never fly one. (Heather)

If you ask a man a question, he'll always have an answer, even if it's the wrong one. (Aisha)

Men do things first, and think about the risks later. (Candy)

Men cannot watch sport on TV and talk to women at the same time. (Mai)

What men say about men

5 Men know that common house spiders aren't as dangerous as rattlesnakes. (Daniel)

Men can drive without looking at themselves in the mirror every ten seconds. (Ron)

Men can watch a whole film without interrupting to ask, 'Who is he?' 'What's her job?' 'Does he like her?' (Alfred)

When men want something, they ask for it instead of making a comment distantly related to the subject and hoping their partner will guess what the real subject is. (Guy)

What men say about women

6 Women couldn't invent weapons that kill, only weapons that make you feel really guilty until you say sorry. (Kent)

While men speak in sentences, women speak in paragraphs. (Sergio)

Women are happy to own twenty CDs, while men need 200. (Steve)

Women order salad, then eat the man's chips. (Kazeem)

What women say about women

7 Women have natural instincts about what is dangerous for babies. (Linda)

Women notice when something is dirty or needs replacing. (Carol)

Only women can understand other women. (Xun)

Women have a calendar in their brains: we remember birthdays and anniversaries easily. (Avril)

VOCABULARY

INTERVIEW ADVICE

1 **Match 1–8 with a)–h) to make advice.**

1 Don't avoid eye
2 The most important thing is to be
3 Make sure you show
4 You must arrive on
5 Shake hands
6 Make sure you dress
7 Don't always answer
8 Before the interview, do

a) some research about the company.
b) briefly. Try to give a full response.
c) smartly. Maybe wear a suit.
d) contact. Look at them during the interview.
e) enthusiasm. Smile and ask questions.
f) firmly with your interviewers.
g) prepared. Think about what they will ask you.
h) time. Don't be late!

FUNCTION

TALKING ABOUT YOURSELF

2 A **Add the vowels to complete the conversations.**

Conversation 1

A: C_ _ld I _sk a q_ _st_ _n?
B: Sure. Go ahead.
A: Will this type of project become common?
B: In my _p_n_ _n, architecture will become more environmentally friendly.

Conversation 2

A: Th_r_ _r_ a c_ _pl_ _f th_ngs I'd l_k_ t_ _sk _b_ _t.
B: OK.
A: How do you see your future in our company?
B: F_r m_, th_ m_st _mp_rt_nt th_ng is to keep developing and learning the job.

Conversation 3

A: I h_v_ a q_ _ry.
B: Yes? Go ahead.
A: A lot of people criticised you because of the cuts in funding for education. Did you ever think about resigning from the government?
B: One th_ng I'd l_k_ t_ s_y _s th_t compared to other governments, we invested a lot of money in education.

Conversation 4

A: Earlier, you mentioned your latest film. C_n I _sk you _b_ _t th_t?
B: Yes, of course.
A: Was it difficult not being the star?
B: I'd h_v_ t_ s_y 'yes'. In my last four films I always had the biggest part.

B **Match pictures A–D with conversations 1–4 in Exercise 2A.**

LEARN TO

USE TWO-WORD RESPONSES

3 **Circle the correct option to complete the conversations.**

1 A: Is it OK if I check my emails?
B: ______ . That's fine.
a) Go ahead **b)** That's right **c)** I understand

2 A: Are you interested in free medical insurance?
B: ______ . How do I sign up?
a) You're correct **b)** Yes, definitely **c)** No problem

3 A: My dog is ill, so I can't come to work today.
B: ______ . Will you be in tomorrow?
a) You're correct **b)** Please continue **c)** I see

4 A: Hi, Nazir. I'm going to be about fifteen minutes late.
B: ______ . There's no hurry.
a) Yes, definitely **b)** That's right **c)** No problem

5 A: I can't travel in June – my wife's expecting a baby.
B: ______ . We'll make sure there's no travel until at least August.
a) I understand **b)** Go ahead **c)** You're welcome

6 A: Do you live at 106 West Smith Road?
B: Yes. ______ .
a) That's right **b)** No problem **c)** You're welcome

7 A: Thank you so much for letting me use your motorbike.
B: ______ . Did you have fun?
a) Yes, definitely **b)** I see **c)** You're welcome

8 A: Excuse the interruption. I'm just showing Mr Liu the classrooms. ______ .
B: Oh, OK. So, students, turn to page 33.
a) I see **b)** You're welcome **c)** Please continue

9 A: Are you able to work next weekend?
B: ______ . We need to finish the project, don't we?
a) Go ahead **b)** Of course **c)** I understand

VOCABULARY

TYPES OF STORY

1 A Add vowels to complete the words to describe types of story.

1 Cr_m_ films range from Hitchcock's thr_ll_r *Vertigo* to *Gone Girl*.

2 *The Theory of Everything* is a b_ _p_c of the scientist Stephen Hawking.

3 The most successful ever f_nt_sy film series is *The Lord of the Rings* and *The Hobbit*.

4 I enjoy all film genres, particularly historical or p_r_ _d dr_m_.

5 *Begin Again* is a r_m_nt_c c_m_dy about a woman who goes to New York to work as a musician and meets a man who changes her life.

6 *The Wizard of Oz* is a classic children's _dv_nt_r_ story.

7 *2012*, one of the biggest Hollywood d_s_st_r films ever made, shows the end of the world as we know it. The special effects are truly spectacular.

8 *The Hunger Games* is one of the best ever _ct_ _n films.

9 *The Salt of the Earth* is a d_c_dr_m_ about the life of Brazilian photographer Sebastiao Salgado.

B Which words in Exercise 1A could be used to describe these films?

1 In *What If*, a man falls in love with his best friend but doesn't think he can tell her.

2 *San Andreas* is based on what would happen if there was an earthquake in Los Angeles.

3 *Nowhere Boy* talks about John Lennon while he was at school and art college in 1950s Liverpool.

4 *World War Z* is set some time in the future when a virus has turned much of the world's population into zombies.

5 *Die Hard* stars Bruce Willis as a policeman battling against terrorists.

6 *Murder on the Orient Express*: When his train is stopped by deep snow, detective Hercule Poirot is called on to solve a murder when the body of one of the passengers is discovered.

GRAMMAR

PRESENT PERFECT AND PAST SIMPLE

2 Underline the correct alternatives.

1 A: *I've never been/didn't go* to Hollywood.
B: Haven't you? I *went/'ve been* there last year.

2 A: How many films *have you acted/did you act* in so far?
B: *I've acted/acted* in seven films up to now.

3 A: He's only twenty-two years old, but he *travelled/has travelled* all around the world.
B: Which countries *did he visit/has he visited*?

4 A: She *has won/won* four Oscars for her performances.
B: That's right. She *has won/won* an award for Best Actress last month.

5 A: They *have lived/lived* in California for twenty years.
B: When *did they move/have they moved* to Texas?

6 A: *Have you been/Were you* here long?
B: Yes. I *arrived/have arrived* over an hour ago.

7 A: We*'ve been married/were married* for forty years now.
B: Do you remember the day we*'ve met/met*?

8 A: *Did you enjoy/Have you enjoyed* the film?
B: I *didn't have/haven't had* time to watch it yet.

3 Rewrite the second sentence so that it means the same as the first. Use the correct form of the words in capitals.

1 I met Ella ten years ago. KNOW
I *'ve known* Ella for ten years.

2 She went to Mumbai four weeks ago. BE
She ____________ in Mumbai for four weeks.

3 They started the business in 2009. WORK
They ____________ together since 2009.

4 We moved into the house six months ago. LIVE
We ____________ this house for six months.

5 This is my third visit to London. GO
I ____________ three times.

4 A 2.1 Listen and complete the conversations.

1 A: Have you been here before?
B: Yes, ____________ Naples a few times.

2 A: Have you had time to see the museum yet?
B: No, ____________ time.

3 A: Did you find your hotel OK?
B: Yes, ____________ the hotel without any problems.

4 A: Have you got your guidebook?
B: Oh no. I ____________ it in my room.

5 A: Have you had any lunch?
B: Yes, ____________ eaten.

6 A: Have you enjoyed your stay?
B: Yes, ____________ a wonderful time.

B Listen again and shadow the answers.

VOCABULARY PLUS

PREPOSITIONS

5 Underline the correct preposition to complete the sentences.

1 I'll see you *at/on/in* lunchtime.
2 We often cook outside *at/in/on* the summer.
3 I start work at 8.30a.m. *at/on/in* Monday.
4 I try not to go out alone *at/on/in* night.
5 I just heard it *at/on/in* the radio.
6 *At/On/In* the end, we decided to take a taxi.
7 I'm sorry. I took your coat *at/by/in* mistake.
8 Please be quick. We're *at/by/in* a hurry.
9 Wait there. I'll be with you *at/on/in* a moment.
10 We found the museum completely *at/by/in* chance.
11 I'm afraid Mr Reeves is away *at/on/in* business. Can I help?
12 Nobody wanted to come with me, so I went *at/on/in* my own.

READING

6 A What do you know about James Dean? Are the statements true (T) or false (F)?

1 James Dean became famous for his role in the film *Rebel Without a Cause*.
2 He died in a car accident when he was just twenty-one years old.
3 He was speeding in his car at the time of the accident.
4 When he was younger, he nearly died in a motorcycle accident.
5 His favourite drink was whisky.

B Read the article on the right and check your answers. Correct the false statements.

C Circle the correct option to answer the questions.

1 Why do people come to Hollywood?
  a) Because it's dangerous.
  b) To follow their dreams.
  c) To meet other actors.
2 Why was James Dean nicknamed 'America's Rebel'?
  a) He played a teenager in the film *Rebel Without a Cause*.
  b) He was friends with another actor, Ronald Reagan.
  c) Teenagers respected his rebellious attitude.
3 What did he do before he arrived in Hollywood?
  a) He performed dangerous stunts on television.
  b) He raced motorbikes.
  c) He worked in a restaurant.
4 Why did Dean argue with his father?
  a) His father caught him drinking whisky.
  b) He crashed his father's car.
  c) His father didn't want him to be an actor.

FOREVER YOUNG:

THE HOLLYWOOD HERO WHO DIED YOUNG

'Dream as if you'll live forever; live as if you'll die tomorrow.'

1 The dream is the same for everyone: actors, dancers, singers, film-makers. They go to Hollywood looking for money, success, fame and power. And many come to Hollywood as young people, barely out of their teens. But Hollywood can be a dangerous place, and some of Hollywood's heroes even lose their lives because of it. But although they die young, they are heroes forever, immortalised in film history.

2 One such hero was James Dean. Dean once said 'Dream as if you'll live forever; live as if you'll die tomorrow'. Arriving in Hollywood as a young man, James Dean quickly became a star. In the film *Rebel Without a Cause*, Dean showed teenage angst at its best, and he captured the world with his casual style and rebellious attitude. It was an attitude that he held both on-screen and off, and teenagers everywhere found a hero they could both respect and admire. Soon, he was more popular than even his own screen idol, Marlon Brando, and he was nicknamed 'America's Rebel' by Ronald Reagan.

3 Always the rebel, Dean was afraid of nothing. Before becoming famous, he worked as a stuntman for a TV show. Dean loved his car, a silver Porsche 550 Spyder, and it was in this car that on September 30, 1955, Dean crashed and died from his injuries. He was just twenty-four years old. Even though his career in Hollywood was short, he only made three films, he made a lasting impression on everybody who watched him, and even on future generations. James Dean will be forever young.

4 There are many myths about James Dean, but only some of them are true. James Dean loved speed. When he was younger, he had a motorcycle accident and lost his two front teeth. People assumed that Dean was speeding at the time of his car crash – he had been stopped by police for speeding just two hours earlier. But experts now believe that Dean was travelling at 55 mph, and that the accident was just unlucky. As a young man, Dean was a rebel at home. He was thrown out of his father's house when they argued about Dean wanting an acting career, rather than a career in law. And finally, on-screen James Dean is shown getting into a fight after drinking whisky, but off-screen his favourite drink was coffee.

D Find words or phrases in the text to match definitions 1–5.

1 still very young/in their early twenties (paragraph 1) ________
2 made famous for a long time (paragraph 1) ________
3 opinions or behaviour which are against authority (paragraph 2) ________
4 an opinion or feeling about someone/something that you have for a long time (paragraph 3) ________
5 thought something was true (paragraph 4) ________

LISTENING

1 A Read the introduction to a radio programme. Are the statements true (T) or false (F)?

1 A 'flashbulb memory' is a memory of an important event.
2 You do not usually remember small details with a flashbulb memory.

FLASHBULB MEMORIES – WHERE WERE YOU THEN?

Do you remember where you were when an important event occurred? Can you remember who you were with? Then you may have what is called a 'flashbulb memory'. In 1977, two psychologists, Roger Brown and James Kulick, used the term 'flashbulb memories' to talk about people's recollections of the John F. Kennedy assassination. They suggested that, like a camera's flashbulb, when a truly shocking event happens, the brain 'takes a picture' of the moment when you learn about the event. This enables us to remember, sometimes in great detail, events of an emotional significance to us. Tune in to Radio 6 *Real Lives* and listen to some of the stories.

B 2.2 Listen to the stories. Match pictures A–D with speakers 1–4.

A ___

B ___

C ___

D ___
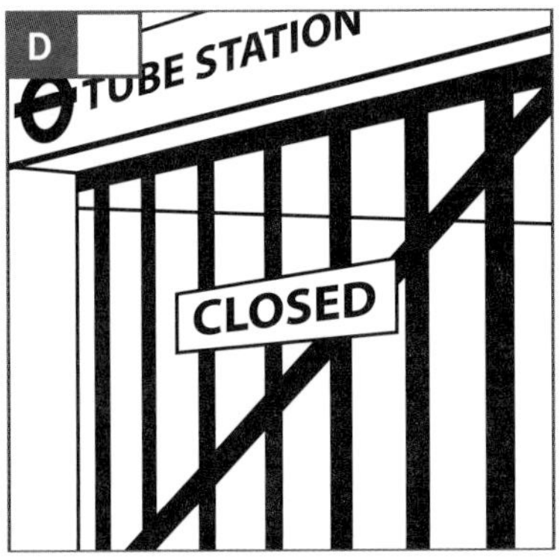

C Listen again and answer the questions.

1 Who was angry about not getting to a meeting on time? ________
2 Who watched the news on a black and white television? ________
3 Who got up to make everyone coffee? ________
4 Who were trying to talk on their mobile phones? ________
5 Who thought that maybe what they remembered was just a dream? ________
6 Who wanted peace for everyone? ________

GRAMMAR

NARRATIVE TENSES

2 Circle the correct option to complete the sentences.

1 Simon was feeling exhausted because
 a) the baby wasn't sleeping all night.
 b) the baby hadn't slept all night.
2 We were driving to the hospital to visit Sam when
 a) they called to say she had gone home.
 b) they were calling to say that she was going home.
3 By the time we got to the beach
 a) the rain had stopped.
 b) the rain stopped.
4 Juan was feeling excited because
 a) he wasn't seeing his parents for ten years.
 b) he hadn't seen his parents for ten years.
5 She was singing an old folk song
 a) which I hadn't heard for years.
 b) which I didn't hear for years.
6 Everyone was dancing because
 a) Porto had just won the match.
 b) Porto were just winning the match.

3 Complete the conversations with the correct form of the verbs in brackets.

Conversation 1

A: What [1] ________ (happen) to you on Saturday night? We [2] ________ (wait) for ages, but you [3] ________ (not come).
B: I'm really sorry. I [4] ________ (drive) back from Aga's house when my car [5] ________ (break) down.
A: Why didn't you call?
B: My phone [6] ________ (run out) of battery.

Conversation 2

A: [7] ________ you ________ (enjoy) your dinner last night?
B: No. Actually, I [8] ________ (hate) it.
A: Why? What happened?
B: Well, we [9] ________ (book) a table, but I [10] ________ (not realise) it was right by the door. People [11] ________ (come) in and out all evening and it was freezing. Then, when the waiter [12] ________ (pour) my wine, he [13] ________ (spill) it down my dress. And also, we [14] ________ (order) fish, which they [15] ________ (say) was fresh. But when it [16] ________ (arrive) it [17] ________ (taste) terrible!

VOCABULARY

THE NEWS

4 A Complete the headlines with the words in the box.

crash	demonstration	attacked	strikes
earthquake	fugitive	floods	hostages

1 Plane ________ in the Mediterranean

2 Thousands killed and more homeless in huge ________ in Haiti

3 Pirates take families as ________

4 HEAVY ________ DESTROY HOUSES AS RIVER WATER RISES

5 ________ arrested at airport

6 Thousands attend anti-war ________

7 PRIME MINISTER ________ WITH EGGS AND ROTTEN FRUIT DURING CONFERENCE

8 Train workers' ________ cause delays

B Circle the correct option to complete the sentences.

1 We need to check our flights. The airport workers are planning ________.
 a) strikes b) demonstrations
2 Protesters ________ the building when they were locked out and caused a lot of damage.
 a) demonstrated b) attacked
3 Police were congratulated when the ________ was finally arrested.
 a) hostage b) fugitive
4 If the rain continues, more ________ are expected.
 a) floods b) earthquakes
5 The driver ________ because he had turned the corner too fast.
 a) crashed b) attacked

WRITING

A NEWS REPORT; LEARN TO USE TIME LINKERS

5 A Put the sentences/paragraphs in the correct order to complete three news reports, A–C. Each report should have three parts:

1 an introductory statement to say what happened
2 background information
3 a concluding statement (or an opinion in quotes).

REPORT A

a ____ The pupils mark their fingerprints [1]*while/as soon as* they enter the church. They will be monitored over three years.

b ____ [2]*During/Until* that time, if they attend 200 masses, they will be excused from taking one exam.

c ____ A Polish priest has installed an electronic reader in his church in Warsaw for school children to leave their fingerprints when they attend mass.

REPORT B

a ____ But Kiyotaka Yamana, a Tokyo resident who started the 'Love Message Yelling Event' after his marriage failed, said that didn't mean they were unromantic. 'The dominant image of Japanese men is of overworked businessmen, but I wanted to tell people around the world that Japanese men are actually very romantic,' Yamana told reporters.

b ____ [3]*While/During* they are on stage, yelling 'I love you' or 'Let me be with you', they are filmed and the event is broadcast on national television. [4]*Until/By the time* recently, Japanese men have usually chosen not to talk very openly about love.

c ____ Love is really in the air in Tokyo at the 'Love Message Yelling Event'. [5]*While/During* the event, dozens of people stand on a stage in Hibiya Park in central Tokyo and shout out love messages to their partners.

REPORT C

a ____ However, [6]*by the time/until* they reached the ruins, the area had been cut off by floods and mudslides and they had to wait [7]*as soon as/until* army helicopters could come and airlift them to safety.

b ____ The travellers had finished the difficult 45-km (28-mile) trek along Peru's Inca trail to see the famous Machu Picchu ruins.

c ____ Over a thousand tourists had to be evacuated from Machu Picchu last week.

B For each report, answer the questions.

1 What happened?
2 Where was it exactly?
3 Why did it happen?

C Underline the correct time linkers to complete the reports.

D Write a short news report (80–120 words) describing a recent news event in your country.

VOCABULARY
SAY/TELL

1 Complete the sentences with the correct form of *say* or *tell*.

1 President Obama ______ a joke and everybody laughed.
2 The manager called to ______ she was sorry about what had happened.
3 I still can't believe that he ______ me such a big lie. I'm furious with him.
4 Someone once ______ me a story about that.
5 Listen. Why don't you just ______ what you mean?
6 As Jodie walked past the table, the young man looked up and ______ 'hello'.

FUNCTION
TELLING A STORY

2 Underline the correct options to complete the story.

STUCK IN THE SNOW

[1]*This happened when/All of a sudden* I was snowboarding with a few friends in Italy. [2]*Before long/Well*, most of the group were really good skiers, [3]*so/in the end* one day we went to the top of this difficult run. [4]*In the beginning/Anyway*, the field was full of fresh snow and in the middle a tree had fallen down and was covered in snow. It made a perfect jump, so soon everyone was queuing up to perform tricks. [5]*Well/Before long* it was my turn. Well, I went as fast as possible and jumped up ready to do a back flip. But I forgot to bend my knees. [6]*So/The next thing I knew*, I was pointing down, like an arrow. I went head-first into the snow, right up to my waist. My legs were sticking up in the air and I couldn't move. [7]*In the end/Before long*, they had to dig me out. [8]*Anyway/All of a sudden*, we've all laughed about it ever since.

LEARN TO
SHOW INTEREST

3 Complete the conversation with the words in the box.

what	Really	no	then	amazing
happened	Oh	kidding		

A: You'll never guess what happened to Mukul.
B: No. What happened?
A: Well, you know he's working as a taxi driver to help pay for his medical studies.
B: Yes, I know.
A: Anyway, he took a family who were on holiday from Italy in his taxi. And one of his passengers was a seventy-two-year-old grandmother.
B: Yes, so what [1]______?
A: Well, she left her handbag, with more than $21,000 of the family's travelling money, some very valuable jewellery and some of their passports, in the back of his taxi.
B: Oh [2]______. You're [3]______. So, [4]______ did he do?
A: Well, he looked in the bag to see who it belonged to.
B: Yes, …
A: And he found an address that was fifty miles away. So, he drove all the way there.
B: And what happened [5]______?
A: Well, there was no one in …
B: [6]______ dear.
A: So he left a note and his telephone number. And when the family called him, he went back and returned the bag.
B: [7]______?
A: Yes. As you can imagine, the family were overjoyed and they offered him a reward.
B: How much?
A: I don't know. He didn't take it. He said he couldn't accept it. He was just happy that he'd done the right thing.
B: I don't believe it. That's really [8]______.

VOCABULARY LANGUAGE

1 **Complete the sentences.**

1 Sarah uses a lot of ____________ and informal words when she speaks – she's a typical teenager.
2 I thought he was British – his English is so good he sounds like a ____________.
3 His story was written well but the ____________ wasn't good – he made lots of spelling mistakes.
4 I wish I were ____________! It must be great to speak two languages from childhood!
5 Living in a ____________ country is a great way to learn the language.
6 The teacher was impressed by her ____________ and how easily she spoke.

GRAMMAR QUESTION FORMS

2 **A** **Complete the interview questions. Use the same verbs as the answers.**

A: Who [1] ____________________________?
B: I work for a small publishing company called Calinet.
A: What type of things [2] ____________________?
B: I do a lot of things – some editing, contacting authors.
A: What problems [3] ______________________?
B: I deal with problems concerning the manuscripts: mistakes, wrong length, wrong style.
A: When [4] ____________________ working there?
B: I started working there in 2007.
A: [5] ______________________________ the job?
B: Yes, I do enjoy it. It's great.
A: So why [6] ____________________ for this job?
B: I applied because it's a great company.

B R1.1 **Listen and repeat the questions with the correct intonation.**

VOCABULARY RELATIONSHIPS

3 **A** **Match the sentences with the people in the box.**

classmate boss team-mate partner mentor employee

1 'Please finish this report for me by tomorrow morning.' ____________
2 'Ian, can I borrow your pen? I forgot to write my name on my homework.' ____________
3 'Come on! Together we can win this game!' ____________
4 'Let's look at this together; I can give you some ideas.' ____________
5 'I have a meeting in the office with my manager at 6.00.' ____________
6 'We'll split the costs 50/50, OK?' ____________

B **Mark the stress on the words in the box.**

GRAMMAR REVIEW OF VERB TENSES

4 **Put the verbs in brackets into the correct tense to complete the introduction to a speech.**

Hello, everybody! My name is Shane Towers. I [1] ____________ (be) a teacher, but at the moment I [2] ____________ (take) a year off to finish my Master's Degree. I [3] ____________ (not start) working with children until 2005, but now I [4] ____________ (love) it.

Today I'm going to talk about Theatre of the Oppressed. I first [5] ____________ (see) the name when I [6] ____________ (look) through some articles for my degree. I [7] ____________ (read) an article about drama in education and suddenly the name [8] ____________ (jump) out at me: 'Theatre of the Oppressed'. In my country, the theatre [9] ____________ (not be) usually for or about the oppressed; it's for rich or middle-class people. I [10] ____________ (want) to find out more ...

VOCABULARY PLUS COLLOCATIONS

5 **Complete the sentences with *go*, *take*, *get* or *do*. Use the present simple or the past simple.**

1 I *did* a lot of research before I *got* my degree.
2 A year ago she ____________ up a new hobby: acting. Then she ____________ part in her first play.
3 Last night we ____________ some work on the proposal and then we ____________ for a meal.
4 Can you ____________ me a favour? Can you help me to ____________ this test?
5 You ____________ after your father. I hope you don't ____________ grey when you're twenty-five, too!
6 Eventually I ____________ off Jane because she always ____________ angry for no reason.

VOCABULARY INTERVIEW ADVICE

6 **Circle the correct option to answer the questions.**

1 How should you dress before an interview?
a) messily **b)** brilliantly **c)** smartly
2 How should you shake hands with someone?
a) nicely **b)** firmly **c)** heavily
3 When should you arrive for an appointment?
a) on time **b)** quickly **c)** late
4 What shouldn't you avoid in an interview?
a) foot contact **b)** head contact **c)** eye contact
5 What should you do before an interview?
a) some research **b)** a job **c)** the washing
6 What should you show in an interview?
a) your CV **b)** your photos **c)** enthusiasm

FUNCTION TALKING ABOUT YOURSELF

7 **Read the conversation between Ian and his boss, John. Which lines are correct? Which have an extra word?**

I: John, could I to ask a question?	**1** *to*
J: Of course. What would you like to know?	**2** ✓
I: There are but a couple of things.	**3** ______
J: Yes, go ahead.	**4** ______
I: I am have a query about the website.	**5** ______
J: Yes. You know it isn't finished yet?	**6** ______
I: Can I to ask you when it will be finished?	**7** ______
J: It's for me, the most important thing is to get it right.	**8** ______
I: I understand, but when will it be ready?	**9** ______
J: I'd have really to say, websites have been a big problem for this company.	**10** ______
I: In the my opinion, they've been the biggest problem. But when will it be ready?	**11** ______
J: One thing I'd like for to say is that we are working hard on the website.	**12** ______
I: So you don't have a date?	**13** ______
J: Er ... no. Sorry.	**14** ______

LEARN TO USE TWO-WORD RESPONSES

8 **Put the words in the boxes into pairs to make two-word responses. Then complete the conversations with the correct responses.**

of problem welcome course no you're

1 **A:** Thank you so much.
B: ______.
2 **A:** Sorry about that.
B: ______.
3 **A:** Can I leave early, please?
B: ______.

ahead correct see I go you're

4 **A:** I think the answer is 'Paris'.
B: ______.
5 **A:** Can I tell you what happened?
B: ______.
6 **A:** I couldn't come because I was ill.
B: ______.

I right that's please understand continue

7 **A:** Is your name John Brown?
B: ______.
8 **A:** Sorry I didn't finish it.
B: ______.
9 **A:** So, I was telling you about ...
B: ______.

VOCABULARY TYPES OF STORY; THE NEWS

9 **Complete the descriptions of films with the words in the box.**

fantasy fugitive demonstrations strike biopic science earthquake period thriller violent crash attack disaster comedy

1 This ______ describes the life of Cesar Chavez, the leader who organised a workers' ______ so that people could work under fair conditions.
2 This psychological ______ tells the story of a ______ who hides from the police while trying to prove that he is innocent.
3 This is a very funny romantic ______ that tells the story of two people who fall in love when their cars ______ on a small road.
4 This ______ fiction film describes what happens when aliens ______ planet Earth, attempting to destroy everything.
5 This children's ______ begins when a hole opens up in the ground after an ______ and a giant, friendly creature comes out to rescue everybody.
6 This ______ movie tells the story of a ______ storm that destroys the city.
7 This ______ drama tells the story of women fighting for the vote and their ______ on the streets of London in the early 1900s.

GRAMMAR PRESENT PERFECT AND PAST SIMPLE

10 **Read the phrases in italics and correct the ones that are wrong.**

1 The Berlin Wall *has fallen* in 1989.
2 *Have you been* to any of the Caribbean islands?
3 I started work at 6a.m. but I still *haven't finished.*
4 What time *have you gone* to bed last night?
5 It's so dry here. It *hasn't rained* for weeks.
6 Did you hear about Casey? He's *broken* his leg!
7 Van Gogh *hasn't sold* many paintings during his lifetime.
8 You're a good guitar player. *Have you played* for long?

11 R1.2 **Listen and tick the sentence you hear.**

1	**a)** I stopped.	**b)** I've stopped.
2	**a)** We made it.	**b)** We've made it.
3	**a)** He helped me.	**b)** He's helped me.
4	**a)** They killed it.	**b)** They've killed it.
5	**a)** You worked hard.	**b)** You've worked hard.
6	**a)** I thanked her.	**b)** I've thanked her.

VOCABULARY PLUS PREPOSITIONS

12 **Complete the diary entry with the correct prepositions.**

I went [1]__________ a run in the morning while listening to some music [2]__________ Eminem. I hate running [3]__________ the winter, especially [4]__________ Monday morning. It's too cold! Unfortunately, Kim is away [5]__________ business and only gets back late [6]__________ night, so I had to run [7]__________ my own. It was hard work running six miles, but I did it [8]__________ the end. Had breakfast [9]__________ a hurry and managed to get to work [10]__________ time. Problems with the bus so I went [11]__________ train, which was quicker. [12]__________ chance, I heard [13]__________ the radio that the new film [14]__________ Roger Graves, an old friend of mine, was coming out [15]__________ June. It's about a man who runs every morning and hates it!

GRAMMAR NARRATIVE TENSES

13 **Complete the sentences with the past simple, past perfect or past continuous form (positive or negative) of the verbs in the box. Use each verb once.**

turn on	finish	eat	open	do	leave	stay	listen	wear	go

1 She went to Hotel Buena Vista, but I __________ in Hotel Primavera!
2 As Bilal closed the door, he realised he __________ the keys in the car.
3 Yannick __________ to music when someone knocked on the door.
4 When I got to work, I saw that I __________ one black shoe and one brown shoe!
5 When we arrived, it was cold because Dad __________ the heating.
6 Bella started the course last year, but she __________ it.
7 Goa was new to us because we __________ there before.
8 It was too hot so I __________ the window.
9 The police want to know what you __________ between 6.30a.m. and 7.00a.m. yesterday.
10 The food tasted horrible, so we __________ it.

VOCABULARY SAY/TELL

14 **A** **Complete the phrases with *say* or *tell*.**

1 __________ jokes
2 __________ 'hello'
3 __________ a white lie
4 __________ sorry
5 __________ stories
6 __________ what you mean

B **Complete the sentences with the correct form of phrases from Exercise 14A.**

1 When I was young, my father always __________ before we fell asleep.
2 Most comedians __________ but his face alone makes you laugh!
3 I explained that I didn't mean to break the window! I __________!
4 She isn't very friendly, is she? She never __________ when I see her in the street.
5 He didn't want to make her cry, so instead of telling the truth, he __________.
6 Instead of talking for hours around the issue, why don't you just __________!

FUNCTION TELLING A STORY; SHOWING INTEREST

15 **Underline the correct alternatives.**

A: [1]*Happened this/This happened* when I was on holiday in Portugal last year. There were three of us renting this old, scary house in the countryside. It was miles from anywhere.

B: So what [2]*happened/did happen*?

A: We'd had a really nice evening. My friend is a good cook and she'd made this lovely meal, so we were feeling very content and full. [3]*In anyway/Anyway,* that night, just after we'd all gone to bed, we heard this kind of scratching sound at the door. [4]*To/In* the beginning, we just thought it was the wind and we went to sleep and forgot about it. But then the following night, the same thing: scratch, scratch at the door.

B: [5]*But no/Oh no*!

A: [6]*Well/Very well,* we were all in separate rooms but [7]*after/before* long we were all sitting together in the living room, really scared. [8]*So/So on* we talked and talked, trying to work out what to do.

B: And what [9]*did you do/you did*?

A: [10]*Final/Finally* we decided to get a knife or another weapon and go outside together to see what it was. [11]*The next thing/The near thing* I knew, I was at the front of three frightened girls, carrying the kitchen knife and about to unlock the front door.

B: [12]*Dear/Oh dear*!

A: It went really quiet again. And then, all of [13]*the sudden/a sudden,* there was the scratching sound.

B: So what [14]*happened then/then happened*?

A: I opened the door and a cat jumped back and ran off into the night. All that panic and [15]*for/in* the end it was just a cat!

B: That's really [16]*funny/fun*!

A: Well yes, we all laughed afterwards, but it was very scary at the time!

CHECK

Circle the correct option to complete the sentences.

1 Jose is ____________ – he speaks Spanish and English.
a) monolingual **b)** bilingual **c)** multilingual

2 Where ____________ last summer?
a) have you go **b)** do you go **c)** did you go

3 What music ____________?
a) do you listen **b)** you listen to **c)** do you listen to

4 Who ____________ you with this homework?
a) helped **b)** did help **c)** was helped

5 ____________ she like pasta?
a) Is **b)** Does **c)** Do

6 I'm ____________ a novel.
a) writing **b)** be writing **c)** already written

7 What ____________ between 4.00p.m. and 4.30p.m.?
a) did you do **b)** were you doing **c)** you were doing

8 We are ____________ of a tennis club.
a) team-mates **b)** partners **c)** members

9 They ____________ in a concert.
a) did **b)** took place **c)** took part

10 Can you ____________?
a) make me a favour **b)** do me a favour **c)** do me favour

11 You have excellent ____________ and learn quickly.
a) learning strategies **b)** learning styles **c)** learning systems

12 I ____________ research before I started the project.
a) did a **b)** took some **c)** did some

13 I ____________ about this topic.
a) could question **b)** ask a question **c)** have a query

14 Why don't you ____________ and tell your story?
a) go ahead **b)** be ahead **c)** go forward

15 ____________ me, the most important thing is to be honest.
a) By **b)** For **c)** According

16 I love films about the future, especially ____________.
a) fiction science **b)** science fiction **c)** period drama

17 We ____________ to Italy yet.
a) didn't go **b)** not have been **c)** haven't been

18 ____________ Paul last night?
a) Were you see **b)** Did you see **c)** Have you seen

19 What ____________ to your hair?
a) have you done **b)** you have done **c)** you did

20 I didn't want to work ____________ my own.
a) in **b)** on **c)** by

21 She fired the gun ____________ mistake.
a) by **b)** on **c)** at

22 He realised he ____________ Janine before.
a) met **b)** was meeting **c)** had met

23 The alarm went off while we ____________.
a) sleep **b)** were sleeping **c)** had slept

24 I was nervous because I ____________ a speech before.
a) wasn't giving **b)** didn't give **c)** hadn't given

25 When I ____________ her, she didn't know who I was.
a) had met **b)** was meeting **c)** met

26 The kidnappers wanted a million dollars for each ____________.
a) hostage **b)** fugitive **c)** flood

27 That boy is always ____________ lies.
a) speaking **b)** saying **c)** telling

28 If you did something wrong, you should ____________ sorry.
a) ask **b)** say **c)** tell

29 All ____________, the rain came down.
a) in the end **b)** very sudden **c)** of a sudden

30 That's impossible – you ____________ joking!
a) must to be **b)** must be **c)** must

RESULT	/30

VOCABULARY
ORGANISATION

1 A Match 1–5 with a)–e) to make sentences.

1 Will you be able to **meet**
2 Well I'm ready! Shall we **get**
3 Do you think she's going to **put things**
4 My son always **gets**
5 I'm going to **use my time**

a) **started** and open the meeting?
b) **distracted** when he's doing his homework.
c) **off**? She already has a lot of work to do.
d) **wisely** and check my luggage while I'm waiting for the taxi.
e) **the deadline** on this job or will you be late?

B Match the sentences in Exercise 1A with the responses below. Complete the responses with the words in the box.

ahead	prioritising	multitasking
leave	waste	

1 Don't worry. I'll finish. I don't usually ____________ time.
2 Tell him to finish it all ____________ of time and then it won't be such a problem.
3 I don't think so. She probably wants to get it done fast and she is pretty good at ____________.
4 Good idea as we have limited time. I'd like to start by ____________ our most important tasks.
5 Yes, better not to ____________ things to the last minute or you'll miss your flight.

LISTENING

2 A 3.1 Listen to three people talking about planning things. Who thinks he/she:

a) is a procrastinator? ____________
b) is a good planner? ____________
c) plans too much? ____________

B Listen again and circle the correct option.

1 Where is Ruth planning to stay?
  a) in city hotels
  b) in youth hostels
  c) in hostels and cheap hotels
2 What does she plan to do in Lodz?
  a) go out and find artwork
  b) do a city tour
  c) shop in the city centre
3 What has Kieron done to prepare for his trip?
  a) packed his sports bag
  b) booked his bus ticket
  c) written a list of things to pack
4 What does he think he will forget?
  a) his bag
  b) his boots
  c) the tickets
5 What type of party is Amber organising?
  a) a beach party for a diving group
  b) a birthday party at a swimming pool
  c) a birthday party with diving
6 What does Amber enjoy about her job?
  a) arranging large events
  b) scuba diving
  c) meeting new people

C Match the underlined words and phrases in extracts 1–5 with meanings a)–e).

1 I'm afraid I have to organise things in massive detail …
2 … you see them as you wander around the city.
3 I'm going to a sports tournament next week …
4 … we've made it to the final matches.
5 I think planning comes naturally to me.

a) walk around slowly in a relaxed way with no specific purpose
b) be successful in or achieve something
c) do something easily without learning it
d) a competition with different matches leading to a winning team
e) a large amount

GRAMMAR

THE FUTURE (PLANS)

3 Underline the correct alternatives to complete the conversation.

A: [1]*Do you go/Are you going* anywhere this weekend?
B: Yes, we [2]*'re going/'ll go* up to Edinburgh to see some of the sights.
A: That's nice. Where [3]*are you going/might you* to stay?
B: I don't know yet. I [4]*have/'m going to have* a look online later.
A: I've got some friends in Edinburgh. They [5]*might/are going to* have some space. I [6]*'ll give/'m going to give* you their number.
B: Thanks. That's great. What about you? [7]*Do you do/Are you doing* anything exciting?
A: No, I think I [8]*'ll spend/'m spending* the weekend watching DVDs.

4 Complete the email. Use the present continuous, *will/might* or *be going to*. There may be more than one possibility.

Hi Ros

[1] ____________ (you/do) anything at the weekend? Do you want to come out with us? Danny and I [2] ____________ (go out) on Saturday night. It would be great if you could come. We [3] ____________ (try) one of the restaurants in Trastevere – it's really nice round there.

One thing we've planned is we [4] ____________ (meet) up with a few people from the course for a drink first, in Piazza Santa Maria. Do you know it? We [5] ____________ (be) outside Café Marzo from about 6.30, if you want to join us. I'm not sure how late we [6] ____________ (be). If anyone still has enough energy at the end of the evening, a DJ friend of mine [7] ____________ (play) at the Gioia Music Restaurant, so we [8] ____________ (go) there and dance a bit afterwards. We'll see how things go. I [9] ____________ (call) you tomorrow to see what your plans are.

Speak soon,
Silvia

5 A 3.2 Listen to the sentences. Which words are stressed? Circle the option you hear.

1 a) They're <u>going</u> to <u>play squash</u>.
b) <u>They</u>'re going to play <u>squash</u>.
2 a) I'm <u>going</u> to buy a <u>new phone</u>.
b) I'm going to <u>buy</u> a new <u>phone</u>.
3 a) She's <u>going</u> to <u>spend</u> a week in <u>Greece</u>.
b) She's going to spend a <u>week</u> in <u>Greece</u>.
4 a) He isn't <u>going</u> to eat <u>anything</u>.
b) He <u>isn't</u> going to <u>eat</u> anything.
5 a) Are you <u>going</u> to <u>walk</u> to the <u>station</u>?
b) Are <u>you</u> going to <u>walk</u> to the station?
6 a) <u>He's</u> going to change his <u>job</u>.
b) He's going to <u>change</u> his <u>job</u>.

B Listen again and repeat. Focus on the pronunciation of *going to* in fast speech.

WRITING

MESSAGES; LEARN TO USE NOTE FORM

6 A Match messages 1–6 with situations a)–f).

a) a brother leaving a message for his sister
b) a mother leaving a message for her son
c) a secretary leaving a message for his/her boss
d) a colleague leaving a message for other colleagues
e) a son leaving a message for his mother
f) a person leaving a message for self as a reminder

B Which words have been deliberately left out of the messages? Rewrite the messages in full.

1 ____________
2 ____________
3 ____________
4 ____________
5 ____________
6 ____________

C Write notes for these situations.

1 To your boss: Tell him that Mr Ali telephoned and that you have arranged for them to meet at Mr Ali's office tomorrow morning at 9a.m.
2 To your brother: Invite him out to the cinema this evening.
3 To your colleague: Say that you have gone home and will be back in the office tomorrow.

READING

1 **Read the text and choose the best heading.**

a) Famous inventions
b) Man and the planet – what's next?
c) Science in the future: discoveries

2 **Read the text again and answer the questions.**

1 Where has space travel taken us?

____

2 What kind of energy will we produce?

____

3 How will we control the locks and lights in our homes?

____

4 What can American scientists already do?

____

5 Why will skin and bone grown in a laboratory help people?

____

6 Why do some people disagree with space exploration?

____

3 **Complete the text in Exercise 1 with the following sentences. Write the correct letter in gaps 1–5.**

a) We will no longer need to be physically present to control what happens in our homes.
b) Some people would prefer technology to be used differently.
c) Of course at the moment the equipment is large and inconvenient.
d) These changes will make life easier for people but will offer other advantages, too.
e) It is hard to believe that only a few years ago computers were not an everyday part of life.

4 **Find words in the text to match definitions 1–4.**

1 important (paragraph A) ____________
2 clever and complex (paragraph D) ____________
3 damage to a part of the body such as a hole or cut (paragraph E) ____________
4 searching for and finding out about a place (paragraph F) ____________

A 1__________ We now take tablets, mobile communication and other types of new technology for granted. We can speak to friends on the other side of the world as if they were in the same room and see their faces on instant-messaging systems. Space travel is no longer unusual as we explore Mars and beyond. Medical science has produced new ways of curing disease and helped build robotic hands. In the last fifty years, technology has changed the world beyond recognition. Leading scientists believe that technology will continue to change our lives in significant ways. So what can we expect in the next 20 years or so?

B Firstly science will continue to change our homes and the world around us. 2__________ Scientists believe that technology will be key in helping us to protect the environment. New systems will allow cities to become environmentally 'clean'. Resources will be recycled and we will produce energy that does not pollute the environment.

C Houses themselves will become 'smart' with water, electricity and doors being controlled via the internet or our phones. 3__________ We already have the technology to control locks, lights and alarms via phone apps. These will become normal as people use their mobile devices to turn on heating or air conditioning and check security from miles away or even other countries.

D We will continue to use technology to communicate. It is likely that broadband will become so sophisticated we will be able to project images of our friends like holograms when we talk to them. Scientists in the USA have already found a way to project 3D images using sensors, mirrors and video-conferencing pods. 4__________ But they believe that the technology will eventually be good enough and small enough for people to use every day and people will be able to project an image of themselves to wherever they want – a business meeting for example.

E Medicine will continue to improve. Doctors will be able to grow skin, bone tissue and even organs in laboratories to help repair wounds. As scientists understand more about human genes they will be able to cure or prevent illnesses by using this knowledge.

F Of course not everyone is impressed by these developments. 5__________ In fact many people believe that science should only be used to prevent hunger, war and disease, and the money spent on computers, space exploration and weapons should be used to improve the world as it is now.

VOCABULARY

FUTURE TIME MARKERS

5 A Complete the predictions with the words in the box.

term	next	~~future~~	in	time	short

1 In the near *future* I'm going to travel around Europe. I just need to save a bit more money.
2 The economy is weak now, but it will improve in the long ____________.
3 In the ____________ term we expect our profits to increase by about 3 percent.
4 I'm planning to get married to my boyfriend ____________ a year or two. Then we'll start a family.
5 In ten years' ____________ I hope to be a doctor working with children somewhere in Africa.
6 I'm starting a new job ____________ month. If all goes well, I'll keep working for the company until I retire.

B Which predictions are about things that will happen soon? Which are about things that will happen more than three years in the future?

GRAMMAR

THE FUTURE (PREDICTIONS)

6 Rewrite the second sentence so that it has the same meaning as the first sentence. Use the words in capitals.

1 There's a possibility that I will study in Spain. MAY
I *may study in Spain*.
2 Where do you plan to stay? WILL
Where ____________________?
3 Will you speak to Ted tomorrow? GOING
Are ____________________?
4 Janine probably won't pass her exam. UNLIKELY
Janine ____________________.
5 The weather forecast predicts a storm. GOING
There's ____________________.
6 He has a chance of becoming the champion. COULD
He ____________________.
7 Scientists will probably find a cure for cancer one day. LIKELY
Scientists ____________________.
8 I don't think we'll be able to attend the meeting. MAY
We ____________________.
9 There isn't time for us to go shopping. WON'T
We ____________________.
10 There's an opportunity to meet next week. COULD
We ____________________.

7 Complete the text with one word in each gap. Contractions are one word.

THE FUTURE OF LANGUAGE LEARNING

In the future we [1] ____________ going to see more and more people using technology to learn languages. There will [2] ____________ software that gets computers to read texts aloud and translate them. And we [3] ____________ only talk on the computer; we will also talk with the computer in any language we choose.

We will also begin to understand the importance of the five senses in language education, and researchers and publishers are likely [4] ____________ look at children's toys for inspiration. Music is going [5] ____________ play an increasing role in language learning. Short texts and phrases will be set to music and this will help students to remember the words, just as *The A, B, C Song* helps children learn the alphabet.

Textbooks may [6] ____________ unrecognisable when compared to today's books. They will come with microchips that produce smells and sounds. So if we are learning the word *bread*, when we touch that part of the page it will smell of bread. If we are learning the word *cry*, when we touch the word it [7] ____________ make a crying sound.

At first, these books [8] ____________ likely to be expensive, but market economics will drive prices down. So get ready for fun and games while you learn another language – these changes could happen sooner than you think!

VOCABULARY PLUS

IDIOMS

8 Underline the correct alternatives.

'I always put my [1] *foot/hand* in it when I speak to people. Socialising is really not my cup of [2] *tea/coffee*. I love my friends, they're really close to my [3] *head/heart*, but I'm quite shy with strangers.'

'I joined the [4] *mouse/rat* race last year when I became a project manager. I have to keep my [5] *ear/eye* on three or four projects at the same time. We're always [6] *working/running* against the clock and quite often we [7] *work/run* out of time. My friend said I was constantly multitasking and he [8] *kicked/hit* the nail on the head – there is always something to do.'

'I thought an online course would be a [9] *piece/bit* of cake, but I soon found myself in [10] *cold/hot* water. It was really difficult. I work hard but, let's [11] *face/eye* it, sometimes that isn't enough. So I asked for some advice from another guy. He was an A student and he gave me a [12] *foot/hand* with one of the assignments and I passed the course.'

FUNCTION

DEALING WITH MISUNDERSTANDINGS

1 **Put the underlined words in the correct order to complete the sentences.**

1 I tried to call you but wrong it number was the.

____

2 Sorry! realise didn't I it was your birthday!

____

3 He was late because date he wrong the got.

____

4 I didn't know it was you – recognise didn't voice your I.

____

5 We emailed but in fact different was a it person with the same name.

____

2 3.3 **Cover Exercise 3. Listen and match pictures A–C with conversations 1–3.**

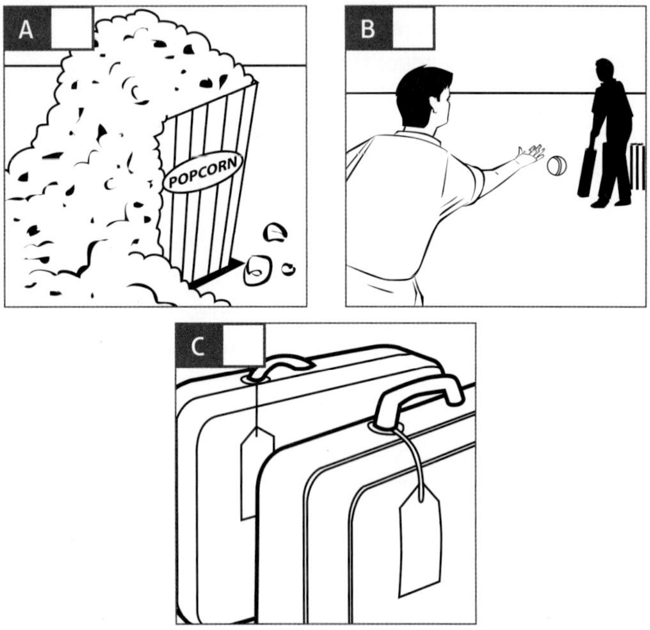

LEARN TO

REFORMULATE

3 **Listen again and complete the conversations.**

Conversation 1

A: Hello? I'm trying to find my lost luggage.

B: Ah, OK.

A: My bags went missing in Montevideo in Uruguay, after a flight from Curitiba, Brazil.

B: [1] ______ you say that [2] ______? Montevideo?

A: I flew from Curitiba to Montevideo and my bags went missing.

B: Have you reported it already?

A: Yes, the name is Anders Kleeburg.

B: Hang on. Could you [3] ______ the last name? Anders … ?

A: Kleeburg. K-l-e-e-b-u-r-g.

Conversation 2

A: OK, so cricket. So this is the bowler, OK? He runs up and bowls at the batsman.

B: [4] ______ exactly do you [5] ______? What's a bowler?

A: A bowler is the person with the ball in his hand, OK? And he tries to get the batsman out. Get him off the field.

B: Do you mean to [6] ______ he tries to kill the batsman with the ball?

A: No!

Conversation 3

A: Did you read this?! About popcorn. In 1948, two American scientists found some popcorn in a cave in New Mexico and dated it. It was over five thousand years old.

B: I didn't [7] ______ any of that. Are you talking about popcorn?

A: Yeah, it's an ancient food. Popcorn is thousands of years old.

B: I don't [8] ______ what you're [9] ______. You mean the popcorn we ate in the cinema yesterday is thousands of years old!

A: No! Popcorn in general. People have eaten it for thousands of years.

4 **Put B's words in the correct order to complete the conversations.**

Conversation 1

A: I'm afraid you have to wear a tie in this nightclub.

B: we / can't / saying / in / you're / so / come

____

____

Conversation 2

A: The show starts at nine o'clock.

B: you / at / it / starts / didn't / ten / o'clock / say / ?

____

____

Conversation 3

A: The pass mark for this exam is seventy percent.

B: what / failed / mean / so / we / you / is

____

____

Conversation 4

A: This type of car is twice as expensive as the other one.

B: me / do / costs / to / that / tell / you / it / mean / €50,000 / ?

____

____

Conversation 5

A: No other team can catch us.

B: the / words, / we / in / are / other / champions

____

____

VOCABULARY

PERSONAL QUALITIES

1 A Complete the words about personal qualities.

1 He won the election because he is a g__________ c__________. People enjoy listening to him talk.
2 Susan's h__________-w__________ nature helped her through university, when she had to study a lot.
3 Tim started at the bottom of the company, but he was a__________. He knew that one day he would be the manager of the whole organisation.
4 Lucy's a very g__________ l__________. She listens to people and then decides what's best for everyone to do.
5 He hates to lose a race. He's very c__________.
6 I find it difficult to make decisions. I'm a bit i__________.
7 You need to be more creative and think o__________ t__________ b__________.
8 They are a group of very m__________ students. They are keen to work hard.
9 Being a racing driver, Anton has to be a r__________ t__________. He isn't afraid of danger.

B Find words or phrases in Exercise 1A which have the opposite meaning to 1–8.

1 makes decisions easily *indecisive*
2 not interested in competing with others __________
3 lazy __________
4 thinks the same as everyone else __________
5 doesn't communicate well __________
6 not good at organising a team of people __________
7 doesn't like dangerous situations __________
8 not interested in becoming successful __________

GRAMMAR

MUST/HAVE TO/SHOULD (OBLIGATION)

2 Match sentences 1–10 with sentences a)–j). Then underline the correct alternative.

1 We *don't have to/shouldn't* wear a uniform at work.
2 You *shouldn't/have to* stay up all night studying.
3 I think you *should/mustn't* talk to your boss.
4 You *don't have to/mustn't* drink and drive.
5 I think he *mustn't/should* start his own company.
6 Nurses *have to/should* work long hours.
7 You *don't have to/mustn't* cheat during the exam.
8 I *must/don't have to* leave at 4 o'clock.
9 You *should/don't have to* apologise for his behaviour.
10 We *should/must* remember to book the tickets today.

a) He's very ambitious.
b) You need to find out why he shouted at you.
c) It wasn't your fault.
d) You'll be thrown out of the college.
e) We can wear whatever we want.
f) It'll be too late if we wait until tomorrow.
g) It's against the law.
h) Otherwise I'll miss my train.
i) You'll be too tired tomorrow.
j) It's no good if you want a nine-to-five job.

3 Correct one mistake in each sentence.

1 You must ~~to~~ tell him as soon as possible.
2 I've finished this exercise. What I should do now?
3 The clients don't has to come to the office. We can meet them at the restaurant.
4 I shouldn't to tell you this, but the boss is leaving on Monday.
5 Do we have wear a uniform?
6 Everybody must leaving the building by 6p.m.
7 She have to be at work by 7.30a.m.
8 I think you should to check what time the film starts.
9 You don't must use a mobile phone in the classroom.
10 We have wait until the IT man comes to fix the system.

LISTENING

4 A Look at the pictures. What qualities do you think are important for these jobs?

A

B

C

D

E

F

B ▶ 4.1 Listen to six people talking about their jobs. Match pictures A–F above with speakers 1–6.

C Listen again. Who says these things? Write the number of the speaker next to each statement.

1 You have to be organised and have a good memory, too.
2 And you need to pay attention to detail.
3 You shouldn't get stressed too easily.
4 You have to care about the people you're looking after.
5 You always have to be on time.
6 And you have to be able to work well under pressure.
7 You must be very accurate and observant. *1*
8 You have to be able to stay calm.

VOCABULARY PLUS

CONFUSING WORDS

5 A Complete the conversations with the words in the box.

job work remember remind forget leave hear listen fun funny

1 A: Oh no, ____________ to that. It's raining and I don't have an umbrella.
B: Why not? Did you ____________ it at home?
A: Yes, I did.
B: Here. Use mine.

2 A: Can you ____________ me to post that letter on the way home?
B: Sure. Just ____________ to bring it with you.

3 A: Did you have a good night last night?
B: Yes, it was really ____________. We danced until two in the morning, but today I feel terrible.

4 A: I got the ____________, by the way.
B: Congratulations! That's brilliant news.
A: Yes, I'm so excited. Finally, I'm going to earn a proper salary.
B: That's great. Well done.

5 A: I've got to go to ____________ now. I'll see you later.
B: Yes, don't ____________ we're meeting Chaz at 7.30.
A: Don't worry. I'll be there.

6 A: Did you ____________ the joke about the scarecrow?
B: No.
A: He won an award for being outstanding in his field.
B: That's not even ____________.

B Complete the sentences with words from Exercise 5A.

1 Can you ____________ me to call my brother later? It's his birthday.
2 Did you ____________ about that couple who won millions of pounds on the Euro lottery?
3 I don't get paid enough. I need to get a new ____________.
4 We're having a meeting tomorrow morning. Don't ____________!
5 I really enjoy my ____________. I find it interesting, and the people I work with are good ____________.
6 He's so ____________. He always makes me laugh.

DREAM JOB turns into NIGHTMARE

1 It was advertised as the best job in the world. And it certainly looked good. You would be paid ($189,000 for six months) to surf, sail and swim. The job came with a beachside mansion, with its own swimming pool, and fantastic views of the ocean. All you had to do was look after tiny Hamilton Island, situated off the coast of Queensland. Duties included feeding the fish and writing a blog of your experiences to help encourage tourism in the area. There were more than 34,000 applicants for the job from all over the world, so Ben Southall was delighted when he beat them all and won the contract.

2 But, as it turned out, it wasn't quite the dream job that some people might have expected. Firstly, it was incredibly busy. Ben found himself working seven days a week and up to nineteen hours a day. He had a busy schedule of events to attend, with promotional events, press conferences, training courses and administrative duties. 'It has been very busy, busier than most people would have imagined, and certainly busier than I had imagined,' Mr Southall told reporters when he finished his contract.

3 In fact, during his six months, Ben visited ninety 'exotic locations', made forty-seven video diaries and gave more than 250 media interviews – including a chat with popular US TV host Oprah Winfrey. He also posted more than 75,000 words in sixty separate blogs, uploaded more than 2,000 photos and 'tweeted' more than 730 times.

4 That didn't leave much time for surfing, sailing or simply relaxing and enjoying the sea views. And when he did get the chance to try out his water sports, things didn't always go well. On one trip, Ben was stung by a deadly jellyfish. Irukandji jellyfish are transparent and very small, so they are very difficult to see in the water.

5 In his blog, Ben describes how he was enjoying jet skiing with some friends, when as he climbed off the jet ski, he felt a sting on his arm. Within thirty minutes, Ben was feeling the venom. He was hot and sweaty, with a headache, pains in his chest and high blood pressure. Ben had to be rushed to a doctor who diagnosed the symptoms and gave him some medication. Luckily, Ben was fine, but it was an unwelcome end to his stay in paradise, and not how he expected to spend his last few days on Hamilton Island. Ben was lucky to survive.

6 However, he still insists that he enjoyed himself immensely. In fact, Tourism Queensland is offering him a new contract, and he will also write a book about his experiences.

READING

1 A Ben Southall got a 'dream job': looking after Hamilton Island, off the coast of Queensland, Australia. The article describes how the job turned into a nightmare. Which of these problems do you think it will mention?

loneliness	free time	feeling bored
problems with animals	illness	
money	other	

B Read the article to see if you were right. Then answer the questions.

1 What three things help to make the job 'the best job in the world'?

______

2 Why was the job not as 'ideal' as it seemed at first?

______

3 What happened to Ben towards the end of his contract?

______

4 What is he going to do now?

______

2 Tick the things which Ben did as part of his job.

1 gave speeches
2 made video diaries
3 managed a big team of people
4 gave interviews
5 attended press conferences
6 learned a new language
7 met politicians
8 wrote a novel
9 wrote a blog about his experiences
10 learned to surf and sail

3 Find words or phrases in the text to match definitions 1–8.

1 a large house by the sea (paragraph 1) ______
2 a plan that includes a lot of things to be done in a short time (paragraph 2) ______
3 meetings at which someone answers questions asked by people from newspapers, television, etc. (paragraph 2) ______
4 activities involved in managing the work of a company or organisation (paragraph 2) ______
5 posted a comment using the website Twitter (paragraph 3) ______
6 have an opportunity (paragraph 4) ______
7 taken very quickly (paragraph 5) ______
8 very, very much (paragraph 6) ______

VOCABULARY

EXTREME ADJECTIVES

4 Complete the sentences with the correct word.

1 **a)** I thought the show was *brilliant/boiling*.
b) Is the heating on? It's *brilliant/boiling* in here.

2 **a)** Have you heard the news? Isn't it *terrible/furious*?
b) All the trains were delayed. I was *terrible/furious*.

3 **a)** I'd invite you round, but my apartment is *delicious/tiny*.
b) Have you tried these salads? They're *delicious/tiny*.

4 **a)** I can't do it – it's *exhausted/impossible*!
b) I'm going home. I'm *exhausted/impossible*.

5 **a)** It's a(n) *fascinating/enormous* story of naval history.
b) $50,000! That's a(n) *fascinating/enormous* amount of money!

GRAMMAR

USED TO, WOULD

5 Complete the paragraphs. Use one word for each gap.

'I used [1] ____________ work for a big company. I [2] ____________ to work long hours and I [3] ____________ dream of living in a more exotic location, sitting on a beach with my laptop. Now I run my own website business. I don't earn as much money as I [4] ____________ to earn, but I'm much happier.'

'I [5] ____________ to work as a computer programmer. Most of the time, I [6] ____________ enjoy it. But I didn't [7] ____________ to like being in an office all day. So, I decided to get a job working outdoors. Now, I train people in forestry skills, so I'm outside most of the time. And my lifestyle is much healthier than it [8] ____________ to be.'

6 A Rewrite the sentences with *used to*.

1 Did you spend your holidays by the sea?

____

2 We didn't have a dog when I was a child.

____

3 I loved reading in the evening, but now I'm too tired.

____

4 I remember how I sat in my grandfather's studio and watched him paint.

____

5 Children always played around on the streets in the old days, but there's nobody here now.

____

6 They lived in a big house, but they had to move.

____

B Tick the sentences in Exercise 6A where you could replace *used to* with *would*.

7 A Look at the underlined words. Are they pronounced with a /s/ or /z/ sound?

1 I <u>used</u> to be very sporty.
2 Can I <u>use</u> your phone?
3 He never <u>used</u> to worry about it.
4 I <u>used</u> to live in the USA when I was 18.
5 This stuff is <u>used</u> to kill insects.
6 I don't <u>use</u> the car much any more.
7 We <u>used</u> to love going there on holiday.
8 I didn't <u>use</u> to live in Europe.

B ▶ 4.2 Listen and check. Then listen and repeat. Focus on the pronunciation of /juːstə/.

WRITING

A COVERING LETTER; LEARN TO ORGANISE YOUR IDEAS

8 A Put the covering letter in the correct order.

☐ Thank you for your consideration. If you require any further information, please do not hesitate to contact me. I can be reached at vinniej22@dmail.com or 07788 922 123. I look forward to hearing from you [1]<u>soon</u>.

1 Dear Ms Nelson,

☐ I believe that my communication skills, customer service abilities and positive work ethic would make me an asset to the shop.

☐ I am currently studying English at Exeter University and I am looking for summer work to help me finance my studies. [2]<u>I think I would be good at this job</u>. Firstly, I am both hard-working and organised, and I have excellent communication skills. Secondly, I have [3]<u>shown that I am good at</u> customer service. In my previous job, on the reception desk at Queen's Hospital, I had [4]<u>practical</u> experience of providing quality customer service and working with all types of people.

☐ Yours sincerely,

☐ I am writing to you [5]<u>about</u> the summer position at SunnySam's Electronics, advertised on www.summerjobs4students.com. [6]<u>I want to apply</u> for the post. I attach my CV, application form and all the information required in the advertisement.

☐ Vinnie Jessop

B Replace the underlined sections 1–6 in the letter with the phrases in the box. Write the correct number.

hands-on ☐ at your earliest convenience ☐
regarding ☐ proven ability at ☐
I would like to submit an application ☐
I believe I meet all the requirements of the post ☐

C Write a covering letter (120–180 words) for a summer job working as a restaurant/shop manager.

VOCABULARY

BUSINESS

1 A Circle the correct options to complete the text.

Hi Lucy,

I'm just writing to tell you about my new job. Remember when I had to go for [1] __________ last month? Well, I got the job. I'm so pleased about it, because I heard a lot of people were [2] __________ for it, probably because it has quite a high [3] __________.

The people in the office are really good fun and it is such a relief not to be out of [4] __________ any more. My new boss is in [5] __________ of the whole marketing department and she [6] __________ it really well. She has lots of really interesting business [7] __________ and encourages us to try and do the same. The only problem now is that I still arrive late for work all the time. I hope I don't get [8] __________.

Let me know how you're getting on at work.

Speak soon.

Becca

1	**a)** an interview	**b)** a job	**c)** a work
2	**a)** working	**b)** attempting	**c)** competing
3	**a)** salary	**b)** money	**c)** holiday
4	**a)** work	**b)** salary	**c)** employ
5	**a)** control	**b)** charge	**c)** lead
6	**a)** works	**b)** is	**c)** runs
7	**a)** thoughts	**b)** ideas	**c)** posts
8	**a)** interview	**b)** boss	**c)** fired

B Use the phrases in Exercise 1A to complete the sentences.

1 I'm lucky to work there – lots of people __________ to get jobs there.
2 Would you prefer to earn a high __________ or do something interesting?
3 My boss __________ the business very successfully and it's growing every day.
4 He behaved so badly I'm not surprised that he was __________.
5 I hate it when I have to do an __________ – I get nervous.
6 My cousin has been out of __________ for ages. She doesn't have any money.

FUNCTION

REACHING AGREEMENT

2 Complete the conversation with the phrases in the box.

not sure that I agree · suggest we think about · see what you mean · see things · that's a good idea · How about if we · That's fine

A: The way I [1] __________, the first thing we need to do is update the website.
B: Yes, [2] __________. But we haven't decided what information to put there.
A: I know. I [3] __________ what should be on the site and then decide who's going to work on it.
B: [4] __________ by me.
C: I'm [5] __________, actually. I think we need to look at the finances first. We don't know how much money we can spend on the website yet.
B: I [6] __________, but I'm not sure what to do. [7] __________ decide what we would like first and then look at how much it will cost?
C: Fine. That sounds good to me.

LEARN TO

MANAGE A DISCUSSION

3 Complete the sentences with the words in the box.

on (x2) · all · recap · to · up

1 Let's focus __________ the main problems and talk about the rest if we have time.
2 OK, but first of __________, we need to look at the notes from the last meeting.
3 Moving __________ to the next point. What are we going to do about salaries?
4 So, let's __________ on the main ideas we've discussed and then we'll stop for lunch.
5 I think we need to come back __________ the decision to relocate.
6 Let's sum __________ what we've talked about.

GRAMMAR THE FUTURE (PLANS)

1 Circle the correct option to complete the sentences.

1 I'm working hard so that I ________ the deadline.
a) meet
b) do
c) find

2 Let's ________ started and not waste time.
a) make
b) try
c) get

3 I usually prioritise ________ at the start of the day.
a) tasks
b) time
c) job

4 I hope you aren't going to ________ off doing that!
a) put
b) place
c) stop

5 Concentrate please! Don't ________ distracted.
a) been
b) get
c) have

6 Who ________ invite?
a) will you
b) will you going to
c) you might

7 Peter ________ fifty on Saturday!
a) is being
b) is going to be
c) might be

8 ________ a Thai curry. I'm expecting about twenty people.
a) I'm going to cook
b) I will to cook
c) I'm cooking

VOCABULARY ORGANISATION; FUTURE TIME MARKERS

2 A Complete the sentences with the words in the box.

~~meet~~ gets multitask last get distracted of prioritise time use

1 I always try to *meet* my deadlines and finish my work without delays.
2 My friend usually leaves things till the ________ minute.
3 Can you get your homework done ahead ________ time if possible?
4 She is a great manager. She always ________ meetings started on time.
5 Don't waste ________ with small jobs – focus on the most important ones.
6 I like to ________ things done as well as possible.
7 He is really easily ________ from the main task.
8 If you can ________ your time wisely, you will get more done.
9 If you have small children, you have to learn to ________ and do several things at once.
10 I don't know which tasks to ________ in this project.

B Underline the correct alternatives.

1 We'd like to buy our own house in a *term/year* or two.
2 In the long *term/year*, I think she made the right decision.
3 I'd like to start my own business at some point in the future, but that will be a *short/long* time from now.
4 In the *short/long* term, over the next few weeks, we want to see business improve.
5 In ten *next/years'* time, I hope to be a surgeon.
6 *Next/Years'* month, we will celebrate twenty years of marriage.

GRAMMAR THE FUTURE (PREDICTIONS)

3 Underline the correct alternative to complete the text.

THE FUTURE OF DRIVING

So, with improvements in technology and people becoming more and more environmentally aware, what is the future of motorised transport? We asked some experts for their opinions.

Matthew G – car salesman, USA

'Honestly? I think things [1]*aren't likely to/are going to* change a lot. People [2]*may/might not* like it, but governments [3]*may/aren't going to* introduce more laws and taxes to 'punish' people who use their own cars instead of public transport. This [4]*is going to/isn't going to* force people to leave their cars at home and some people might even sell their cars. It's already happening and I think in the future this trend [5]*won't to/is likely to* continue.'

Ian M – bus driver, UK

'I think the future [6]*will/is likely* be very different. Vehicles [7]*couldn't/won't* need people to drive them. I think they [8]*are going/may* have robot drivers, so people like me will have to find different jobs. I think we [9]*are going to/may not* see more and more cities begin to use buses like this. There [10]*might/couldn't* be fewer jobs for lorry drivers, too, as companies won't have to pay people to transport their products.'

VOCABULARY PLUS IDIOMS

4 Write the second sentence so that it means the same as the first. Use idioms which include the words in capitals.

1 It's so easy. CAKE
It's ________.
2 He was in trouble. WATER
He was ________.
3 I said something really inappropriate. FOOT
I put ________.
4 It's an issue which is very important to me. HEART
It's an issue which is ________.
5 He left his job in the city to go and become a coffee farmer. RAT
He decided to leave ________ and become a coffee farmer.
6 Could you help me sort out these papers? HAND
Could you ________ sorting out these papers?
7 I am trying to lose weight. FACE
________, I'm a bit too heavy at the moment.
8 I don't really like R&B music. TEA
R&B music isn't ________.
9 I like to follow what's happening in politics. EYE
I like to ________ what's happening in politics.
10 I'm afraid we have no more time. RUN
I'm afraid we've ________.

FUNCTION DEALING WITH MISUNDERSTANDINGS; REFORMULATING

5 Complete the conversations with the words in the box.

saying mean catch get other repeat what say exactly lost

1 **A:** The picture dates back to the sixteenth century when it was …
B: I didn't ________ any of that.
2 **A:** So, you take the third turning on the right, go straight on for 200 metres, turn left, take the first right again and it's straight in front of you.
B: I'm sorry. You've ________ me.
3 **A:** If you don't have a pink stripe on your ticket, then I'm afraid staff are not allowed to let you in.
B: Apologies, but I'm afraid I don't ________ what you're saying.
4 **A:** We had a very minor incident involving your new car.
B: What ________ do you mean?
5 **A:** We are sorry to report that all trains have been cancelled.
B: Do you ________ to say we can't travel today?
6 **A:** I've come to collect a parcel for Mr Wainwright.
B: Can you ________ that again?
7 **A:** There's one stop-over, for twenty-four hours, in Bahrain.
B: Could you ________ the last thing you said?
8 **A:** This desk is now closed.
B: So, you're ________ that we need to move to another desk?
9 **A:** I'm afraid you need to vacate the premises.
B: So ________ you mean is we need to go?
10 **A:** We anticipate inconveniences along the route.
B: In ________ words, we're going to be late.

VOCABULARY REVIEW

6 Complete the words in the sentences.

1 He always wants to win. He's very co________.
2 Part of being a good le________ is being able to listen to people.
3 It's one of the most am________ films I've ever seen. It's very moving.
4 I have to go to bed as soon as possible. I'm absolutely ex________.
5 To be a successful entrepreneur, you need to be a ri________ ta________.
6 It's minus ten degrees outside. It's fr________!
7 It's a fa________ story, really interesting. It's about a man who …
8 I love my job, but I should be earning a much bigger sa________.
9 He was always telling the bo________ what to do and in the end, he got fi________.
10 I'm very nervous, because I've got to go for this job in________ tomorrow.
11 I can't believe how angry he was. He was absolutely fu________.
12 I'm sure she'll do well in her new job. She's very ha________-wo________.

7A Put the words in the box into the correct place in the table according to the stress pattern.

~~amazing~~ ~~salary~~ tasty competitive successful leader interview furious delicious boiling difficult freezing exhausted impossible

oOo	Ooo
amazing	*salary*
Oo	**oOoo**

B R2.1 Listen and check.

GRAMMAR *MUST/HAVE TO/SHOULD* (OBLIGATION)

8 Complete the sentences with the correct form of *must*, *have to* or *should*. Use the information in brackets to help you.

1 Milo ____________ write three ten-thousand-word essays for his course. (It's necessary)
2 We ____________ tidy up the house. Jenna will be home soon. (It's a good idea)
3 You ____________ park here. You'll get a fine. (obligation not to do this)
4 You ____________ pay for children. They can come in for free. (It isn't necessary)
5 The sign says you ____________ keep your dog on a lead. (It's necessary)
6 You ____________ smoke anywhere in the building. It isn't allowed. (obligation not to do this)
7 You ____________ wear a helmet when you ride your motorbike. It's the law. (It's necessary)
8 Do children ____________ go to school on Saturdays? (Is it necessary?)
9 You ____________ wear jeans to a job interview. (It isn't a good idea)
10 You ____________ pay for the coffee. It's free. (It isn't necessary)

VOCABULARY PLUS CONFUSING WORDS

9 Complete the sentences with the words in the box.

listen	funny	remember	remind
hear	fun	forgotten	left

1 I'm sorry. I can't ____________ your name. Is it Sarah or Sue?
2 I've ____________ how this machine works. Please can you show me again.
3 It's in my bag, which I've ____________ in the car.
4 You never ____________ to what I'm saying.
5 Sorry, the music's too loud. I can't ____________ you.
6 Can you ____________ me to stop at the bank on the way home?
7 I always laugh at his stories. He's so ____________.
8 Why don't you come with us to the restaurant? It should be ____________!

GRAMMAR *USED TO, WOULD*

10 A Complete the text with *used to* or *would* and the verbs in brackets. Where both *used to* and *would* are possible, use *would*.

FIVE YEARS AGO

Greg and Emily Bishop [1]____________ (live) on a small island in the Caribbean. They had a wonderful life. Greg [2]____________ (work) as a teacher in a local school, and Emily [3]____________ (study) for an online course at a university. They [4]____________ (have) a house on the beach and after school, the children [5]____________ (play) on the beach with their friends. At the weekends, they [6]____________ (enjoy) surfing, sitting on the beach and eating delicious tropical fruit, like mangoes and pineapples. But when Greg's father became ill, the family decided to move back to the UK.

B Read about Greg and Emily's life now. Then complete sentences 1–6 with *used to* or *would*.

NOW

Greg runs his own taxi company and Emily has a job working in a sports centre. The children don't enjoy school as much and say they have to wear too many clothes all the time to keep warm. At the weekends, they all stay inside and watch football on television and eat fish and chips.

1 Greg ____________ (not have) his own business.
2 Emily ____________ (not work) in a sports centre.
3 The children ____________ (enjoy) school more in the Caribbean.
4 The children ____________ (not wear) so many clothes to keep warm.
5 The family ____________ (not stay) inside at weekends.
6 They ____________ (eat) tropical fruit, not fish and chips.

FUNCTION REACHING AGREEMENT

11 A Complete the phrases in the conversation with the words in the box.

don't	sure	suggest	need	about	what	things	that
me	point	agree	should				

A: OK. As you all know, we had record sales last year, and we'd like to organise a celebration for all the staff. Any ideas for what we could do?
B: Well, I feel [1]____________ we should have a party here in the office.
A: That's OK by [2]____________.
C: I'm not sure that I [3]____________, actually. I think we [4]____________ think about going somewhere else. The way I see [5]____________, we spend every day in the office. Why [6]____________ we do something different to celebrate?
D: That's a good [7]____________. How [8]____________ if we go on a trip somewhere?
B: Yes. Or we could do a course together. There's a place where you can go and make chocolates, or bake bread or something like that.
D: I'm not [9]____________ that's a good idea. I [10]____________ we focus on things we all enjoy doing, like sport. [11]____________ about spending a day playing golf?
C: Golf! I don't think so.
A: OK. I think we [12]____________ to focus on whether we have a party of some kind or go on a trip somewhere.

B Which phrases are used to give opinions? Which are responses to a suggestion or idea?

CHECK

Circle the correct option to complete the sentences.

1 Hi, Jake. What __________ this evening?
a) you doing b) are you doing c) will you doing

2 I'm not sure. I think I __________ stay at home and study.
a) will to b) might c) going to

3 We __________ Italy for our holidays. We love it there.
a) are going to b) will go c) might going

4 I always want to __________ things done as quickly as possible. I hate time wasting.
a) have b) make c) get

5 I hate doing my banking so I'm very easily __________.
a) prioritised b) distracted c) changed

6 He's changing his job in a month or __________.
a) term b) year c) two

7 I think it will be better for everyone in the long __________.
a) year b) term c) time

8 Look at the sunshine! You __________ have a great time at the beach.
a) 're going to b) 're likely to c) may

9 We __________ never see him again.
a) aren't likely to b) may c) won't

10 Yes, we're working against the __________ to finish in time.
a) pressure b) life c) clock

11 I was really late home even though my dad told me not to be. I'm in really __________ water.
a) dark b) hot c) dirty

12 We don't know much about him. He's a dark __________.
a) horse b) dog c) fish

13 She's very lazy. The boss told me to keep an __________ on her and check she's working.
a) sign b) note c) eye

14 I'm sorry. I didn't __________ you were busy.
a) recognise b) remind c) realise

15 I'm afraid I didn't __________ that. Can you say it again?
a) catch b) take c) do

16 André is very __________. He wants to sell his designs all over the world.
a) lazy b) ambitious c) indecisive

17 Françoise is a good __________. People really listen to what she has to say.
a) risk taker b) listener c) communicator

18 The doctor said I __________ take these pills.
a) has to b) have to c) haven't to

19 Help yourself to anything you want. You __________ ask.
a) don't have to b) have to c) must

20 It's a wonderful __________. I enjoy it a lot.
a) work b) study c) job

21 I can't believe how big your kitchen is. It's __________.
a) tiny b) big c) enormous

22 The interview was __________. I'll never get the job.
a) brilliant b) awful c) exhausting

23 When I told my boss, he was __________.
a) furious b) terrible c) impossible

24 As children, we __________ play at the bottom of the garden.
a) used b) use to c) would

25 My mother __________ live in the mountains.
a) used to b) use to c) would

26 If we work as a __________, we'll get the job done faster.
a) boss b) businessman c) team

27 More than a hundred people had to __________ for a single job.
a) compete b) decide c) get fired

28 The way I see __________, we need to start again.
a) point b) things c) idea

29 That's OK __________ me.
a) on b) at c) by

30 I think we need to sum __________ what we've learned.
a) up b) on c) at

RESULT /30

LISTENING

1 A ▶ 5.1 Listen to Mia, Tom and Owen answering the following questions. Write M (Mia), T (Tom) or O (Owen) next to the question they answer.

1 How has your country changed in the last thirty years? ___________

2 Is the world getting better or worse? ___________

3 How has your life changed in the last thirty years? ___________

B Circle the correct option to complete the sentences.

1 Mia thinks that thirty years ago ___________.
   a) life was simpler
   b) the pace of life was faster
   c) people were happier

2 Mia thinks that email puts pressure on people because ___________.
   a) people's computers crash
   b) emails sometimes don't arrive
   c) we are expected to give an instant response

3 Tom says that Beijing has grown because people ___________.
   a) don't have as much money as before
   b) came from around the world to get rich
   c) came from all over China to make money

4 Tom says that life in the countryside ___________.
   a) has changed enormously because of new technology
   b) will never change because they do not have access to technology
   c) has not changed that much, but people have more technology

5 Owen says that living conditions around the world ___________.
   a) are improving, even though many people are still living in terrible poverty
   b) are terrible and are going in the wrong direction
   c) are not improving, and more and more people are living in poverty

6 Owen thinks that there are ___________.
   a) fewer wars than before, but weapons are getting more dangerous
   b) more wars than before, and weapons are getting more dangerous
   c) the same number of wars as before, and weapons are getting safer

C Listen again and check.

GRAMMAR

COMPARATIVES AND SUPERLATIVES

2 Complete the conversation with the correct form of the adjectives in brackets.

A: I love my new digital camera. It was [1]___________ (expensive) my last one, but the pictures are much [2]___________ (good) quality and it's [3]___________ (easy) to use.

B: But it's much [4]___________ (big). Isn't it [5]___________ (heavy) to carry around with you?

A: Actually, it was one of [6]___________ (light) models in the shop. Although you can get [7]___________ (small) and [8]___________ (cheap) cameras, they're not as good as this one.

3 Underline the correct alternatives.

WHAT'S YOUR FAVOURITE GADGET IN THE KITCHEN?

My favourite gadget in the kitchen is the dishwasher. It's [1]*much/a lot more* faster than me at washing up. The problem is that I'm getting [2]*a slightly/a little bit* lazier. **Yuri**

The toaster. Morning is [3]*by far/slightly* the best time of the day for me. I enjoy a relaxing breakfast. And toast is [4]*a lot/more* tastier than bread. I love it. **Katia**

I don't cook very much, because I'm too busy. I have a microwave, which I find makes it [5]*more/a bit* easier. Now, I eat [6]*slightly/a little far* better than I did before. **Nguyen**

VOCABULARY

TECHNOLOGY

4 A Underline the correct alternative.

1 He's six months old. He's been to the doctor to get his *genetic engineering/vaccinations*.

2 We are running out of coal, so the government is looking at new ways of making *electricity/computer networks*.

3 The government is planning to build new *nuclear power/genetic engineering* stations, but many people are worried that they are too dangerous.

4 The company has just invested thousands of dollars in its new *computer network/antibiotics* to improve communication between employees.

5 It sounds like you've got a chest infection. I think you need some *solar power/antibiotics*.

6 NASA has decided to restart its *communications satellites/space travel* programme and try to send people to Mars.

7 They rode their *commercial aeroplanes/motorbikes* right up through to the United States and Canada. The trip took several weeks.

B **Match words in italics from Exercise 4A with definitions 1–8.**

1 The science of changing the genes of a living thing ______

2 The energy created when you split or join two atoms ______

3 Drugs used to kill bacteria and cure infections ______

4 Power carried by wires and used to make lights and machines work ______

5 Exploration of the area beyond Earth where the stars and planets are ______

6 Machines that are sent into space and travel around the Earth, sending radio and television signals ______

7 Energy from the sun ______

8 An injection given to someone to protect them from a disease ______

5 A **Put the words in the correct column according to the pronunciation of the underlined letter *a*.**

~~space~~ ~~antibiotics~~ nuclear travel machine communications satellites vacuum commercial aeroplanes solar vaccinations

/eɪ/ make	/æ/ apple	/ə/ polar
space	*antibiotics*	

B 5.2 **Listen and check. Then listen and repeat.**

WRITING

AN ADVANTAGES/DISADVANTAGES ESSAY; LEARN TO USE DISCOURSE MARKERS

6 A **Look at the task below and the notes a student has made. Tick the advantages and cross the disadvantages.**

Discuss the advantages and disadvantages of studying English online, as opposed to in a classroom.

1 flexibility – can study where and when you want, don't have to travel to a school
2 lack of interaction with your teacher or students
3 more choice – can choose to skip parts of the course, focus on other parts
4 IT problems – need to be confident with how the technology works, have good connections to the internet, etc.
5 discipline and time management – have to stay motivated
6 materials are technologically advanced – use a variety of multimedia materials

B **Look at the two plans, A and B, for the essay. Which is better? Why?**

Plan A

Many people now study English online. There are lots of good materials on the internet for doing this. As the technology improves, more and more people will try online learning.

But there are some problems, too. Online learning is boring because you are on your own. It's difficult to be motivated.

My opinion – I have tried online materials and they are very good. But going to a class is a better way to improve your English.

Plan B

Introduction:
Improvement in technology means many people are now choosing to study English online, not in classrooms.

Advantages:
- increased flexibility
- increased choice of materials

Disadvantages:
- lack of interaction with teacher and students
- difficulty with motivation and discipline
- IT problems

Conclusion:
- Online courses offer students more choice and flexibility, but are more impersonal.
- Language is about communication, so face-to-face interaction with people in a classroom is a better way to learn.
- Online courses might be a good way to supplement your learning.

C **Look at the essay one student wrote. They forgot to use any discourse markers to link their ideas. Rewrite the essay, including discourse markers from the box where you see an asterisk (*).**

One of the main advantages is that Another disadvantage is The problem is that However, (x2) In my opinion, And another thing,

With the improvement in technology, many people are now choosing to study English online, rather than in the classroom. It's easy to see that there are many advantages to online courses. * There are also disadvantages.

* When you study online, you have increased flexibility to study when you want to and where you want to. You have an increased choice of the materials you want to study, because you can choose them yourself.

* When you study online, there is a lack of interaction with your teacher and students. * You might find it difficult to stay motivated and be disciplined with your studies. * You might experience computer problems, which make your study difficult.

* Online courses offer students more choice and flexibility. * They are more impersonal. As language is about communication, face-to-face interaction with people in a classroom is a better way to learn.

VOCABULARY

INFORMATION

1 Cross out the alternative which is not possible in each sentence.

1 The class had a really good *debate/discussion/~~reply~~* about the environment.
2 He's sure he's right so if you disagree with him, he will *argue/quarrel/inquire* about it.
3 You should try to *respond to/argue/reply to* emails as quickly as possible.
4 I *questioned/looked into/inquired about* renting a car, but it was too expensive.
5 My brother and I always *argued/quarrelled/replied* about everything when we were young.
6 I've always *wondered about/questioned/quarrelled* this man's motivation.
7 The *look into/research/investigation* was a waste of time; we found no solutions.
8 His newspaper column *debates/inquires/discusses* the issues of the day.

2 Add the missing letters to complete the text.

WHO GOES FIRST?

Everyone involved in medical [1]re*search* is eventually faced with a difficult [2]qu__________: who will be my guinea pig? Who will be the first person to try this new medicine before we know if it works?

If we [3]l__________ i__________ the history of drug testing, we find that many researchers not only [4]de__________ this issue, but that a few have a surprising [5]re__________; they use themselves as guinea pigs.

When scientist Jonas Salk was [6]in__________ a new polio vaccine in the 1950s, he tried the drug on himself, his wife and children. It worked. Someone later [7]in__________ about who held the patent (the right to sell the medicine). Salk's [8]re__________ showed his character: he [9]wo__________ why anyone wanted to make money from something that the world needed.

GRAMMAR

QUESTION TAGS

3 Underline the correct alternative.

1 You're from France, *aren't you/weren't you*?
2 She broke a world record, *hasn't she/didn't she*?
3 They haven't seen us, *have they/haven't they*?
4 Don won't tell anybody, *does he/will he*?
5 That house looks nice, *isn't it/doesn't it*?
6 We didn't see that film, *did we/saw we*?
7 It hasn't rained for months, *has it/have it*?
8 You will come tomorrow, *won't you/will you*?
9 The shop doesn't open at 6a.m., *will it/does it*?
10 You stopped smoking last year, *didn't you/you didn't*?

4 Read the situations and write questions. Use the correct question tags.

1 You think your friend is in love.
You *really like Mary, don't you*? (really like / Mary)
2 You leave the cinema laughing together.
That film ____________________? (be / funny)
3 Your friend's younger brother is going to borrow your car.
He ____________________? (not crash / the car)
4 You leave the football stadium after a boring match.
It ____________________? (not be / very good / game)
5 You say goodbye to your friend at the airport.
You will ____________________? (write / to me)
6 You want to check that your friend got home safely last night.
You ____________________? (not miss / the last bus)
7 A tourist thinks you speak French.
You ____________________? (speak / French)
8 You have lost your watch.
You ____________________? (not see / my watch)

5 A Read the conversations. Which responses are genuine questions (where Speaker B really doesn't know the answer)?

1 A: Have you met Yinka's parents?
B: Only once. They're doctors, aren't they?
2 A: There isn't a cloud in the sky.
B: I know. It's a beautiful day, isn't it?
3 A: Are you looking for the scissors?
B: You haven't seen them, have you?
4 A: Have you read Jhumpa Lahiri's new book?
B: Yeah, she's a great writer, isn't she?
5 A: I've got my final exam tomorrow.
B: You'll pass, won't you?
6 A: I think this is the wrong address.
B: Yes, we've made a mistake, haven't we?

B 5.3 Listen and check. Then listen again and repeat the responses. Use the same intonation in the question tags.

READING

6 A Read the introduction to the article. Which questions can you answer? Which can only be answered by experts?

I NEVER KNEW THAT!

What is worse for you: boredom or stress? Why is sea air good for you? If you throw water into the air during the Russian winter, will it come back down as ice? What three foods should you take to a desert island?

People love trivia*. In 2005, a book called *Does Anything Eat Wasps?* was a surprise hit. It was a collection of questions and answers from readers of a magazine called *New Scientist*. We at *Lynx Mag* decided to come up with our own questions and then we asked a panel of experts for answers.

**trivia*: unimportant facts

B Read the rest of the text to find the answers.

1: You are going to stay on a desert island for several months and you can only choose three foods to take with you. Which do you choose, and why?
Broccoli, walnuts and orange juice. Broccoli has a chemical which helps detoxify your liver. It's also a superfood. Walnuts have protein and plenty of healthy fats. Orange juice is a source of clean water, and the orange contains Vitamin C. *Dr Leah Morecombe*

2: What's worse for you: boredom or stress?
Boredom. Stress can have benefits. Weightlifting is a type of stress. So are other sports and pressures at work. All of these are good for you in small doses. Boredom means you have no purpose in life, and no dose of boredom is good for you. *Dr Samran Naipaul*

3: Why is sea air good for you?
It isn't particularly. It got a reputation for being good for you in Victorian times because there was so much unhealthy smog in big cities. *Dr Robina Whitman*

4: Why do flies like rotting food?
Flies like rotting food because soft environments provide perfect conditions for breeding. When a fly's eggs hatch, the larvae live in and eat the rotting food until they grow into adult flies. *Dr Kelvin Marsh*

5: If you throw water into the air during the Russian winter, will it come back down as ice?
It depends where you are in Russia and what the temperature is at the time. But, potentially, yes. At a temperature of -30°C, small amounts of water will turn into ice almost immediately. *Immanuel Kanevsky*

C Complete the questions for the answers.

1 Q: ______ helps detoxify your liver?
A: Broccoli.

2 Q: What does the writer say ______?
A: It can be good for you, while boredom can't.

3 Q: Who thought sea air was ______?
A: The Victorians.

4 Q: What creatures live in and ______?
A: Fly larvae.

5 Q: At -30°C, when will a small ______?
A: Almost immediately.

D Find words in the text in Exercise 6B that match meanings 1–5.

1 remove dangerous chemicals or poison from something (paragraph 1) *detoxify*
2 measured amounts of something that you experience at one time (paragraph 2) ______
3 unhealthy air that is full of smoke and pollution (paragraph 3) ______
4 going bad; becoming soft and useless (paragraph 4) ______
5 when an egg breaks and a baby bird, fish or insect comes out (paragraph 4) ______

VOCABULARY PLUS

WORD BUILDING: ADJECTIVES

7 Complete the text with the correct form of the words in brackets.

THE PNEUMATIC TYRE: HOW DID IT START?

John Dunlop, a Scottish vet, was [1] ______ (response) for one of the world's great inventions.

Dunlop's young son kept falling off his tricycle because the bumpy streets were [2] ______ (hope) for cycling. Dunlop thought of a [3] ______ (create) solution: filling the rubber tyres with air. This, he realised, would be an [4] ______ (ease) way to make the tricycle more stable. He was right: it turned out to be a very [5] ______ (effect) solution. Lots of cyclists copied the idea and the air tyre became very [6] ______ (success). French car makers realised it was a [7] ______ (value) idea and produced air-filled car tyres. The tyres also became very [8] ______ (profit); Dunlop Tyres is still a huge company today.

VOCABULARY

PROBLEMS AND SOLUTIONS

1 Complete the sentences with the words in the box.

memory switching crashed sort work print down order recharging fixing

1 I'm on the motorway and my car's broken ______.
2 My phone isn't working. The batteries need______.
3 We can't use the machines here because they're out of ______.
4 Can you call the maintenance department and tell them that the photocopier needs ______?
5 If it still doesn't work, try ______ it off and on again.
6 I don't believe it! My laptop's just ______ again!
7 Have you got another pen? This one doesn't ______ any more.
8 Don't worry about that now. I'll ______ it out later.
9 OK. First, you'd better save the documents onto a ______ stick.
10 I've got a copy on my computer. Do you want me to ______ you a copy?

FUNCTION

POLITE REQUESTS

2 A 5.4 Listen to eight conversations. What does the person want each time? Match pictures A–H with conversations 1–8.

B 5.4 Listen again. Complete the conversations with one word in each gap.

1 A: Excuse me, ______ you tell me the way to the swimming pool, please?
B: Yes, of ______ I can. You keep going this way, until you get to the traffic lights. Then, …
2 A: Hello. Do you ______ what time the bank opens?
B: I'm not ______. I'll just ask someone.
3 A: Do you want us to bring anything?
B: That would be great. Could ______ bring some salad, and maybe something for dessert?
A: Yes, ______ course. Anything else?
B: No, that'll be fine.
4 A: Could you ______ me with my bags?
B: I'm ______, I can't. I've got my hands full.
5 A: Would you mind ______ the door for me?
B: Of course ______. There you are.
A: Thank you. That's very kind.
6 A: Could you ______ me what time the show starts?
B: ______ me have a look. The afternoon show starts at 3p.m.
A: Thanks very much.
7 A: Would you ______ coming to get me from the station?
B: OK. ______. Wait outside and I'll be there in ten minutes.
8 A: Do you know ______ there's a post office near here?
B: Yes, ______ is – there's one just along this road.

LEARN TO

RESPOND TO REQUESTS

3 Put the words in the correct order to make responses.

1 A: Would you mind saying that again?
B: of / not / no, / course
______
2 A: Do you know how to get there?
B: sure. / not / I'm / look. / me / have / a / let
______
3 A: Could you phone Tilly for me?
B: course / yes, / of
______
4 A: Could you finish doing this for me?
B: can't / I / afraid / I'm
______
5 A: Could you take these folders for me?
B: I / yes, / can
______

GRAMMAR COMPARATIVES AND SUPERLATIVES

1 Rewrite the second sentence so that it means the same as the first. Use the prompts in brackets.

1 (slightly / warm)
The sea isn't as cold as it was yesterday.
The sea ________________ than yesterday.

2 (far / expensive)
These black trainers are much cheaper than those white ones.
Those white trainers ________________ these black ones.

3 (delicious)
I have never eaten a meal as good as that one.
That was ________________ I've ever eaten.

4 (lot / easy)
I expected the exam to be more difficult.
The exam ________________ I had expected.

5 (simple)
All the other solutions to the problem are more complicated.
It's ________________ solution to the problem.

6 (much / happy)
I felt terrible yesterday, but today I feel much better.
I'm ________________ today than I was yesterday.

7 (bit / short)
My brother is slightly taller than me.
I'm ________________ my brother.

8 (bad)
Grandad thinks the world was a better place when he was young.
Grandad thinks the world is ________________ it was when he was young.

VOCABULARY TECHNOLOGY

2 Add vowels to complete the words.

1 I don't believe it. The __l__ctr__c__ty has gone off again.
2 He had to have a v__cc__n__t__ __n against measles.
3 I think sp__c__ tr__v__l is a complete waste of money.
4 I worry about g__n__t__c __ng__n__ __r__ng. I don't think we know enough about it.
5 We've put two huge s__l__r p__n__ls on the roof.
6 They're putting in a new c__mp__t__r n__tw__rk to improve communication.
7 N__cl__ __r p__w__r is dangerous because people make mistakes.
8 The region has much more tourism now that c__mm__rc__ __l __ __r__pl__n__s can fly here.

VOCABULARY INFORMATION

3 Underline the correct alternative.

1 I'd like to *discuss/inquire* this with my boss.
2 He didn't *quarrel/respond* to my email.
3 We need to *look/question* into the problem.
4 I'm *wondering/responding* if he'll take the job if we offer it to him.
5 I need to do some *research/argument* before buying a new computer.
6 The police are going to *wonder/investigate* the burglary.
7 We're getting a lot of *inquiries/question* about the new service.
8 It was a very interesting *debate/discuss* about immigration.

GRAMMAR QUESTION TAGS

4 Complete the questions with question tags.

1 We can walk there, ________________?
2 They've already left, ________________?
3 We'll see you later, ________________?
4 You don't like jazz, ________________?
5 The film was great, ________________?
6 You spoke to Mr Johnston earlier, ________________?
7 You won't need the car, ________________?
8 You haven't lost your keys again, ________________?

VOCABULARY PLUS WORD BUILDING: ADJECTIVES

5 Complete the words with the correct suffix.

1 His shoulder is very pain______. He says it hurts a lot when he tries to move it.
2 Unfortunately, the number of home______ people living on the streets has increased.
3 I'm afraid I'm not respons______ for what happened. It wasn't my fault.
4 He's one of Japan's most creat______ film directors. His work is very original and exciting.
5 The situation seemed hope______. What we were trying to do was impossible.
6 It's a very effect______ way to teach reading – we've had excellent results.
7 Don't worry about the car, I'm just thank______ that nobody was hurt.
8 She was always a mess______ child. She just loved getting dirty!

VOCABULARY PROBLEMS AND SOLUTIONS

6 **Put the words in the correct order to make sentences.**

1 car's / down / the / broken

____

2 phone / recharging / my / needs

____

3 out / it's / order / of

____

4 printer / fixing / the / needs

____

5 it / switching / off / try / and / again / on

____

6 this / it / strange / making / noise / keeps

____

7 more / work / doesn't / any / it

____

8 out / have / it / we / sort / to

____

FUNCTION MAKING AND RESPONDING TO POLITE REQUESTS

7 **Underline the correct alternatives.**

1 **A:** Could you *tell/to tell* me where I can find the manager?
B: Yes, *of course/afraid*.

2 **A:** Do you know *if there's/if is there* a supermarket near here?
B: I'm not *afraid/sure*.

3 **A:** Would you mind *checking/to check* the system for me?
B: Of *course/sure* not.

4 **A:** Could you *see/to see* if anyone has arrived yet?
B: Let me have a *look/course*.

CHECK

Circle the correct option to complete the sentences.

1 Houses in the area have become much _______________ recently.
a) more affordable **b)** more cheaper **c)** expensiver

2 People are able to work far _______________ hours than before.
a) most flexible **b)** more flexible **c)** the more flexible

3 The saxophone is _______________ to learn than some other instruments.
a) slightly the hard **b)** slightly easy **c)** slightly harder

4 Could you go and get the _______________? I need to clean the floor.
a) communications satellite **b)** washing machine **c)** vacuum cleaner

5 Nowadays you can have a _______________ to protect you from influenza.
a) antibiotic **b)** vaccination **c)** genetic engineering

6 That's a very good _______________.
a) wonder **b)** inquire **c)** question

7 I'm doing _______________ into how computers affect children.
a) a research **b)** some research **c)** some investigate

8 You don't want to come with us, _______________?
a) would you **b)** did you **c)** do you

9 You've brought the camera with you, _______________?
a) did you **b)** haven't you **c)** didn't you

10 She _______________ one of the best players in the world, isn't she?
a) 's **b)** will be **c)** was

11 I couldn't do anything to make things better. I felt _______________.
a) effective **b)** painful **c)** useless

12 He's a very _______________ puppy.
a) lovable **b)** creative **c)** biological

13 My computer's _______________. Can you help me?
a) needs fixing **b)** doesn't work **c)** crashed

14 Could you tell me _______________?
a) what is the problem **b)** what the problem is **c)** what the problem

15 Sure. Let me _______________.
a) look for **b)** have a look **c)** look at

RESULT /15

UNIT 1 Recording 1

1 When's the best time to learn a language?
2 Who taught you English first?
3 Where's the dictionary?
4 Why did people stop speaking Latin every day?
5 What did you learn last lesson?
6 What does your name mean?

UNIT 1 Recording 2

Maria
My mum and dad didn't speak any other languages at home, only German. But when I started school they were really keen for me to learn English – my mother said it would give me a lot of job opportunities. Luckily, I think I had a natural talent and it's something I was interested in anyway so I enjoyed my lessons. I think my mum encouraged me because she liked travelling so much. We used to visit different countries every year, mostly in Europe, but one year we went to Thailand and I absolutely loved it. Everything was so different. It was a culture shock but in a good way! That's probably why I became a translator, actually, because of my mum encouraging me to learn other languages and visit other countries. I'm pleased she did. I feel very lucky that I meet people from all around the world.

Ahmed
Well, Lebanon is a beautiful country and living in Beirut always felt very cosmopolitan. I mean when you walk down the street you hear Arabic, French, English – all sorts. A lot of the population there speak more than one language. I like that. It's a great experience, I think. You understand that the world is full of different people and different cultures. And it's pretty similar in the Netherlands too, I guess. When I moved there to work I couldn't speak Dutch or Flemish. I mostly communicated in English to start with. To be honest, it didn't actually cause many problems because people there are usually fluent in English. But I did some part-time Dutch lessons at college in the evenings and by the end of the first year I could get by. I hope I'm pretty fluent nowadays but you'd have to ask my Dutch friends!

Jessie
I think in the UK we aren't brilliant at learning new languages. I think people would like to learn but because English is so common everywhere people don't always feel a pressure to speak other languages. And when Brits travel they can generally use English, which is a shame because practice is so important with that kind of thing. I only learnt Japanese because I was living in Japan for a while. I worked for an international company and spent a couple of years in Tokyo. I didn't have lessons. I picked it up in my day-to-day life. To begin with I could only use the basics – *hello, how are you*, that kind of thing. But I gradually built up my knowledge. I wasn't fluent when I left but I had basic communication skills and I could do most day-to-day things – shopping, arranging to meet people, everyday stuff.

UNIT 1 Recording 3

1 He was an employee here.
2 I had a wonderful mentor.
3 All pupils wear a uniform.
4 We were team-mates for years.
5 Have you met my fiancée?
6 Talk to your partner.
7 She's my godmother.
8 That club is for members only.

UNIT 2 Recording 1

1 A: Have you been here before?
B: Yes, we've visited Naples a few times.
2 A: Have you had time to see the museum yet?
B: No, we haven't had time.
3 A: Did you find your hotel OK?
B: Yes, we found the hotel without any problems.
4 A: Have you got your guidebook?
B: Oh no. I've left it in my room.
5 A: Have you had any lunch?
B: Yes, we've already eaten.
6 A: Have you enjoyed your stay?
B: Yes, we've had a wonderful time.

UNIT 2 Recording 2

1 Christine
A lot of friends were staying in my apartment. We'd had a party the night before, and in the morning, one friend, Danny, got up to make everyone some coffee. While he was making the coffee, he heard the news on the radio. He came back into the room and told us that John Lennon had died. Someone had shot John Lennon. We were all really shocked. It was a very strange feeling. We couldn't believe it. We had all grown up with the music of John Lennon and The Beatles. We had played his music the night before. And now, suddenly, he was dead. There was a huge feeling of loss. He was such a peaceful man, who had wanted peace for everyone. It was a terrible way for him to die.

2 Rob
I was travelling to a meeting on the Tube that morning and there were delays everywhere. They closed the Underground station. At first, I was really angry, and worried about not getting to my meeting on time. But gradually, we started to realise that something terrible had happened. People outside the station were trying to talk on their mobile phones but the networks were all down because of the panic. Some people started to get news and soon we discovered there had been bombs all over London. It was a strange and terrible feeling. There were crowds of people outside shops, watching the news on the televisions.

3 Gino
I was sitting in the kitchen of my house in Italy with my family and I was only a child. Everyone was watching television. I remember the black and white pictures. I watched as this man landed on the Moon. And I can remember thinking how amazing it must be to be an astronaut and what an exciting job it was. Until then, I had wanted to be a train driver, but for a few years afterwards, I definitely wanted to be an astronaut.

4 Marianne

I was staying in Los Angeles with some friends and I was only about eighteen years old. In the night I suddenly woke up and the whole house was shaking. I had never felt an earthquake before, but I knew that was what was happening. It was very frightening. But after a few seconds it stopped, everything went quiet and I went back to sleep. When I woke up in the morning, I thought perhaps it had all been a dream. But when I went downstairs and turned on the radio, I heard the news. The quake was in San Francisco and it had done a lot of damage. So, I was lucky really. But I will never forget that feeling.

R1 Recording 1

1 Who do you work for?
2 What type of things do you do?
3 What problems do you deal with?
4 When did you start working there?
5 Do you enjoy the job?
6 So why did you apply for this job?

R1 Recording 2

1 I've stopped.
2 We made it.
3 He helped me.
4 They've killed it.
5 You've worked hard.
6 I thanked her.

UNIT 3 Recording 1

Ruth

I'm going to backpack around Poland next month with my friend so I've already started making plans. I'm afraid I have to organise things in massive detail or I get worried. I do everything ahead of time. My friend says I plan too much but that's just me. We're travelling by ferry and bus and then doing a lot of walking so it'll be reasonably cheap. We might stay in hotels if we can find some cheap ones but we'll probably try and find youth hostels most of the time. I've booked our travel tickets and now I'm making a list of the best hostels in the cities we're visiting. Actually I really want to visit Lodz – it's the third biggest city in Poland and there's a lot of unusual street art there on the walls of buildings. I'm a graphic designer so I'm really interested in art. And these pictures are huge – on the sides of buildings – so you see them as you wander around the city. I'm organising a route around the streets so I see the best artwork. I think it's going to be fantastic. I'm going to take loads of photos, too.

Kieron

I'd like to think I'm well organised, meet deadlines and so on. For example, I'm going to a sports tournament next week – I've been playing rugby for a long time and this year we've made it to the final matches. So I've got started and written a list of things to pack, the sports kit I need and where to meet the team bus and so on. But the truth is I'm good on paper and then I procrastinate in real life. So I know that I'll put off packing until the last minute despite my plans. I'm going to try and organise myself earlier but if I'm honest I'll probably end up doing it about an hour before I leave, even though the list has been ready for a week. And I'll probably get distracted and forget something really important like my rugby boots.

Amber

I've recently started work as a party planner. We arrange unusual or specialist events, the kind of thing people can't do easily themselves. In my own life I don't plan that much to be honest, I prefer to just let things happen without worrying too much. But at work I'm pretty good at organising things and multitasking. My first big event is happening next week. It's an eighteenth birthday party for a boy who really likes scuba diving. So his parents asked us to organise his party at the beach and arrange for all the guests to dive. I even went and tried it out myself! I think it'll be quite an interesting party. We'll have a diving teacher to help people who want to try it, drinks and then a barbecue and cake and so on. I hope it'll be successful, especially as it's my first party. I think planning comes naturally to me and I love meeting new people so this job suits me perfectly. Even when I was a child I used to love organising things for other people – I used to drive my mum mad because I was so bossy. But I try to keep it balanced. I don't plan much at all for myself. I just see what happens and go with that!

UNIT 3 Recording 2

1 They're going to play squash.
2 I'm going to buy a new phone.
3 She's going to spend a week in Greece.
4 He isn't going to eat anything.
5 Are you going to walk to the station?
6 He's going to change his job.

UNIT 3 Recording 3

Conversation 1

A: Hello? I'm trying to find my lost luggage.
B: Ah, OK.
A: My bags went missing in Montevideo in Uruguay, after a flight from Curitiba, Brazil.
B: Can you say that again? Montevideo?
A: I flew from Curitiba to Montevideo and my bags went missing.
B: Have you reported it already?
A: Yes, the name is Anders Kleeburg.
B: Hang on. Could you repeat the last name? Anders …?
A: Kleeburg. K-l-e-e-b-u-r-g.

Conversation 2

A: OK, so cricket. So this is the bowler, OK? He runs up and bowls at the batsman.
B: What exactly do you mean? What's a bowler?
A: A bowler is the person with the ball in his hand, OK? And he tries to get the batsman out. Get him off the field.
B: Do you mean to say he tries to kill the batsman with the ball?
A: No!

Conversation 3

A: Did you read this?! About popcorn. In 1948, two American scientists found some popcorn in a cave in New Mexico and dated it. It was over five thousand years old.
B: I didn't catch any of that. Are you talking about popcorn?
A: Yeah, it's an ancient food. Popcorn is thousands of years old.
B: I don't get what you're saying. You mean the popcorn we ate in the cinema yesterday is thousands of years old!
A: No! Popcorn in general. People have eaten it for thousands of years.

UNIT 4 Recording 1

1 I work in a busy airport in France. I am responsible for a small group of people. In my job you need to know what you are doing. You must be very accurate and observant. And you have to be able to work well under pressure and be a good decision maker.
2 I work in a pizza restaurant. In my job you need to have a friendly, relaxed manner. It's important to be friendly to customers, and patient. You have to be organised and have a good memory, too.
3 In my job you have to be a really good communicator. You need to be able to listen carefully to customers and find out what the problem is. And then you have to be able to think outside the box sometimes to see if you can find a solution to the problem which will keep everybody happy. You have to be able to stay calm, even if the customer starts getting angry.
4 I work in a lawyer's office. You have to have good organisational skills, I think, and you shouldn't get stressed too easily. You have to be quite hard-working as well. And you need to pay attention to detail.
5 I work in a children's hospital. I think the most important quality for my job is that you must be a caring person. You have to care about the people you're looking after. And you have to get on with children. That's very important.
6 You need to be very patient in my job, especially when there's a lot of traffic. And you have to be a good timekeeper as well. You always have to be on time.

UNIT 4 Recording 2

1 I used to be very sporty.
2 Can I use your phone?
3 He never used to worry about it.
4 I used to live in the USA when I was 18.
5 This stuff is used to kill insects.
6 I don't use the car much any more.
7 We used to love going there on holiday.
8 I didn't use to live in Europe.

R 2 Recording 1

amazing
successful
delicious
exhausted
salary
interview
furious
difficult
tasty
leader
boiling
freezing
competitive
impossible

UNIT 5 Recording 1

Mia
Well, it's changed a lot, goodness, enormously. I mean thirty years ago, I was still at school. I was ten years old. Life was a lot simpler then. All I had to think about was doing my homework and enjoying my free time with friends. I think life was simpler for everybody then. We didn't have all this technology and I think the pace of life was slower. At work, when someone sent a letter, it could take a week or two even before they would get a reply. Nowadays, people email and they expect an instant response. On the same day or within an hour or two. That puts a lot of pressure on people. We say that technology has saved us time, but it just speeds things up, and we're expected to do so much more. It's non-stop. We have mobile phones and BlackBerries, iPhones. So we don't just turn off and relax.

Tom
That's an interesting question. It's changed a lot. I live in Beijing. So there has been a huge advancement of technology and huge growth. There are more people, with more money. There has been an economic explosion here, so the city has grown. All the offices and high-rise buildings, lots of those weren't here thirty years ago. And it's very multicultural nowadays. People from all over the world live in Beijing. People came from everywhere to see if they could get rich, and many of them did get rich. They made millions. I think in a lot of places out in the countryside, things haven't changed that much. Life is quite similar to how it was before for farmers and their families. I suppose they have more technology now. They have mobile phones, and televisions, and the internet, so they know a lot more about the wider world and what is going on. Thirty years ago, they just had a radio and it was difficult to find out information. That's much easier now.

Owen
Oh, well, both probably. The world is getting better in many ways. I think if we look at living standards across the world, obviously there are still millions of people living in terrible poverty, but I think the situation is getting better. People have better access to food and medicines and education. So, these are all things which are improving. Medicine is improving, so people live longer and we can fight infectious diseases. People's lives have improved because of technology, so life is easier now than it was before. A lot of manual work is done by machines. But in some ways, the world is getting worse. War, for example, is a bigger problem all the time. There are more and more wars, which is surprising. And weapons are becoming even more dangerous. I think the environment is definitely suffering, so we are polluting more than we used to because of all the industrialisation. And I think also, socially, things are getting worse. Because people are less social now than before. They spend more time on their own, with computers and computer games, and less time talking to others, working together, and I think that is a great shame and a problem for the future, too.

UNIT 5 Recording 2

/eɪ/ make
space
communications
aeroplanes
vaccinations
/æ/ apple
antibiotics
travel
satellites
vacuum
/ə/ polar
nuclear
machine
commercial
solar

UNIT 5 Recording 3

1 **A:** Have you met Yinka's parents?
B: Only once. They're doctors, aren't they?
2 **A:** There isn't a cloud in the sky.
B: I know. It's a beautiful day, isn't it?
3 **A:** Are you looking for the scissors?
B: You haven't seen them, have you?
4 **A:** Have you read Jhumpa Lahiri's new book?
B: Yeah, she's a great writer, isn't she?
5 **A:** I've got my final exam tomorrow.
B: You'll pass, won't you?
6 **A:** I think this is the wrong address.
B: Yes, we've made a mistake, haven't we?

UNIT 5 Recording 4

1 A: Excuse me, could you tell me the way to the swimming pool, please?
B: Yes, of course I can. You keep going this way, until you get to the traffic lights. Then, …

2 A: Hello. Do you know what time the bank opens?
B: I'm not sure. I'll just ask someone.

3 A: Do you want us to bring anything?
B: That would be great. Could you bring some salad, and maybe something for dessert?
A: Yes, of course. Anything else?
B: No, that'll be fine.

4 A: Could you help me with my bags?
B: I'm sorry, I can't. I've got my hands full.

5 A: Would you mind opening the door for me?
B: Of course not. There you are.
A: Thank you. That's very kind.

6 A: Could you tell me what time the show starts?
B: Let me have a look. The afternoon show starts at 3p.m.
A: Thanks very much.

7 A: Would you mind coming to get me from the station?
B: OK. Sure. Wait outside and I'll be there in ten minutes.

8 A: Do you know if there's a post office near here?
B: Yes, there is – there's one just along this road.

UNIT 1

1.1

1A

2 fluency
3 mother tongue
4 foreign
5 native speaker
6 slang
7 jargon
8 learning strategies
9 skill
10 accuracy

B

2 fluent
3 accurately
4 mother tongue
5 foreigner
6 slang
7 skills
8 native speaker

2A

1 b **2** b 3 b 4 b 5 a 6 a 7 b

B

b 5 c 7 d 1 e 6 f 3 g 4

3A

1 When's the best time to learn a language?
2 Who taught you English first?
3 Where's the dictionary?
4 Why did people stop speaking Latin every day?
5 What did you learn last lesson?
6 What does your name mean?

4A

Maria
Which? English
How? In lessons at school
Ahmed
Which? Dutch
How? In evening classes (at college in the Netherlands)
Jessie
Which? Japanese
How? In day-to-day life informally

B

1 Thailand
2 A translator
3 The Netherlands
4 He spoke English.
5 Because English is commonly used and they don't feel pressure to learn another language.
6 Japan

C

1 d 2 a 3 f 4 c 5 b 6 e

5A

Email 2 needs to be formal.

B

1 Hi Pilar
2 How are you?
3 thought I'd
4 really like
5 can't wait to stay
6 Hope
7 Dear members
8 I am writing to introduce myself
9 I would like to take this opportunity
10 I will explain
11 I look forward to working with you all
12 Yours sincerely

1.2

1A

1 employee, boss
2 classmate, pupil
3 fiancée, fiancé, godfather, godmother
4 team-mate, member

B

1 fiancée
2 classmate
3 boss
4 member
5 pupil
6 employee
7 godfather
8 team-mate

2A

1 employee
2 mentor
3 pupils
4 team-mates
5 fiancée
6 partner
7 godmother
8 members

3

1 are, found
2 won, was sleeping
3 don't like, didn't (you) tell
4 Did (you) hear, were driving
5 Do (you) need, 'm staying
6 'm reading, didn't finish
7 get up, leave
8 're waiting, was looking

4

2 **a)** ii **b)** i
3 **a)** i **b)** ii
4 **a)** ii **b)** i
5 **a)** ii **b)** i

5A

1 men – said by women
2 men – said by women
3 women – said by women
4 women – said by women

C

2 Mai
3 Guy
4 Sergio
5 Linda
6 Avril

D

1 spatial perception
2 equip
3 further
4 distantly
5 instincts

6

2 go
3 take
4 do
5 do
6 get
7 go
8 do
9 take
10 get
11 take
12 go

1.3

1

1 d 2 g 3 e 4 h 5 f 6 c 7 b 8 a

2A

Conversation 1
Could I ask a question?
In my opinion
Conversation 2
There are a couple of things I'd like to ask about.
For me, the most important thing
Conversation 3
I have a query.
One thing I'd like to say is that
Conversation 4
Can I ask you about that?
I'd have to say

B

A 4 **B** 1 **C** 2 **D** 3

3

1 a 2 b 3 c 4 c 5 a 6 a 7 c
8 c 9 b

UNIT 2

2.1

1A

1 Crime, thriller
2 biopic
3 fantasy
4 period drama
5 romantic comedy
6 adventure
7 disaster
8 action
9 docudrama

B

1 romantic comedy
2 disaster
3 biopic
4 fantasy
5 action / thriller
6 crime

2
1 've never been, went
2 have you acted, 've acted
3 has travelled, has he visited
4 has won, won
5 lived, did they move
6 Have you been, arrived
7 've been married, met
8 Did you enjoy, haven't had

3
2 's / has been
3 've / have worked
4 've / have lived in
5 've / have been to London

4A
1 we've visited
2 we haven't had
3 we found
4 've left
5 we've already
6 we've had

5
1 at
2 in
3 on
4 at
5 on
6 In
7 by
8 in
9 in
10 by
11 on
12 on

6A/B
1 T
2 F (He was twenty-four years old.)
3 F (He wasn't speeding at the time of the accident.)
4 F (He had a motorcycle accident and lost two teeth.)
5 F (His favourite drink was coffee.)

C
1 b 2 c 3 a 4 c

D
1 barely out of their teens
2 immortalised
3 rebellious attitude
4 a lasting impression
5 assumed

2.2

1A
1 T 2 F

B
A 3 B 4 C 1 D 2

C
1 Rob
2 Gino
3 Danny, a friend
4 people outside the station
5 Marianne
6 John Lennon

2
1 b 2 a 3 a 4 b 5 a 6 a

3
1 happened
2 waited
3 didn't come
4 was driving
5 broke
6 had run out
7 Did (you) enjoy
8 hated
9 had booked
10 hadn't realised / didn't realise
11 were coming
12 was pouring
13 spilled
14 ordered
15 had said / said
16 arrived
17 tasted

4A
1 crash
2 earthquake
3 hostages
4 floods
5 Fugitive
6 demonstration
7 attacked
8 strikes

B
1 a 2 b 3 b 4 a 5 a

5A
Report A
a 2 b 3 c 1
Report B
a 3 b 2 c 1
Report C
a 3 b 2 c 1

B
Report A
1 A priest installed an electronic fingerprint reader in his church.
2 Warsaw, Poland
3 He wants to monitor whether the children attend mass or not.
Report B
1 There was a 'Love Message Yelling Event'.
2 Hibiya Park in central Tokyo, Japan
3 Kiyotaka Yamana started the event after his own marriage failed, to encourage people to be more romantic.
Report C
1 More than a thousand tourists had to be evacuated from Machu Picchu in helicopters.
2 Machu Picchu, Peru
3 The ruins had been cut off by floods and mudslides.

C
1 as soon as
2 During
3 While
4 Until
5 During
6 by the time
7 until

2.3

1
1 told
2 say
3 told
4 told
5 say
6 said

2
1 This happened when
2 Well
3 so
4 Anyway
5 Before long
6 The next thing I knew
7 In the end
8 Anyway

3
1 happened
2 no
3 kidding
4 what
5 then
6 Oh
7 Really
8 amazing

REVIEW 1

1
1 slang
2 native speaker
3 accuracy
4 bilingual
5 foreign
6 fluency

2A
1 do you work for
2 do you do
3 do you deal with
4 did you start
5 Do you enjoy
6 did you apply

3A/B
1 boss
2 classmate
3 team-mate
4 mentor
5 employee
6 partner

4

1 'm
2 'm taking
3 didn't start
4 love
5 saw
6 was looking
7 was reading
8 jumped
9 isn't
10 wanted

5

2 took, took
3 did, went
4 do, take
5 take, go
6 went, got

6

1 c 2 b 3 a 4 c 5 a 6 c

7

3 but
4 ✔
5 am
6 ✔
7 to
8 It's
9 ✔
10 really
11 the (my opinion)
12 for
13 ✔
14 ✔

8

1 You're welcome
2 No problem
3 Of course
4 You're correct
5 Go ahead
6 I see
7 That's right
8 I understand
9 Please continue

9

1 biopic, strike
2 thriller, fugitive
3 comedy, crash
4 science, attack
5 fantasy, earthquake
6 disaster, violent
7 period, demonstrations

10

1 fell
4 did you go
7 didn't sell

11

1 b 2 a 3 a 4 b 5 b 6 a

12

1 for
2 by
3 in
4 on
5 on
6 at
7 on
8 in
9 in
10 on
11 by
12 By
13 on
14 by
15 in

13

1 stayed
2 had left
3 was listening
4 was wearing
5 hadn't turned on
6 didn't finish
7 hadn't been
8 opened
9 were doing
10 didn't eat

14A

1 tell
2 say
3 tell
4 say
5 tell
6 say

B

1 told stories
2 tell jokes
3 said sorry
4 says 'hello'
5 told a white lie
6 say what you mean

15

1 This happened
2 happened
3 Anyway
4 In
5 Oh no
6 Well
7 before
8 So
9 did you do
10 Finally
11 The next thing
12 Oh dear
13 a sudden
14 happened then
15 in
16 funny

CHECK

1 b 2 c 3 c 4 a 5 b 6 a 7 b
8 c 9 c 10 b 11 a 12 c 13 c
14 a 15 b 16 b 17 c 18 b 19 a
20 b 21 a 22 c 23 b 24 c 25 c
26 a 27 c 28 b 29 c 30 b

UNIT 3

3.1

1A

1 e 2 a 3 c 4 b 5 d

B

1 1, waste
2 4, ahead
3 3, multitasking
4 2, prioritising
5 5, leave

2A

1 Kieron
2 Amber
3 Ruth

B

1 c 2 a 3 c 4 b 5 c 6 c

C

1 e 2 a 3 d 4 b 5 c

3

1 Are you going
2 're going
3 are you going
4 'm going to have
5 might
6 'll give
7 Are you doing
8 'll spend

4

1 Are you doing
2 are going out
3 might try / are going to try
4 're/are meeting / 're/are going to meet
5 'll / will be
6 're / are going to be
7 is playing
8 might go
9 'll / will call

5A

1 a 2 b 3 b 4 b 5 a 6 b

6A

1 d 2 c 3 f 4 b 5 a 6 e

B

1 **I've** gone to lunch. **I'll be** back soon.
2 Mr Jackson called **(earlier)**. **He didn't leave a** message. **(He said that) He** will call again later.
3 **My** dentist appointment **has been** cancelled. **I** need to rebook.
4 **I'm** at the cinema. **Your** dinner **is** in the oven. **I'll** see you later.
5 **I'm** going **(to go)** swimming after school – **do you** want to come **(with me)**?
6 **I'm** sorry, **I** didn't tidy **my** bedroom – **I** was late for school.

3.2

1

c

2

1 Mars and beyond
2 clean energy
3 via phone apps
4 project 3D images
5 They can be used to repair wounds.
6 They think money should be spent on improving the world not on space travel.

3

1 e 2 d 3 a 4 c 5 b

4

1 significant
2 sophisticated
3 wound
4 exploration

5A

2 term
3 short
4 in
5 time
6 next

B

1, 3, 4 and 6 are about things that will happen soon.
2 and 5 are about things that will happen more than three years in the future.

6

2 will you stay
3 you going to speak to Ted tomorrow
4 is unlikely to pass her exam
5 going to be a storm
6 could become the champion
7 are likely to find a cure for cancer one day
8 may not be able to attend the meeting
9 won't have time to go shopping
10 could meet next week

7

1 are
2 be
3 won't
4 to
5 to
6 be / become
7 will
8 are

8

1 foot
2 tea
3 heart
4 rat
5 eye
6 working
7 run
8 hit
9 piece
10 hot
11 face
12 hand

3.3

1

1 it was the wrong number
2 I didn't realise
3 he got the wrong date / the date wrong
4 I didn't recognise your voice
5 it was a different person

2

A 3 B 2 C 1

3

1 Can
2 again
3 repeat
4 What
5 mean
6 say
7 catch
8 get
9 saying

4

1 So you're saying we can't come in.
2 Didn't you say it starts at ten o'clock?
3 So what you mean is we failed.
4 Do you mean to tell me that it costs €50,000?
5 In other words, we are the champions.

UNIT 4

4.1

1A

1 good communicator
2 hard-working
3 ambitious
4 good leader
5 competitive
6 indecisive
7 outside the box
8 motivated
9 risk taker

B

2 competitive
3 hard-working
4 thinks outside the box
5 good communicator
6 good leader
7 risk taker
8 ambitious

2

1 e, don't have to
2 i, shouldn't
3 b, should
4 g, mustn't
5 a, should
6 j, have to
7 d, mustn't
8 h, must
9 c, don't have to
10 f, must

3

2 I've finished this exercise. What ~~I should~~ **should I** do now?
3 The clients don't ~~has~~ **have** to come to the office. We can meet them at the restaurant.
4 I shouldn't ~~to~~ tell you this, but the boss is leaving on Monday.
5 Do we have **to** wear a uniform?
6 Everybody must ~~leaving~~ **leave** the building by 6p.m.
7 She ~~have~~ **has** to be at work by 7.30a.m.
8 I think you should ~~to~~ check what time the film starts.
9 You ~~don't must~~ **mustn't** use a mobile phone in the classroom.
10 We have **to** wait until the IT man comes to fix the system.

4B

A 3 B 1 C 6 D 5 E 4 F 2

C

1 2 2 4 3 4 4 5 5 6 6 1 7 1 8 3

5A

1 listen, leave
2 remind, remember
3 fun
4 job
5 work, forget
6 hear, funny

B

1 remind
2 hear
3 job
4 forget
5 work, fun
6 funny

4.2

1B

1 good salary, beachside mansion, fantastic views of the ocean
2 Because Ben was too busy and there wasn't much time to relax.
3 He was stung by a deadly jellyfish.
4 He is planning to write a book about his experiences, and he might accept a new contract with Tourism Queensland.

2

2, 4, 5 and 9

3

1 a beachside mansion
2 a busy schedule
3 press conferences
4 administrative duties
5 tweeted
6 get the chance
7 rushed
8 immensely

4

1 a) brilliant	b) boiling
2 a) terrible	b) furious
3 a) tiny	b) delicious
4 a) impossible	b) exhausted
5 a) fascinating	b) enormous

5

1 to
2 used
3 would
4 used
5 used
6 would
7 use
8 used

6A

1 Did you use to spend your holidays by the sea?
2 We didn't use to have a dog when I was a child.
3 I used to love reading in the evening, but now I'm too tired.
4 I remember how I used to sit in my grandfather's studio and watch him paint.
5 Children always used to play around on the streets in the old days, but there's nobody here now.
6 They used to live in a big house, but they had to move.

B

Sentences 1, 4, 5

7A

1 /s/ 2 /z/ 3 /s/ 4 /s/
5 /z/ 6 /z/ 7 /s/ 8 /s/

8A

2 I am writing to you about …
3 I am currently studying English …
4 I believe that my communication skills, …
5 Thank you for your consideration. If you require …
6 Yours sincerely,
7 Vinnie Jessop

B

1 at your earliest convenience
2 I believe I meet all the requirements of the post
3 proven ability at
4 hands-on
5 regarding
6 I would like to submit an application

4.3

1A

1 a 2 c 3 a 4 a 5 b 6 c 7 b 8 c

B

1 compete
2 salary
3 runs
4 fired
5 interview
6 work

2

1 see things
2 that's a good idea
3 suggest we think about
4 That's fine
5 not sure that I agree
6 see what you mean
7 How about if we

3

1 on
2 all
3 on
4 recap
5 to
6 up

REVIEW 2

1

1 a 2 c 3 a 4 a 5 b 6 a 7 b 8 c

2A

2 last
3 of
4 gets
5 time
6 get
7 distracted
8 use
9 multitask
10 prioritise

B

1 year
2 term
3 long
4 short
5 years'
6 Next

3

1 are going to
2 might not
3 may
4 is going to
5 is likely to
6 will
7 won't
8 may
9 are going to
10 might

4

1 a piece of cake
2 in hot water
3 my foot in it
4 close to my heart
5 the rat race
6 give me a hand
7 Let's face it
8 my cup of tea
9 keep an eye on
10 run out of time

5

1 catch
2 lost
3 get
4 exactly
5 mean
6 say
7 repeat
8 saying
9 what
10 other

6

1 competitive
2 leader
3 amazing
4 exhausted
5 risk taker
6 freezing
7 fascinating
8 salary
9 boss, fired
10 interview
11 furious
12 hard-working

7A

oOo: successful, delicious, exhausted
Ooo: interview, furious, difficult
Oo: tasty, leader, boiling, freezing
oOoo: competitive, impossible

8

1 has to
2 should
3 mustn't
4 don't have to
5 must / have to
6 mustn't
7 must / have to
8 have to
9 shouldn't
10 don't have to

9

1 remember
2 forgotten
3 left
4 listen
5 hear
6 remind
7 funny
8 fun

10A

1 used to live
2 used to work
3 used to study
4 used to have
5 would play
6 would enjoy

B

1 didn't use to have
2 didn't use to work
3 used to enjoy
4 didn't use to wear
5 didn't use to stay
6 would eat

11A

1 that
2 me
3 agree
4 should
5 things
6 don't
7 point
8 about
9 sure
10 suggest
11 What
12 need

B

opinions: I feel that, I think we should think about, The way I see things, Why don't we, How about if we, I suggest we focus on, How about, I think we need to focus on
responses: That's OK by me, I'm not sure that I agree, That's a good point, I'm not sure that's a good idea

CHECK

1 b 2 b 3 a 4 c 5 b 6 c 7 b
8 a 9 b 10 c 11 b 12 a 13 c
14 c 15 a 16 b 17 c 18 b 19 a
20 c 21 c 22 b 23 a 24 c 25 a
26 c 27 a 28 b 29 c 30 a

UNIT 5

5.1

1A

1 T 2 O 3 M

B

1 a 2 c 3 b 4 c 5 a 6 b

2

1 more expensive than
2 better
3 easier
4 bigger
5 heavier
6 the lightest
7 smaller
8 cheaper

3

1 much
2 a little bit
3 by far
4 a lot
5 a bit
6 slightly

4A

1 vaccinations
2 electricity
3 nuclear power
4 computer network
5 antibiotics
6 space travel
7 motorbikes

B

1 genetic engineering
2 nuclear power
3 antibiotics
4 electricity
5 space travel
6 communications satellites
7 solar power
8 vaccination

5A

/eɪ/ **make:** communications, aeroplanes, vaccinations
/æ/ **apple:** travel, satellites, vacuum
/ə/ **polar:** nuclear, machine, commercial, solar

6A

1 ✔ 2 ✘ 3 ✔ 4 ✘ 5 ✘ 6 ✔

B

Plan B is better because it is more clearly organised into advantages and disadvantages. The paragraphs are planned and there is an introduction and a conclusion.

C

However, there are also disadvantages.
One of the main advantages is that when you study online, you …
The problem is that when you study online, there is … students. **Another disadvantage is** you might find it difficult … your studies. **And another thing,** you might experience …
In my opinion, online courses offer students more choice and flexibility
However, they are …

5.2

1

Not possible:
2 inquire
3 argue
4 questioned
5 replied
6 quarrelled
7 look into
8 inquires

2

2 question
3 look into
4 debate
5 response
6 investigating
7 inquired
8 reply
9 wondered

3

1 aren't you
2 didn't she
3 have they
4 will he
5 doesn't it
6 did we
7 has it
8 won't you
9 does it
10 didn't you

4

2 was funny, wasn't it
3 won't crash the car, will he
4 wasn't a very good game, was it
5 write to me, won't you
6 didn't miss the last bus, did you
7 speak French, don't you
8 haven't seen my watch, have you

5A

1, 3, and 5 are genuine questions.

6C

1 Which food
2 about stress
3 good for you
4 eat rotting food
5 amount of water turn into ice

D

2 dose
3 smog
4 rotting
5 hatch

7

1 responsible
2 hopeless
3 creative
4 easy
5 effective
6 successful
7 valuable
8 profitable

5.3

1

1 down
2 recharging
3 order
4 fixing
5 switching
6 crashed
7 work
8 sort
9 memory
10 print

2A

A 3 He wants to know if they have to bring anything.
B 4 She wants someone to hold something for her.
C 7 She wants someone to pick her up from the station.
D 2 He wants to know what time the bank opens.
E 1 She wants to know the way to the swimming pool.
F 8 She wants to know if there is a post office near there.
G 6 He wants to know what time the (afternoon) show starts.
H 5 She wants someone to open the door for her.

B

1 could, course
2 know, sure
3 you, of
4 help, sorry
5 opening, not
6 tell, Let
7 mind, Sure
8 if, there

3

1 No, of course not.
2 I'm not sure. Let me have a look.
3 Yes, of course.
4 I'm afraid I can't.
5 Yes, I can.

REVIEW 3

1

1 is slightly warmer
2 are far more expensive than
3 the most delicious meal
4 was a lot easier than
5 the simplest
6 much happier
7 a bit shorter than
8 a worse place than

2

1 electricity
2 vaccination
3 space travel
4 genetic engineering
5 solar panels
6 computer network
7 Nuclear power
8 commercial aeroplanes

3

1 discuss
2 respond
3 look
4 wondering
5 research
6 investigate
7 inquiries
8 debate

4

1 can't we
2 haven't they
3 won't we
4 do you
5 wasn't it
6 didn't you
7 will you
8 have you

5

1 painful
2 homeless
3 responsible
4 creative
5 hopeless
6 effective
7 thankful
8 messy

6

1 The car's broken down.
2 My phone needs recharging.
3 It's out of order.
4 The printer needs fixing.
5 Try switching it off and on again.
6 It keeps making this strange noise.
7 It doesn't work any more.
8 We have to sort it out.

7

1 tell, of course
2 if there's, sure
3 checking, course
4 see, look

CHECK

1 a **2** b **3** c **4** c **5** b **6** c **7** b
8 c **9** b **10** a **11** c **12** a **13** c
14 b **15** b

NOTES

NOTES